THE QUEEN'S DAUGHTERS

THE QUEEN'S
DAUGHTERS

A STUDY OF WOMEN-SAINTS

By

C. C. MARTINDALE, S.J.

SHEED AND WARD
LONDON AND NEW YORK

FIRST PUBLISHED 1951
BY SHEED AND WARD, LTD.
110/111, FLEET STREET,
LONDON, E.C.4
AND
SHEED AND WARD, INC.
830 BROADWAY,
NEW YORK, 3

PRINTED IN GREAT BRITAIN BY
THE CHISWICK PRESS, NEW SOUTHGATE, N.11

Never in the course of the history of humanity have events required on the part of woman so much initiative and daring, so much fidelity, moral strength, spirit of sacrifice and endurance of all kinds of sufferings—in a word, so much heroism . . .

PIUS PP. XII.

These words were sent to Rawalpindi on the occasion of the opening of the new Holy Family Hospital there, March 25, 1950. The Hospital is in the care of the Medical Mission Sisters (p. 182 n.2).

CONTENTS

INTRODUCTION

SOME YEARS ago a small book was published called *What are Saints?* It consisted of a few quarter-of-an-hour broadcast talks about men who had become known as "Saints", and I had hoped to follow it with a similar book about women-Saints. This became impossible, and I regret it the less because of apparently unsurmountable difficulties that would have been encountered. First, a high proportion of canonized women-Saints were cloistered nuns, and of these, many were notable chiefly because of their penances and ecstasies; and while it would have been unfair to omit them, it would have been impossible to explain them in brief broadcast talks. The exterior life of St. Teresa, for example, could have been related and would have been picturesque; but, by itself, it would have exhibited neither her personality, nor her doctrine, nor her real work. Again, when speaking of the men, one could take examples from almost every period of history, whereas there are whole tracts of history in which very few women-Saints are known, or well enough for a "personality" to be properly exhibited. And I have felt it a duty not to "embellish" the historical evidence by the use of "legends", however charming. It may indeed be that certain legendary details have found their way into these pages, but that was not intentional. And in a simple book like this it was impossible to add references to all its sources. I am almost certain to have made various mistakes, or omitted really unusual or characteristic details for which there would have been room, and express my regret for this beforehand. On the other hand, the book as it progressed turned out in no way to be a "companion" to *What are Saints?*, if only because it did not have to consist of thirteen "parts", each of a certain length. At first I chose some outstanding figures and did

indeed try to write of them more or less as the men had been
written of; but then I found that the chapters became
longer; and it was more and more distasteful to omit any
of the lovely characters encountered as it became easier
to learn facts about them and indeed as we passed into the
period of photography and we had a much better chance of
knowing what the Saints looked like; after all, you cannot
help making some "image" of them, and if you start by
picturing a Saint as a fragile flower and she turns out to have
been exceptionally plump and stalwart, you are apt to make
much graver misjudgments about her. What I sincerely
hope is that no one belonging to this or that Congregation
will think I have omitted her Foundress from failure to
respect or admire her: indeed, there are so many who have
been recently beatified that it is impossible even to know
them all—why, during this Holy Year people are being
beatified of whom one had not even heard. But among them
is, I fear, no Englishwoman; in fact, apart from the Blessed
Margaret Clitheroe and Blessed Anne Lyne, who were
martyrs, have we had any women-Saints (or, for the matter
of that, men-Saints) since the Reformation? This is partly
why I have included Mary Ward, though I do not know
whether she is moving towards canonization: but then, I
have added a few more names of women who, we hope, may
be canonized, a task made easy by the existence of an
excellent book, *Kommende deutsche Heilige*, compiled by
A. Köhler and J. Sauren (Essen, 1936); would that there
were similar books for every country; would that there were
one for ours, showing at least that we know what sanctity
means, and aspire to seeing our land become once more
"the island of Saints" and fit to be Mary's Dowry. Are we
not by now convinced that it is not learned argument and
certainly not compromise that will bring Christians together
into one fold, but that it is the "Note" of Holiness which may
have a supremely "evidential" value? Yet even so, the
divine light has to shine through the clouded glass of our
poor humanity, and the Saints themselves will not always

be just what we might have expected. After all, they had to *win* their battles, and were often wounded in the winning them. Not everything in the Saints will be equally attractive! May God grant us the truly "seeing eye".*

LONDON, 1950

* Fr. F. Breymann, S.J.'s, *Holiness of the Church in the Fourteenth Century*, trans. by Fr. C. Kempf, S.J. (New York, 1916) has been of great help.

PROLOGUE

CHRIST IS the source of all sanctity, and every form of sanctity finds something in His all-holy life to originate, sanction and explain it. No one man or woman can reproduce that all-inclusive perfection. I do not know that there are qualities which should be called *in themselves* more "feminine" than others. We dare not say, for example, that initiative or business capacity are the monopoly of men—tenacity certainly is not—or that gentleness and insight belong exclusively to women. But, in a woman, *all* virtues are *womanly*. If we detect a certain elemental passionateness in St. Helena and in her son Constantine, it will not be in her in a masculine way nor in him in a feminine way. Whatever be said of St. Teresa's masculinity ("I fear only two men in Spain—the King and Teresa!"), who was a more womanly woman than she? For all his extreme sensitiveness and even childlikeness, St. John of the Cross reveals himself all through his history as a true man. Hence we shall study these women-Saints with no preconceived ideas about what we ought to find.

Women played their various and happy parts throughout our Lord's life. There is a special sweetness in the encounter of His very young Mother with the aged St. Elizabeth, and the still older prophetess Anna in the Temple; nor can we imagine that when the Bethlehem shepherds told everyone of what they had seen, their wives and daughters failed to visit Mary, to delight in, as all women would, her Child. Women appear—perhaps momentarily, yet how vividly!—throughout that history: Peter's mother-in-law; the mothers of the boy who had died at Naim and of Jairus's daughter; the Canaanitess; the woman whom many doctors could not heal but who was fain to touch the hem of His garment; the woman at the well; the woman taken in the very act of sin; she whom "Satan had bound for eighteen years"; the mother of John and James; Martha and Mary, those two sisters so like and so unlike; the women of the Passion, even Pilate's wife; and those who wept on the Way of the Cross and who anointed hastily Christ's Body on the Friday and returned on the Sunday to finish their work, only to find Him risen; and, more than any save one, the Magdalen. It would be pleasant to know more of those women and their future; but even as it is, they do much to bring the gospel scenes to life.

It was, of course, into His own Mother that Christ poured His fullest grace; we hope to end this book by a renewed expression of our veneration and our love. Here it shall be enough to have mentioned her name, and to have asked her help as we proceed to write of those "Daughters of God's House" who have followed in the train of their Queen and their Mother.

CHAPTER I

THE CHURCH IN THE PAGAN EMPIRE

ST. BLANDINA (A.D. 177); SS. PERPETUA AND FELICITAS (A.D. 202-203)

DURING the very earliest age of the Church a few names of women are mentioned. Some are to be found in the Acts of the Apostles and the Epistles of St. Paul, but nothing more is known of them than their existence. A very few names belonging to the sub-apostolic era are known— St. Prisca, St. Praxedes, St. Thekla; but even the legends surrounding these are very tenuous. There was more going on within the Church during those first 300 years than suffering; there were active charity, and thoughtful writing. But naturally martyrdom stands out as something more dramatic. In the official records of martyrdoms, again, there are a few names of women; but these records contain only brief sentences; answers made by the accused to their accusers; and though these, like the inscriptions scrawled on the soft stone of Catacombs, have an infinite pathos of their own, they do not supply us with enough to offer a picture of *personalities*. Two documents of incomparable value, however, have come down to us, and it is these that we begin by using.

It had always been easy to rouse popular opinion against the early Christians. They were aloof and seemed morose; they celebrated mysterious rites at night; they refused, above all, to worship the Roman Emperor, the sole real link that held the Empire together, and branded themselves thus as the foes of civilization itself. And they are always disliked who refuse to share in the amusements and the vices of their fellow-men.   Persecution was sometimes stimulated by popular outcry; but also, should a local governor want his extreme loyalty to be brought to the notice of higher authority, he would trade on popular emotionalism so as to escape from the appearance of arbitrary cruelty.   Thus in the year A.D. 177 the Emperor Marcus Aurelius initiated a fierce anti-Christian persecution.   It raged hotly in Gaul, where the only fully-constituted church so far was at Lyons. Among the Christians there were many of Asiatic origin and these wrote a letter to their brethren in Asia Minor which has been preserved to us by the historian Eusebius.

i

The official persecution was preceded by a "popular movement", spontaneous, or, as we suggested, engineered. It began with a boycott: Christians could enter neither private houses, nor the baths, nor the markets. However, "hastening to go to Christ", they endured being shouted at, pelted with stones, and having their homes looted.   The governor himself was absent; civil and military officials initiated a preliminary interrogation.   All the old fables were repeated— Christians ate the flesh of children; they lived incestuously, and committed crimes "such", says the Letter, "that it would be wrong for us to mention or even think about them, and indeed we do not believe that anyone at any time did such things".   These accusations were mostly made by slaves, hoping thus themselves to escape suspicion.

Of all who were seized, only about ten apostatised.   All were, of course, tortured, especially the "deacon of Vienne"; Sanctus, a quite recent convert; Maturus; Attalus, a "pillar and foundation" of the Asiatic church of Pergamum, and a young slave-girl, Blandina.   "Through her, Christ showed that those who in the eyes of men appear cheap, ugly and contemptible, are treated by God with great honour because of their love for Him, which displays itself in power and not mere outward boasting. For while we were all of us trembling and her earthly mistress (who was herself contending along with the martyrs) was in torment lest Blandina, so frail in body, should not be strong enough to acknowledge her faith frankly, the child was filled with such strength that the torturers, who followed one another in relays and tormented her from morning to night with every kind of torture, acknowledged that they were beaten and had nothing more that they *could* do to her." Any one of their tortures, they said, ought to have killed her, and they could not understand how so pierced and tattered a body still could breathe. As for her, she seemed to draw fresh life by constantly repeating: "I am a Christian, and nothing wrong is done amongst us." Sanctus, too, would answer no enquiries about his family and birthplace, save: "I am a Christian." This stood, in his eyes, for everything. Even when they had placed red-hot sheets of bronze to the most sensitive parts of his flesh; even when his body was nothing but wounds and weals, and so contracted and shrivelled that it had lost the very form of humanity, "*Christ suffering in him* exhibited great glories . . . showing that nothing is frightening where the love of the Father is; nothing painful, where the glory of Christ remains." Even after further torturing, when they thought that "not even the touch of a hand" would be tolerable to his swollen and inflamed wounds, "his body stood itself upright" and new agonies seemed to serve merely for its healing. Meanwhile, the sufferers were kept in a horrible dungeon, their feet in stocks and "extended to the fifth hole"; this means that five pairs of holes were bored in a beam of wood; when the feet were drawn apart to be fastened to the outermost holes, the body was nearly wrenched asunder. As for the Bishop, Pothinus, who was over ninety, he was dragged both to and from the tribunal among yells and kicks and blows of the fist and struck by stones thrown by those at a distance. He was scourged, and after two days died in prison. It is interesting to learn that recent converts,

B

who had not yet learnt endurance, were apt to die thus in prison; and, that the mob jeered at apostates; still, for the most part, they recovered their faith and ended by suffering too.

About now, the governor returned; he had written to the Emperor, who replied that apostates should be let go; the obstinate must be executed. Maturus, Sanctus, Attalus and Blandina were therefore taken to the amphitheatre to be given, as a public spectacle, to the beasts. The first two were tortured again—the populace had gone mad with blood-lust; finally they were placed on the "iron chair" which was heated red-hot, and they died, says the Letter, in the reek of their own roasted flesh. Blandina was fastened to a stake as though to a cross; she prayed aloud, giving much courage to the others, "who beheld with their very eyes, by means of this their sister, Him who had been crucified for them". But the beasts would not touch the child; she was put back into prison. Attalus and a doctor called Alexander were then given to the beasts. On the last day of the show, Blandina was brought out together with a boy of fifteen called Ponticus. They had been forced, daily, to watch the tortures of the others. Ponticus died first, encouraged throughout by Blandina. She, last of all, was scourged, burned, tied up in a net and thrown to a savage bull to be tossed and finally, when no consciousness remained in her save of her faith and hope and charity, she was killed. By a refinement of cruelty, the bodies were left exposed for a week, nor were the Christians allowed to gather the relics. These were burnt, and the ashes cast into the river Rhône.

That amphitheatre has disappeared. But should you stand on the cliff of Fourvières, you can see beneath you the city of Lyons so often swathed in mist, and feel that the huddle of dim houses is not so very different from what you might have seen all those centuries ago; the two great rivers flow where they did, meet, and send their waters forward, turbid and blue, unmingling for quite some distance, as they must always have done; and far upon the horizon are the ever-lasting Alps. It was from here that the aged bishop, and the little slave-girl, and all those strong young priests and laymen, and the boy Ponticus, went triumphant into heaven.

ii

A breathing space. But in 202 the Emperor Septimius Severus issued an edict forbidding anyone to become a Christian, under pain of death. He wished to be the absolute autocrat, and saw that the Christians were becoming powerful, even educationally. At Carthage, today Tunis, that same year, a number of arrests were made, including a group of catechumens, a slave Revocatus and his fellow-slave Felicitas, Saturninus and Secundulus, and a noble lady, Vibia Perpetua. She was only twenty-two, and had a small son still at the breast. Her father was a pagan, her mother, a Christian, and one of her brothers was a catechumen. Soon, a certain Satyrus declared himself a Christian, and by a real miracle of Providence we possess what he and Perpetua wrote just before they suffered, and what was written directly afterwards.[1]

They were actually in the hands of the police-spies when Perpetua's father came to beg her—not precisely to renounce her interior faith, but to abstain from baptism; new baptisms were what the decree forbade. "I said, 'Do you see this?' (It was a little vase.) He said, 'Yes.' I said, 'Could I call it anything but what it is?' And he said, 'No.' 'Neither can I call myself anything but what I am, a Christian'." The poor old man, who loved her passionately, made as though he would tear out her very eyes, but turned helplessly away. They were rapidly baptized and put into a prison which, so crowded was it, was stiflingly hot, "and I was terrified—never yet had I known anything so dark . . ." But above all, the thought of her child tormented her. However, the "good

---

[1] The origin of this account, and even the orthodoxy of the Martyrs, have been disputed, but quite unconvincingly.

deacons, Tertius and Pomponius", bribed the gaolers to allow the prisoners some fresh air, and so Perpetua's mother managed to bring the child to her, and she nursed it, and afterwards was actually allowed to have it with her in the prison, "so that the prison instantly became for me a palace, so much so that I preferred to be there rather than anywhere else." Her brother asked her to obtain a word from God as to their fate. She prayed, and then dreamed that she saw a ladder beset with knives. Only one could climb it at a time. A dragon was at its foot. Saturninus climbed it first, and, turning, said, "Perpetua, I await you. But beware of the dragon." "I said, 'He will not hurt me, in the Name of Jesus Christ'." The dragon raised his head; she trod on him, and climbed. She stepped off into a wide pasture where a Shepherd sat surrounded by His flock. He too raised His head, and said, "Welcome, child!" Then he gave into her joined hands "milk and cheese that He had milked", and "all those standing around answered 'Amen'." At their voice, she woke up, and thereupon ceased to hope anything from this world.[1]

Her father, utterly distraught, visited her again; she remained firm, though heart-broken, for she loved him as he did her. Abruptly, while they were breakfasting, they were haled to the tribunal. Crowds had assembled and again her father came to implore her to recant. The Procurator Hilarianus had him driven off with whips. "It went to my heart as if I had myself been struck." Her father had taken away the baby; she asked Pomponius to beg for it back; her father refused; but, by a kindly grace, the child from then on ceased to need its mother's milk, and Perpetua, to suffer in her breast. And another strange incident and dream. While they were all praying, "my voice broke off suddenly and I called out, 'Dinocrates!' I was amazed that he had never come into my mind till that very moment, and I thought with sorrow of what had happened to him."

---

[1] The symbolism of these dreams, so strange to us, was quite characteristic. Here the Eucharist is certainly intended.

Dinocrates, her young brother, had died at seven, apparently unbaptized, of some facial ulcer that had made "his death a horror to everyone". Perpetua felt she must pray hard for him, and did so. That night she dreamed of him in a dark place, hungry and thirsty, in soiled clothes, and his face disfigured. He was trying to drink out of some vessel that stood too high for him. Perpetua prayed night and day that he might be "granted to her". Some days later, she again dreamed that she saw him, healthy and happy, brightly dressed, drinking a water that never ran dry from a golden cup; and when he had finished he "began to play about happily, as children do". So she knew he was set free.[1] On their last day of life, Perpetua dreamt again, and saw herself led by Pomponius to the amphitheatre; no beast attacked her, but a hideous Ethiopian appeared with whom she had to fight before a celestial umpire. On waking, she knew she would have to fight the devil, but that victory would be hers. Satyrus too had his dream. He and Perpetua were carried by angels to Paradise; there he recognized Jucundus, Saturninus and Artaxius, who had already been burnt alive, and asked "where the rest of them were?" Then they were admitted to the presence of God, joined in the eternal "Sanctus", and after a kiss of peace were told, "Now go and play!" "Then I said to Perpetua, 'You have what you want.' She answered, 'Thank God, I was always merry when in the flesh, and now shall be merrier still'." As they left, they saw the Bishop of Carthage and a priest Aspasius standing separate and sad; these men knelt down and begged the destined Martyrs to reconcile them. "But are you not our bishop and our priest, and do *you* kneel to *us*?" "Perpetua", says Satyrus naively, "talked Greek to them." The reconciliation took place. The dream ended. Meanwhile, in the frightful strain that they were enduring in that prison, Secundulus had died.

---

[1] In such a family, it must clearly have been intended that he should be baptized; so doubtless if he had not been baptized sacramentally, of which there is no hint, he was so "by desire".

As for Felicitas, she was in great distress, for it was forbidden to give a pregnant woman to the beast and she expected to have a child in another month. But she wanted to die with the others, and they too loved her. She prayed, and forthwith the pains of childbirth began. They were severe, and she cried aloud. A woman said, "What will it be, when you are thrown to the beasts?" She said, "Now it is I who suffer. But there, Another will be within me, who will suffer for me, and I for Him." So clearly did these Africans, like the Martyrs of Lyons, understand our incorporation into Christ. Her child was then born, a girl, whom a Christian woman adopted. The eve of the Emperor's birthday arrived. They took their last meal together, making it a love-feast. The gaoler, Pudens, overwhelmed by this spiritual grace and grandeur, accepted Christ. They entered the amphitheatre, when day broke, as though it were heaven— Perpetua moving slowly, like a bride; Felicitas, her sister in Christ, gay as ever. They protested that they came there freely, and freely gave their lives. The populace demanded that they should be scourged; this too they accepted in union with Christ's Passion. A leopard and a bear were set at Saturninus and Satyrus; they were lacerated but not killed. A maddened cow had been kept for the two women, who had first been stripped; but since their tormented, tender bodies made even that maniac crowd shudder, they were dressed in loose robes and brought back. Perpetua was the first to be thrown by the wild cow. She sat up and drew her torn dress about her. Even, she bound up her hair—it was not fit that a Martyr should die with hair dishevelled as though grieving. . . . She stood up, saw Felicitas lying on the ground and went and lifted her. They were taken from the amphitheatre. Rusticus, a catechumen, was by the door; Perpetua, coming to herself as from a dream, said, "When are we to be thrown to that—that—cow?" They had to show her her tattered dress to convince her it had already happened. She then begged her brother and Rusticus to stand firm.

Satyrus meanwhile had been talking to the officer Pudens. He had said that the bear would not harm him, but that he would die from a single snap of the leopard's jaws. And so it was. At the very end, the leopard attacked him. He was so streaming with blood that the crowd yelled at him as men did to those who had been bathing: *Salvum lotum! Salvum lotum!* "Had a good bath? Had a good bath?" And it was for him as a second baptism. Even so, he had not yet died. He said to Pudens, "Goodbye. Think of the Faith and of me, and may this not make you flinch but encourage you." He then asked for the ring on the officer's finger, dipped it in his blood, and gave it back. Then, almost unconscious, he was thrown with the others into the place where the death-stroke should be administered. Even there, they managed to lift themselves a little, and to give to each other the kiss of peace. Satyrus died first, and went to "await Perpetua". When the executioner came to her, he quailed, his hand hesitated and he struck awry. She herself directed him to her heart.

On the hill where the citadel of Carthage then stood, today a cathedral stands. And you can look down to Tunis, shimmering in strong sunlight, and note the lake which once was the circular docks of the great African city that had thought it could rival Rome. But not far down the hill of the citadel lies in wonderful preservation the amphitheatre where the Martyrs suffered, and you can kneel and pray on the very arena where so much blood was spilt. And perhaps it will be sadly that you look further towards the sky-line, across the waving palms and the square Tunisian minarets, and maybe listen first to the muezzin's call to prayer, and then to the Angelus.

The period of persecution is bright with the names of women-Saints—Dorothy, the first of the Saints whose legend is fragrant with the scent of miraculous flowers and fruits from Paradise; St. Lucia of Syracuse, brought into contact with the relics of her exemplar, St. Agatha of

Catania—no wonder their Sicily surrounds them with a loving worship, though for us they are little more than names still popular; St. Cecilia, whose legend inspired Maderna's exquisite statue and who has become patroness of so much lovely music; above all, the child St. Agnes, for whom, as for many another, Pope Damasus (366-384) wrote an inscription still to be seen where the stairs go down to her sepulchre at St. Agnes-Outside-the-Walls; over her too Constantine was to build a basilica; the shrine that you now see was built by Pope Honorius about 630. Lambs are blessed on her feast, and of their wool the palliums are made which the Pope grants to newly-consecrated archbishops.

We have twice used the word "legend". To speak of the "legend" of a Saint (or of any outstanding personage— there was a legend of Napoleon; of Nero) does not at all mean that the Saint did not exist in a firm historical sense. The combination of name, tomb and cultus suffices by itself to establish historicity. But the contemporary accounts of the pre-Constantinian Saints have nearly all perished, either as documents, considered unimportant, do, or, deliberately destroyed by persecuting officials. Then when freedom came, Christians, who found themselves surrounding a holy name and a tomb with homage, wished to know more about the Saint in question, and devout stories crystallized themselves around the name and the place, "legends" were composed, often modelled on favourite stories already in circulation; the fact that a Saint was executed involved his having been tortured, and the tale of the tortures would be embroidered by simple-minded writers for uncritical readers, without any sense of falsification. The legends are on the whole valuable as revealing the mentality of the age in which they were written (often about 600), but cannot be treated as solid historical information. Each must be examined on its own merits so that as balanced a conclusion as possible may be come to. In this little book, then, we are not using legends, or not consciously. A little legendary material may have gathered round St. Helena whom we mention next, and perhaps St. Geneviève; but we shall not be making use of it. We pass, then, out of the first great period of the Church's life—that of the persecutions—into the first period of her freedom.[1]

---

[1] There were women Saints belonging to the East, e.g., the Empress St. Pulcheria (d. 453): but not only the term "Saint" was so loosely used—the very "halo" was put around very unsaintly but imperially important heads—politics were so interwoven with eastern ecclesiasticism, and (my real reason), I know too little about "Byzantine" sanctity which would soon enough lead me into Mohammedan mysticism—in short everything conspires towards dissuading me from distracting my readers from looking towards an East which is all too unfamiliar to them, as to me. And, frankly, we might not derive much inspiration if we did.

CHAPTER II

THE EMPIRE BECOMES
CHRISTIAN

EVERYONE HAS heard of the "Conversion of Constantine".
This event did not mean that the whole Empire forthwith became Christian. In fact, many, perhaps most, of the
powerful ancient families remained "pagan" out of sheer
conservatism, though they had little more than an official
belief in the old gods of Rome. In any case, we can see how
weakened had culture grown, if we compare the clumsy
sculptures on Constantine's arch with those of two hundred
years earlier; if the older education survived at all, it was
more likely to be found in great country-houses far away in
Gaul; classical poetry was making hardly any echo, though
new verse-forms were beginning to exist, though (I hold)
by way of a *reversion* to the original Latin methods of *stress*
and assonance; the amazing anticipations of medieval sentiment and form—the Passion *Pange Lingua* and *Vexilla Regis*
would very soon be resounding, as they still do, in processions
and in churches.

Yet had Constantine remained in Rome, Christianity
would have run worse dangers than it did, for the Faith
would have appeared all too closely linked with the imperial
power, which had been gained by war and was maintained
by wealth. However, Constantine went east and founded
his new "Constantinople" on the site of the immemorial
Byzantium, and there he and his successors did indeed tend
to aspire to spiritual as well as temporal authority. Meanwhile, in Rome itself, there was no danger of a Caesar trying
to be also Pope, but an increasing number of Christian men

and women began to feel that the insane wealth that was
concentrated in the hands of a few—even if those hands
might be their own—and the worldly life of society were
wholly out of keeping with their Faith. There followed a
wave of renunciations, followed soon enough by a wave of
barbarian invasions, and the future of the west became once
more problematic.

Bithynia was a region at the western end of the south shore
of the Black Sea. From the mountains above it, you look
down on the Bosphorus; to north and east lie the open waters.
These snowy mountains contained mines of silver, deep-blue
lapis-lazuli and rose-white marble. Through forests full of
brigands you descended to the rich cities of plain and shore.
The population was quarrelsome, unable to unite, rapidly
changing its allegiance political and even religious; able,
even, at one time, to contain two rival Emperors. Christianity soon entered it; Bithynians are among those to whom
St. Peter addresses his First Letter. Indeed, by A.D. 111
Christians were so numerous that the governor, Pliny, wrote
to ask the Emperor Trajan how he should treat them; the
temples were almost empty; trade was suffering, for no one
bought meat for sacrifice. Trajan hated "secret societies"
as nests of intrigue; such Christians as were denounced and
refused to sacrifice to the gods were disloyalists and must
be severely punished. At the mildest, they were sent to work,
like St. John, in the mines.

Drepanum (now Yalova) was a small town by the sea,
visited for its hot springs. Here Helena was born about
A.D. 250, and became a servant in an inn.[1] Such places
were full of a riff-raff crowd—sailors, muleteers, actors,
vagabonds of all sorts. Antiquity has handed down accounts
of their filth; of the risk of robbery and even murder that
you ran there, and the cheap love to be bought there. A
bill, scratched on marble, shows at how low a price

---

[1] I know that her origin is disputed: she was called "stabularia"; but if
she worked, as I think she did, in such an inn, she quite probably acted as
"groom" as well as barmaid.

each item of degraded entertainment could be bought. Legislation constantly tried, and failed, to control these. Here, then, Helena spent her youth.

About A.D. 270 a soldier called Flavius Constantius and nicknamed Chlorus, Pale-Face, came to this inn and fell in love with the *stabularia*. A soldier was legally allowed only a sort of semi-marriage. He might live quite honourably with one partner, but he must dismiss her if he afterwards wished to marry. Anyhow, such an alliance was a godsend for Helena, and she followed him back to Europe, and they had a son, Constantine. The Pale-Face was a good soldier and won victories in Germany and in Britain; he was honourable; when in need he simply told his richer subjects about it; free gifts poured in which he transmitted to the treasury. In 303 persecution broke out; he applied its edicts mildly; in fact, having told his staff to apostatize, he retained those, precisely, who refused, for, said he, how could a *man* expect fidelity from one who had betrayed his god? He was then governor in northern France; he built fine public monuments, encouraged education and put prisoners of war to open up waste areas.

Already in 286 the Emperor Diocletian had seen that the enormous edifice of Empire was too much for one man. He elected a colleague, Maximian Hercules, as co-Augustus. This proved inadequate. In 293, the two Augusti associated to themselves two "Caesars", Galerius, and Constantius the Pale-Face who had to rule Spain, Gaul and Britain. Marriage was to tie this group more closely together. Constantius was ordered to marry Maximian's daughter Theodora; Helena was sent away. For thirteen years the proud hot-blooded Asiatic lived no one knows where. As for her son Constantine, she saw him no more. He was a dangerous young prince and though only about fifteen might become a claimant. . . . He lived in silken imprisonment and he too took a partner, Minervina, and for their son Crispus, Helena conceived an obstinate, jealous love.

Diocletian grew old, abdicated along with Maximian,

went to grow cabbages in his palace on the Adriatic,[1] and the two Caesars automatically ascended to the rank of Augusti. Galerius had always hated Constantius and his son, and got Diocletian to nominate for Caesars two debauchees. But Constantius kept asking for Constantine. Galerius said he might leave next day. Too shrewd to wait for that, the young man escaped during the night, taking the best horses and ham-stringing the rest. On July 25, 306, he was at his father's deathbed at York. The troops instantly proclaimed him Augustus. Impossible to relate here the confusion that followed. Very soon six men were calling themselves Emperor; one of them, Maxentius, son of Maximian, gave his daughter Fausta to Constantine as wife, thus eliminating Minervina and Crispus, for whom Helena, seeing her own history repeated, developed an even fiercer affection.

Plot followed plot; Maxentius, who had become a mere sexual maniac, fixed himself in Rome, upset Constantine's statues, and got himself hated by even that degraded population. Constantine decided to march against him. But to march on Rome still seemed sacrilegious. The gods were consulted. Their answer was ambiguous. Constantine dreamt that he would conquer if he took the cross of the Christian God for standard. Next day, metal-workers fixed the monogram of Christ to a pole whence a purple strip bearing the portrait of the Emperor hung from a little transverse bar not too unlike a cross. In October, 312, Constantine was at the Milvian Bridge outside of Rome. Maxentius, on the 28th, seventh anniversary of his succession, was at the circus. The disgusted population forced him out against Constantine. The clash came; the bridge broke; Maxentius was drowned. Constantine entered Rome, Christ's name upon his standard.

This section is not about Constantine nor will I discuss his conversion. Hitherto he had presumably been as vaguely

---

[1] The town Split, once Spalato, gets its little name from the expression "eis to palation"—"to the Palace". It was here that the Adam brothers learnt the best of their art. Mass is now offered over the tomb of the last great persecutor.

tolerant as his father. It was customary to invoke one god if another remained deaf; whatever spiritual experience he now had—the records are extremely confused—he became quite sure that the Christian God had given him victory. He remained a soldier, not a theologian, and was not baptized till the very end of his life and then by a heterodox bishop. But he summoned his relatives to Rome; Helena, then about sixty-five, came too. He urged her to embrace the Faith, which she did, says her historian, with such fervour that you would think our Lord Himself had taught her. In due course she was proclaimed "Augusta", the loftiest title in the world —indeed, unique; for though by now there were again only two Augusti, there *were* two, and she stood alone. So far had she travelled. Her coins were struck, and went round the world. She must have been a strong woman; her neck by now was wrinkled, but vigorous; she seems to have liked heavy ropes of pearls; on the other hand, she refused to alter her old-fashioned style of head-dress. How did she, who had learnt no court-elegances, take her place among the patrician millionairesses of Rome? I imagine that the tremendous self-discipline to which she had submitted for so long, her Asiatic blood, enabled her to sweep through obstacles, alert to intrigues, and never showing if sneers could hurt her or flattery insult her. But far worse suffering awaited her.

Constantine and his surviving colleague, Licinius, hated one another. Licinius started an anti-Christian movement in the east. Constantine marched against him; Crispus annihilated his fleet; Licinius and his son were liquidated and Constantine became sole master of the world. But such victories bring no peace. Fausta was madly jealous of Crispus. Crispus, immensely popular, handsome, brilliant captain by land and sea, inexpressibly dear to Helena, stood on the one side; on the other, Fausta, far more elegant than the Augusta, with her five children of whom the eldest was not more than ten, foresaw that Crispus would certainly be heir. Helena saw no less clearly that Fausta was determined to get rid of him. In 326, Constantine celebrated his twenty years of emperorship by a tour ending up at Rome. His fantastic procession—to say nothing of his yellow hair—must have made him look both barbaric and oriental to the populace, who cheered but faintly. Afterwards the Romans had a procession (pagan of course) of their own. He would not walk in it, but stood on the Palatine and mocked. The people were furious. It was easy for Fausta to persuade the suspicious man that Crispus, the popular idol, had provoked these incidents and was aiming at the Empire. Constantine went mad. In but a day or two news came that Crispus had been arrested, and then killed without trial—how, no one ever knew. Helena, who was in the east, came back at full speed and hurled at her son the proofs of his criminal credulity. His brain rocked; in a new access of ferocity he had Fausta suffocated in her bath. Possibly this new "age of Nero", as it was called, was what led Helena definitely into paths of holiness.

Even in her grandest days, she would go to Mass, indistinguishable in sombre dress from the faithful among whom she stood. She invited maidens vowed to God to dine in her palace and waited on them, habited as a slave. True, she could alter neither laws nor hearts, nor check the concentration of wealth in the hands of a few, nor do more than give largesse to the destitute, whose numbers ever grew. Still, she devoted herself to the alleviation of the prisoners who worked in the frightful mines of the time, and obtained that they should not be caged in airless underground dungeons nor wear fetters that injured them. But her career was crowned by her official voyage to Palestine.

The condition of the Holy Places there had become pitiable. A "colony" had been built over Jerusalem; a vast temple-demesne dedicated to Venus held somewhere beneath it Calvary and the Holy Sepulchre; the traditional cave at Bethlehem had vanished beneath a territory sacred to Adonis. Constantine, after the Council of Nicea, wrote to Jerusalem that this must be rectified and by 326 the Holy Sepulchre had been unearthed. The Emperor congratulated the bishop and gave detailed orders about the basilica to be built there, which must have been well in hand when Helena announced that she would go to Palestine in person, though she was nearing eighty. She represented not only Constantine but the whole Christian empire and the treasury had always been at her disposal. Her welcome was everywhere rapturous. In Palestine she gave orders and funds for the building of a basilica at Bethlehem and another on Olivet on the site where our Lord traditionally instructed His disciples.[1] The aged Empress then returned, exhausted; she fell sick and made her will, dividing her wealth between her son and her grandchildren, thereby showing that she had forgiven Fausta. Her life rapidly ebbed away, and in 327 or 328 she died, after so stormy a life, in peace.

Do not be surprised to find in a Saint of 1,600 years ago, and in St. Helena in particular, qualities so unlike what we expect in our time. One could not expect an Asiatic woman to be like even an Italian of that period; nor one who had been transported from scenes of squalid vice into the rough life of semi-barbarian military camps, to be like a cloistered nun; nor that one who abruptly exchanged long years of soul-searing exile for the glories of an Augusta and even then lived in a world of murder mixed with mysticism, should develop a mild and moderate culture. We can rightly put her at the head of that long line of Queens who, each in her own way, held the Cross high before the eyes of their world—and in Helena's time, that "world" was co-extensive with all that was thought of as "civilized". Human passions do not change essentially; and if in our own time we have seen them unchained and ministering to more than we had dreamed possible of hate, cruelty and lust, we must intensify them to

---

[1] The actual church at Bethlehem is an enlargement, parts of which may date from the sixth century. The church on Olivet was destroyed by the Persian Chosroes in the sixth century, restored under Charlemagne and again by the Crusaders, but finally ruined by Saladin. Whenever the Cross was found, it is natural, perhaps, that its discovery should have been connected with Helena's visit: but to my mind there is no evidence for it having been so.

the uttermost if we are to begin to understand the world in which Helena lived. At any rate, thenceforward, the Constantinian basilicas arose, sheathed in splendour, and the Cross was uplifted everywhere in Rome.

*   *   *   *

But now that it had become positively fashionable to be Christian, the quality of Christianity deteriorated. When a man had to give up all for Christ, what must that quality not have been?   But now the Christian name became remunerative, and only a few great patricians held firm, others professed the faith out of opportunism. But the very framework of society made it almost impossible for a whole-hearted Christian to live within it, and indeed there were those who escaped altogether from Italy and went to live in, for example, Egypt, where the monasticism inaugurated by St. Antony was thriving (see *What are Saints?*, Chapter 2). Such, for example, was Antonia Melania, widow of Valerius Maximus, who went to Egypt in A.D. 372, and then to Palestine, to become a nun.   On the Coelian Hill, near the "English Clinic" of today, the Valerian family had a palace.   This family was of incredible antiquity and splendour. Antonia Melania, on her departure, entrusted her son Valerius Publicola, aged six, to a tutor.   He grew up, married, and had one daughter, Melania. She, then, was sole heiress of her father, grandfather and great-grandfather; not the most fantastic fortune of modern times approaches hers. She possessed enormous estates in Italy, Sicily, Gaul, Spain, Britain, Africa, Numidia, Morocco and still further off. Such estates were so large that one of them, near Tagaste, had its own bishop—two in fact; one was a heretic; their produce was not only agricultural, but mineral and industrial.   The palace on the Coelian doubtless contained (much smaller ones did) theatres, temples, immense baths and so forth.   Melania controlled whole societies, nay, populations.

When she was thirteen they married her to the highly eligible Pinianus who was seventeen. She instantly suggested that the marriage should be purely nominal; if he did not like the idea, he could have all her fortune—even the virtuous, if fantastically rich, are apt to judge everyone by financial standards. Pinianus said they must first have two sons. They had a daughter, whom they vowed to virginity; then a son, but he lived only one day and Melania seemed dying too. She made her cure conditional on a life of abstinence; Pinianus agreed, and she recovered. (Note that his ideas were altogether hers; picture no cheated and half-frenzied husband!) Melania's father died, and she and Pinianus gave up their fine clothes and simplified their life so far as possible. Not only the example of her grandmother could inspire her, but a whole "set" of great Roman ladies were "turning ascetic". All Rome was taking sides about this, some, for frivolous reasons: "These women are all mad"; others, more seriously: "They ruin their health by fasting, they fail in their duty of bringing up sons for Rome"; others, quite theologically: "The whole thing smacks of Manichaeism, they treat material things, marriage included, as *bad*."

Anyhow, the struggle to get rid of property began. Melania had an *income*, so far as I can see, of about five million pounds a year, and the immense amount of slave-labour cost almost nothing. The slaves were a frightful problem; Melania's were treated very well, at least where she could keep some sort of an eye on them, in Rome, but abroad it was *impossible* to do otherwise than devolve your responsibilities upon an army of agents and a hierarchy of middle-men, not notorious for justice, not to mention leniency. Well, she would free at any rate her Roman slaves. But the slaves refused point-blank to *be* freed. "They *dared*", exclaimed Melania in all simplicity, "to disobey us!" Who knows how, deprived—thousands at a time—of any work, they would so much as live? They *liked* that family, and transferred themselves *en bloc* to Pinianus's brother. A score of lawsuits were instantly started by relatives arguing that they had a right (and legally they had) to a share in the property. Melania, armed with rich presents, called on Serena, mother-in-law of the Emperor. Overawed by the visit of so very great a lady, Serena obtained a rescript ordering governors throughout the empire to sell the properties in question and to produce the money. But the law about selling property was terribly complicated, especially if you belonged to a senatorial family. The Queen (as she liked to be called) rather turned the tables on Melania and Pinianus, because *after* the interview they brought out their presents and the Queen laughed, saying that they had just got the Emperor to decree that anyone who accepted any of their property was a church-robber, so how could *she* accept anything? And she ordered that no palace official should be given so much as one gold piece as a tip. . . . This was when Melania offered her palace to the Queen, who could not afford it, nor could anyone else. . . . It took fourteen years to sell one estate!

Pinianus was now twenty-four, Melania twenty. Their palace was not only visited by a flood of bishops, priests and laity from overseas, demanding alms, but became a home for innumerable sick, prisoners and exiles whom they personally sought out; and if Melania herself received gifts, she made very sure that the money should be spent exactly as the donor wished. But their difficulties were partly solved when the Visigoths under Alaric invaded Italy in 408. The Emperor fled; Serena was strangled; the pagan prefect of Rome demanded that the fortune being dissipated should be simply seized for the public benefit—but the public itself stoned him . . . and meanwhile Pinianus and Melania had gone to Sicily; in 410 Rome was taken, and the embarrassing palace on the Coelian had been burnt down. But with Alaric's fleet off Messina, Sicily itself was too dangerous; with the aged priest Rufinus they crossed to their African estate at Tagaste. They so flooded this town with benefits that the neighbouring town of Hippo, where St. Augustine was bishop, became jealous. The citizens said Augustine was slow about asking for largesse; they encountered the young couple and the Bishop of Tagaste at Mass in a Hippo church, created a riot, and demanded that Pinianus should be ordained priest on the spot. The bishop's life seemed in danger should he refuse. Augustine obtained a compromise: Pinianus should live for a while in Hippo, but as a layman. But by 417 most of the estates had been sold; Pinianus and Melania were now truly poor, and the populace ceased to be interested in them. (It is rather comforting to know that her denudation sometimes irked Melania; she wondered whether the kingdom of God were worth it. . . .) They therefore went off to Palestine and then Egypt where they visited innumerable anchorets. Finally they returned to Jerusalem, where Melania established herself as a recluse till 431, when her mother (who shared her daughter's ideals) died and was buried on Mount Olivet. Every part of the narrative is full of vivid little incidents. Thus Melania invaded the cell of Abbot Hephaestion and wanted to give him some money. He refused. She hid it in his salt-cellar when he wasn't looking. He found it, ran after her and caught her up when she had crossed a river. "What am I to do with this?" "Give it to the poor!" But there weren't any—the "poor" didn't patronize the desert. So he threw it into the water.

Melania's whole manner of life now changed. She decided to found a monastery and despatched Pinianus to find vocations, which he did in the most improbable places. Hardly was this done, and the Roman rite established with a much gentler rule of life than the Egyptian one or Melania's own, than Pinianus died. He was buried near Melania's mother and she herself lived in a little room near the tomb for four years. She then founded a monastery for men, who should care for the church of the Ascension and continually sing Office for her mother and Pinianus. And a curious interlude. She had an uncle, Volusianus, a pagan, who wrote to her from Constantinople that he was engaged in negotiating the marriage of Valentinian III, Emperor of the West, with Eudoxia, daughter of Theodore II and Eudokia. Since

he had never written to her before, she must have seen some
subtle hint in this, and left at once for Constantinople where
she made the greatest friends with the imperial family. She
then undertook a brisk campaign against the Nestorian
heresy, fell desperately ill, was told that Volusianus was
dying but had been baptized; revived; was carried to his
house, caused him to be given Holy Communion three times
during the night, and assisted him to die, January 6, 437.
"How dear to God", said the Saint, "must be a soul, since
He brought my uncle all the way from Rome and me from
Jerusalem, that we should meet here and he be saved, though
all his life long he never knew Him!" Then she returned
to Jerusalem through Asiatic snow-storms so fierce "that we
saw nothing of the landscape", received next year the
Empress Eudoxia who was fulfilling her promise of visiting
the Holy Places, and saw her off afterwards at Caesarea.
This was too much for her, and in Advent, 438, she felt she
was going to die.

  She went to Bethlehem for her last Christmas and spent
it with her cousin Paula. She returned, and kept the feast of
St. Stephen with the Sisters, reading aloud the account of his
martyrdom in the Acts. They begged her to bless them, that
they might hear her thus read to them on another feast.
She said God would bless them but that they would no more
hear her read. On December 31 she had Mass offered by the
priest Gerontius in the men's monastery, following it from a
little room hard by, and begging him to read louder (but he
was crying) that she might hear. Then she received Communion. Juvenal, Bishop of Jerusalem, arrived and she
entrusted Gerontius and the monastery to him and again
received Communion. Then a great concourse of monks,
nuns and layfolk filed past her. Paula was there, weeping;
Melania consoled her, and to Gerontius in his turn she
entrusted the monastery. Then she said she felt tired and
asked them to pray. After a while, they thought she had
died and were for preparing her for burial. "Not yet", she
said, and agreed to give them a sign. The bishop said: "You

go gladly to the Lord; the angels rejoice, but we, we weep, for all the good you have done to our souls." "As God willed", she said, "so it has befallen." She then received Communion for the third time, kissed the bishop's hand, and died.

*   *   *   *

Now more briefly about the group in which Melania had for a time found herself. Marcella was a wealthy patrician with a palace on the Aventine. As a child she had seen St. Athanasius, a refugee there. She was enthralled by the stories of the Egyptian ascetics and on leaving, Athanasius gave her his Life of St. Anthony (see *What are Saints?*) which so profoundly impressed even the West. She married to please her mother, but in seven months was a widow and nothing would make her marry again. She surrounded herself with other young women—her ward, Principia; Marcellina, sister of St. Ambrose; Fabiola, at first a very worldly young lady who deserted her ill-behaved husband and married someone else—after the death of this new partner she did public penance and built a hospital where she nursed, and even carried the most revoltingly sick men to it; Asella, and Lea whose penances were exceptionally severe, though she became a sort of mother to the whole group; Paula, and others. The house became a mixture of monastery and school, for these ladies devoted themselves to a really deep study of the Scriptures. Paula was born on May 5, 347, and had an almost more tremendous ancestry than even those others, since without counting the gods and heroes who began her race, she undoubtedly united in herself the blood of the Cornelii, the Aemilii, the Scipios and the Gracchi—the very greatest names in Roman history. She married Toxotius and had a son also so called, and four daughters, Blaesilla, Paulina, Eustochium and Rufina. Up to her widowhood she had thoroughly enjoyed her wealth and position. St. Jerome is never tired of telling how startling were her rouge, her powder and her blackened eyelids, and

Blaesilla at any rate followed in her mother's elegant footsteps.

Indeed the arrival of St. Jerome (382) in Rome was of extreme importance for these ladies. Readers who may be unacquainted with this strange man must not base any rapid conclusion about him on what we now write; that would be unkind and unfair. Marcella knew of him as erudite in the Scriptures and insisted that he should teach her and her circle Hebrew and exegesis. As professor, the still-young but fierce Dalmatian will have helped them much; as spiritual "director", less. Marcella herself had to ask him to moderate his sarcasms. Blaesilla was left a widow very young; she threw herself so vehemently into the ascetic life that in 384 she died. Paula went almost off her head with grief and fainted at her daughter's grave; Jerome rebuked her bitterly; *he* would glorify Blaesilla by writing about her. Paula's second daughter, Paulina, married Pammachius, a school-friend of Jerome's; but her children were still-born; she too died; Pammachius became a monk and remained on good terms with Jerome, who, however, had written so violently against the ladies and indeed the clergy of Rome and in other ways so shocked "society" that when Pope Damasus, his protector, died, he went off to Palestine to live in peace. He could not but be a rhetorician; but our taste has completely changed, and we dislike his rancorous writings especially when they are personal. Thus when Melania too went to Palestine and founded houses which could not but be, in a sense, rivals to his and Paula's at Bethlehem, and did not want to submit to his direction, he poured forth a flood of indignation upon her. She may have been, to the end, somewhat autocratic, but her life was as pure and austere as any that Jerome could demand from his own penitents. Marcella, a woman of much good sense and poise, refused to go to Palestine at all, but remained with friends, studying the Scriptures, till in 410 she was brutally beaten by the Goths and died. I think we may say that Jerome was by nature incredibly hyper-sensitive and apt to retaliate ferociously when his suspicions were aroused; that he consistently tried to conquer this; that his stay among these very well-bred, cultured, though independent ladies did something to mellow him—he certainly became much more "understanding" and kindly—so that it would be as ungenerous not to see the real "stuff" of sanctity that was in him, as dishonest to disguise his manifest defects. His rhetoric is so flamboyant as to do a disservice not only to himself but to those of whom he writes; one cannot ever be sure that he reports a conversation correctly—thus I cannot believe that even a Paula illustrated every single sentence she wrote with an appropriate quotation from the Bible. But we *can* be sure that at times he found these ladies—if I dare so put it—rather a handful. They were terribly exacting; their demand for explanations, even for whole treatises, was relentless; they wanted light on everything—the lists of names in the Book of Numbers; the mystical meaning of Hebrew letters; he constantly had to say that he did not know; his correspondence was colossal and he did nearly all of it by dictation to shorthand writers, and did not relish having to sit up all night to hunt for replies to his insatiable scholars.

But we have anticipated. Jerome sailed in August, 385. Soon, Paula, Eustochium and others—"they are mine, in Christ", said Jerome, "whether the world likes it or not"— joined him at Antioch and began that astounding tour of Palestine during which they seem to have visited practically all the places mentioned in the Old Testament—Paula would no more afford a litter and rode on a mule, and fasted all the time. They went on into Egypt where innumerable hermits flocked to see her; she even thought of settling there. However, she established herself at Bethlehem and in three years built a monastery for men, another for women (governed respectively by Jerome and herself) and a hostel for pilgrims. "Mary and Joseph were no more to lack a shelter." We may be surprised that the nuns were divided into three groups according to social status; all had to know the Psalms by heart and each Sister had to sing a whole

Psalm (Rome had not yet copied St. Ambrose's system at Milan where they sang "verse and verse about"). Study of the Scriptures was intense; each took her turn, too, at the roughest work. They heard that the Huns were about to invade Syria and loot Jerusalem; the two communities packed, embarked, but did not sail—the news was false. Fabiola, however, who had thought of staying in Bethlehem, found Jerome involved in such quarrels even with the Bishop of Jerusalem, and so aloof from Melania, that she sailed for Rome to help Pammachius who had opened an enormous hospital at Ostia. Paula herself, harassed by these controversies, kept her heart high, and when Jerome, despondent, talked of leaving Bethlehem, it was she who kept him there.

But in 404 she fell sick; she confided her monasteries to Eustochium and the poor girl went to and fro between her mother's bed and the Cave of the Nativity, asking that if Paula must die, she might die too. Jerome now discovered how much he had depended on Paula. He kept speaking to her; but she, whispering verses from the Psalms, now spoke only to God. The whole of that world knew that she was dying; the Bishop of Jerusalem and an endless procession of monks, nuns and laity filed silently past her. Jerome again asked if she were suffering. She replied, this time in Greek, that all was well and at peace. Her funeral was like a triumphal parade; for three days the Psalms were sung; a tomb was prepared close to the holy Cave. Eustochium's work was enormous; she had not Paula's fabulous prestige; she had not managed a vast Roman household; her temperament was more childlike; there was no more money to be distributed; it had to be begged. Anyhow, the deathblow seemed given to the old Roman world when the Eternal City belied its ancient title by becoming the prey of Alaric in 410.

But a still worse trial had to be endured. The Pelagian heresy invaded Palestine; Jerome was one of its fiercest opponents. Pelagian monks, under arms, attacked the monasteries; there was just time to fly to a tower before all was in flames. This was in 416. Two years later, Eustochium died suddenly, and Jerome in 419; and he, who had composed the memoirs of so many of his friends, found none to write his own.

I would emphasize four points. First, all these ladies had studied the Scriptures intensely, indeed scientifically, before ever St. Jerome arrived. Not many, today, would learn Hebrew just to get the "feel" of the Psalms more truthfully. Nor do we now hear the ploughman singing snatches of Psalms behind his oxen, nor servants humming them as they go about the house. The religious life of that "community" was solidly nourished by the Word of God and ours is the flimsier in proportion as we have deserted it. Second, these ladies encouraged one another. They did not wait till vast numbers of adherents were secured, though they formed a tiny percentage of the Roman population; that did not dishearten them. Third, they did not wait till disaster had forced the "simple life" upon them. They may have exaggerated their self-stripping; but they saw that luxury is always out of place in a Christian, especially when it co-exists with appalling destitution, and still more when it has been shared in and even led by the higher clergy.[1] And fourthly, I do not see how the society of that period *could* have been cured from within. To much, as we have seen, the deathblow was by barbarian rape, fire and massacre; in the provinces, the pagan culture sought to survive behind the façades of great houses where noble, traditional-minded families lived a few more years of dignity; in the *pagi*, remote villages untouched any more by civilization, the ancient cults survived in the forms of an ever more degraded "paganism"; it looked as if every lamp were going out save the little flames that flickered indomitably around the tombs of Martyrs, though new ones were being lit in the great monastic churches and the fortress-like cathedrals.

[1] See the Instructions given by Pope Hadrian VI to his nuncio Chieregati in 1522, and by Cardinal Pole to the Legates at the Council of Trent in 1546. Had the elementary virtues of Christian simplicity and self-denial been consistently practised, different indeed would be the Church's state today.

CHAPTER III

THE CHURCH LOOKS WEST AND NORTH

W HEN ROME fell it seemed to St. Augustine that the end of the world must have come. The end of a civilization —one might well have thought so. The East was paralyzed by the heavy hand of the Emperor until it woke into panic because of the Persian peril; and after no long time was to succumb for the most part to Islam. Meanwhile the Emperors in the East exercised an ever weaker control through their representatives in the West, and devastated Italy and ruined Rome may have seemed to them not worth attending to. As for lands further west, half of them had been overrun by heretic barbarians; the only civilizing forces were the cathedrals and the monasteries; the crisis came when the invading Franks hesitated between their ancestral paganism and Christianity. And if they chose the latter, would they be Catholic, or Arian? Had Clovis not become a Catholic, it is hard to imagine what would have become of that land which had been Gaul and was not yet France. Nor yet what Britain would have become. As it was, Clovis and his Franks did become Catholics, and Gregory I, most justly called "The Great", had ample reason for all-but abandoning any hope from the dying East, and courageously turning to the West and North.

The "barbarians" who broke up the framework of the Roman Empire were not savages (though the Huns and the Vandals left nothing but ruins behind them); they had strong traditions and customs, even if their "natural virtues" could not hold good against Roman luxury which persisted in decadence; and most of them were infected by heresies imported from the East. The Franks, however, were pagans. Their temperament was violent and their passions uncontrolled; they could pass in a moment from religious emotion to cruelty and lust; they had a sly cunning and could interminably pursue an intrigue, and yet behave like children and fall victims to every superstition. They were restless and greedy and yet experienced the charm of poetry and what later was to be called "romance".

Follow the Seine from Paris seaward, and you soon reach Nanterre, where a settlement was known even in the fourth century. Here lived Severus and Gerontia, simple folk, with one daughter, born at latest in 423; her godmother, whose home was in Lutetia (simplest to say "Paris"), called the child Geneviève.

In 429 St. Germanus, Bishop of Auxerre, and St. Lupus, Bishop of Troyes, were sent by the Pope to combat the Pelagian heresy in Britain. ("Pelagianism" was part of a reaction against asceticism, and taught that the human will sufficed to save the soul without need of supernatural grace.) Germanus, passing through Nanterre, noticed Geneviève and asked her if she would consecrate her life to God. He picked up a coin with Constantine's cross upon it and hung it round her neck. Girls who thus dedicated their lives first spent some years in virtuous probation and then received the "veil", a sort of band wound round the head. In the East, the age for this was fixed at twenty-five; but Geneviève apparently received her veil at about fifteen. Aptness took precedence over rules.

Her parents died, and she went to live with her godmother in Paris which was almost wholly on the island where Notre Dame now is; there was already a church there, dedicated to our Lady, but also the cathedral, dedicated to St. Stephen. The city was not insignificant. The boatmen, who took people to and from the island, formed a corporation; south of the city, on the left bank, was a vast palace built by Constantius Chlorus (p. 14) destined to be lived in by a succession of emperors and kings. A few ruins of the camp,

where the Luxemburg Gardens now are, still (I think)
survive. Geneviève lived a life of such prayer and penance
as to become suspected even more than venerated; Germanus,
during a second visit to Britain, corrected this; in 448, when
he was dying, he sent her a message from Ravenna by his
deacon Sedulius.

But the Huns crossed the Rhine and in 451 proposed to
wrest the rich south of Gaul from the Visigoths. Paris
prepared a wholesale evacuation lest the savage Attila should
divert his route thither. Geneviève at first persuaded the men
to stay; but, abruptly changed in mood, they decided she was
mad and prepared to stone her. Just then, Sedulius arrived
and the name of Germanus for a second time rescued her.
Thus began the belief that St. Geneviève protects Paris.
Attila in fact was unable to take Orleans owing to its bishop
St. Agnanus, or Troyes, where he quailed before the
majestic presence of St. Lupus, just as he was to do when
confronted by St. Leo at Rome. Attila, the "Scourge of
God", died in 453, having left nothing but a surname for
those who leave only destruction in their wake. But it is
good to know that the name of Geneviève became familiar
to St. Simeon Stylites in Syria; these solitaries were in touch
with soldiers, traders, politicians, even from distant lands
like Britain, and Simeon can hardly have failed to know the
famous St. Germanus who will have told him about
Geneviève. Meanwhile, it is interesting that the heretics
created nothing.

In 486 the Frankish king Clovis attacked and killed
Syagrius who still represented at Soissons the relics of
Roman authority. Thus ended Roman rule in Gaul. It
looked as though Clovis prepared to starve Paris out.
Geneviève is said to have become practically captain of
eleven barges which slipped out at night, collected grain in
the Champagne, and saved the situation. But soon enough
Clovis was master of the land from Rhine to Loire. When he
entered Burgundy, it was evident that he must make some
arrangement with the Visigoths, and he married the elder

daughter of Chilperic, established at Lyons, Clotilde, who
had been brought up a Christian. She did all she could to
convert him; but if he became a Christian at all, he would
probably become an Arian as two of his sisters had done, if
only to show that he was a good anti-Roman.

By far the most powerful spiritual influence in the land was
now St. Remigius (Rémi), Bishop of Rheims. He recognized
that the Franks had come to stay, and acknowledged Clovis
as king. Clovis too was shrewd enough to see that if he had
the bishops on his side he would have all the Gallo-Roman
population as well. And so impressionable a soul was overwhelmed when it encountered the "Christian character",
especially in its most august development, as in Rémi. So
relations between himself, Rémi and Clotilde were continuous and he allowed his first-born son to be baptized.
But the boy died; the barbarian brain reeled; Clovis regarded
this as a direct vengeance from the gods. A second son was
born, Clodomir; he too fell sick. Was Wotan again in-
furiated? Clotilde and Rémi prayed; the boy recovered.
But the matter was settled by the Alamans, from over-Rhine.
The whole future of "France" depended on which side won.
The Alamans attacked "with their usual ferocity", when
Clovis remembered the god of his wife and promised to be
baptized should he win. He did, and began his catechism.
But what of his people? his special bodyguard? He explained
his intentions; they decided to follow him. Instruction was
given throughout the kingdom. On Christmas Day, 496,
Rheims was so splendidly decorated that Clovis, marching
through it at the head of three thousand Franks, asked if this
were Paradise. "No", said Rémi, "but the first steps towards
it. Adore what thou didst burn; burn what thou didst adore."
Geneviève, invisible in her cell, had fulfilled her destiny; the
Queen retired into the shadows till tragedy summoned her
forth again.

Clovis, alternately ferocious and devout, resolved to build
a basilica near the palace in honour of St. Peter and St. Paul.
Its length should be the distance he could throw his axe, as in

old days all territory struck by Thor's lightning hammer belonged to him. But in 511 he died, aged forty-five, and was buried in the crypt of the unfinished church in a huge stone coffin covered with crosses. And only a few weeks later Geneviève too died and was buried in the same place, having been the living link between the old Celtic-Roman Gaul and the Frankish realm that grew to be "France". The memory of Clovis and the Apostles faded; the church became the shrine of the princess and the peasant. About 630 St. Eloi, goldsmith before he became bishop, made a sheath of gold for Geneviève's relics as he had for St. Martin's. In 857 the Normans burnt the often-restored church; Pope Eugenius put as its guardians monks from the abbey of St. Victor below the hill. The definite restoration was due to Stephen of Tournai (1176-1191), close friend of St. Thomas of Canterbury. A whole town grew up around the basilica, including what became the Paris university. The old cathedral was demolished to make room for Notre Dame (begun in 1194); to preserve the name and the relics, St-Etienne-du-Mont was built and replaced in 1520 by the church actually there. Its nave is curiously out of line because otherwise it would almost have abutted on the basilica. Alas, in 1741 Louis XV came to thank St. Geneviève for a cure; the Canons said the basilica was inadequate; not only a new site was chosen but the old building was practically destroyed. A classical temple with a dome was built instead. Hardly was it finished when the Revolution called it the Pantheon; the remains of Voltaire, Rousseau, Robespierre, Marat and afterwards Zola were placed there. Yet devotion to the Saint seemed ineradicable. When the Bastille was taken, people trooped there to thank her. Even in 1790 the Commune went there officially for Mass. But in 1792 the shrine was removed to St-Etienne—rightly; Geneviève cannot have felt at home among those others. . . . But the Revolution, by now atheist, seized and despoiled the shrine, burnt the relics and threw the ashes into the Seine. Still, in 1803 the curé of St-Etienne found the slab on which the shrine had anciently reposed and this, with a few fragments, has reached us. But only just. In 1807, by another act of insensate barbarity, the remaining ruins of the basilica were destroyed; a lonely tower, Romanesque and Gothic, survives. In 1821 Mass was again offered there; in 1830 the church was again desecrated; in 1852 again re-sanctified; but in 1885 it was once more emptied of all that gave it a meaning and became the frigid shell in which tourists wander, unconscious of souls, even of lost ones.

As for Clotilde, she retained her enormous wealth but could no more control her children. A pernicious law ruled that a kingdom must be divided between the dead king's male heirs; so her sons became boy-kings (the eldest may have been seventeen) holding mock-courts at Paris, Rheims, Soissons and Orleans. Then the Visigoth Amalaric, a fanatic Arian, demanded the Queen's only daughter, also Clotilde, in marriage. Since he and Clovis had been enemies, the girl might be a pledge of peace and was handed over. The Queen had retired to St. Martin's at Tours and was literally alone. Wars soon broke out among the royal kinsfolk. In a battle with a Burgundian cousin of hers, her eldest son Clodomir was killed, and his head, its yellow hair clotted with blood, paraded on a pike. All that she could do was to shelter his three little sons. But her love for them was their doom. What could her next sons think but that she would educate them to be their father's heirs? Evidently they must perish. They got hold of the children and sent shears and a sword to their grandmother. "Shall they be shorn or slain?" Now to be "shorn" meant to become a monk and renounce all claim to thrones. An old fire blazed up in her. "Better dead than shorn!" she cried. The children ran about trying to escape, but two were killed; the youngest, Clodoald—he can hardly have been more than five—was put into a monastery and became venerated as St. Cloud. Clotilde collected the little relics—her sons fled from before her—and buried them in the Paris basilica where they remained till the Revolution offered them the final insult. The Queen seemed now but a ghost, allowed to haunt St. Martin's tomb in peace.

But no. The Arian Visigoth Amalaric was treating the younger Clotilde, his wife, with unbelievable cruelty. She managed to appeal to her brother Childebert who defeated and killed Amalaric. But his sister, exhausted, died on the way home, and Clotilde received but a sealed-up coffin. It remained for her only to pray for her two assassin-sons; she lived at Tours, as widow and penitent—there was so much to expiate! Her ascendancy over vast areas was as incalculable as her beneficence was unlimited; she controlled not only monasteries and the civilization they spread wide and wider around them, but—for once, royal influence was a blessing!—the choice of bishops for Tours. She sought for *worth*—of the first four bishops she chose, the first came from a great senatorial family of Auvergne; the second had been a carpenter; the third was a patrician from the Poitou; the fourth came from quite the poorest class in Tours itself.

At last she felt herself dying. Renouncing all cruel memories, she sent for her two sons who were present at her anointing and Communion and her profession of faith in the Holy Trinity. As she was making it, she died, on June 3, 545. Her biographer relates that a dazzling light then filled the room, together with a fragrance like a heavenly incense; this lasted till the sun rose "in all his strength". And rightly, for it is thus that her memory reaches us from amid the murk and reek of those unhappy years. The mourning city watched her taken away by the two kings to her basilica in Paris, where she was placed beside Clovis and St. Geneviève in the crypt.

England should be specially grateful to Clotilde. It was her granddaughter Bertha who married Ethelbert of Kent and prepared his heart for conversion, and their daughter Ethelburga who in her turn brought her husband Edwin of Northumbria to the Faith. And it was a granddaughter of Clotilde, Clotsinde, who married Alboin, king of the Arian

D

Lombards; St. Nizier of Trèves wrote her a splendid letter concerning his conversion; but she died young. Still, about 589 the Bavarian princess Theodolinda married the Lombard Authari, and so won people's hearts that when he died they said they would accept for king no man but whom she should choose. She therefore married the duke Agiluff, checked his march on Rome, was personally thanked by St. Gregory the Great, who indeed dedicated his *Dialogues* to her, and finally converted her husband, created the cathedral of Monza, the coronation-church and shrine of the Iron Crown, and thus bequeathed the Faith to the Lombards who became sturdily true to it. It would have been pleasant to write of St. Radegunda (d. 587: she is one of the titular Saints of Jesus College, Cambridge); when she obtained a relic of the Cross from Constantinople, Gregory of Tours wrote that majestic hymn, *Vexilla Regis*, which we still sing each year. And were there space we could relate how it was Theodosia, daughter of the Greek governor of Baetica in Spain, who educated in the true Faith Hermenegild and Reccared, sons of the Arian Leovigild, so that in 589 the third Council of Toledo decreed that Spain should be Catholic. Again, it was a woman, Igond, who so strongly encouraged her husband Hermenegild to profess that Faith and, in a sense, to die for it. It was St. Ludmila, converted (about 879) by St. Method, who through her grandson the martyred Wenceslaus gave the Catholic faith to Bohemia; Dubrawa (965) to Poland, and Olga, widow of the national hero Igor, to Russia, when her grandson in his turn became Christian. The Russian liturgy still salutes her, we believe, and bids her rejoice that she made God known there, "for thou art the origin of our alliance with Him".

There is of course a whole constellation of Saints, during these early centuries, who were not so directly responsible for introducing the heavenly light into a land or nation. Enough just to name a very few—back in France, we find the English slave-girl Bathildis who was married by Clovis II and was mother of three sons, each of whom became king.

She was Regent for eight years, and, not forgetting her origin any more than Helena did, with the help of St. Eloi she did much to alleviate the lot of slaves and even to suppress slavery; when her eldest son, Clotaire III, came of age, she became a nun—not even abbess—in the monastery of Chelles, and died in 680. Over her was St. Bertilla as abbess, and along with her, St. Hereswitha, once Queen of the East Angles; Bertilla died in 692. A daughter of another East Anglian king was the very famous Etheldreda (d. 679) who founded two monasteries at Ely, whence arose its cathedral; further off were, for example, St. Brigid, whose memory is interwoven with the whole of Irish history (d. 525); the charming St. Caesaria, sister of St. Caesarius of Arles, who has been called the first of popular preachers—anyhow, his sermons are incredibly vivid and entertaining; she died about 529; back at home, St. Lioba who went from Wimborne to help St. Boniface in his Germanic apostolate and who wrote him such delightful letters and sent him pepper and socks . . . she died in 729. Nor dare we omit St. Matilda, wife of Henry the Fowler and mother of the Emperor Otto I, and of St. Bruno of Cologne, and grandmother of Hugh Capet and thus, ancestress of so long a line of kings; the last part of her long widowhood was spent by her, too, in some convent that she had founded (d. 968). Finally, Saints Adelaide and Cunegunda; Adelaide was married by the Emperor Otto the Great, but cruelly treated by her own son Otto II, and after a life of suffering died in the peace she loved, in 999; Cunegunda was the wife of the Emperor St. Henry II and died, she too, in a convent, 1039. We feel it has been almost foolish to mention these names thus summarily, especially as they cannot represent the ordinary life of holiness, as led by women in or out of convents. But after all, as we said earlier, you cannot help queens becoming notorious, and you are only too glad when their notoriety was a good one! St. Benedict's sister, St. Scholastica, died about 543. And St. Margaret of Scotland, 1093.

CHAPTER IV

THE LIGHT OF MEDIEVAL MYSTICISM

I HAVE OFTEN to remind myself, and must beg readers to remember, that I am not writing an outline of European, or ecclesiastical history, nor even that of the developments of sanctity as such, but am no more than trying to recall—I fear in the sketchiest way—the names and lives of certain women-Saints. Thus I say nothing about the enormous cultural revolution due to the creation of the Holy Roman Empire—Charlemagne was crowned Emperor by the Pope in A.D. 800. But for two hundred years before and after this, there were not a few women who received a local cultus and, I feel sure, could be rescued from obscurity by some competent student. Yet on the whole they do not emerge as "personalities" nor have they influenced the course of Catholic piety. I have constructed a frail bridge of names, though even this does not adequately stretch from one side to the other of the gulf. But when we reach the mid-eleventh century, so new are the phenomena we meet with that we seem at first to find ourselves introduced to a new religion. No, the development has been continuous; the newness resides really in a psychological area: that civilization has undergone vast changes, who shall doubt? And the cultural changes inevitably bring about changes in religious imagination and speech. And though the first examples that I have chosen—Elizabeth of Schönau, Hildegarde, Gertrude—come from the North, only their special colouring, so to call it, was non-Latin; the deepest changes were proper, I think, to the whole of Europe.

We often hear the "Dark Ages" spoken of, and there are

those who seem to regard these as covering everything from
A.D. 500 to 1500; I, were I driven to offer dates, would be
much more inclined to limit the period of darkness to the
space between 850 and 950, though even then the skies were
starry with Saints. But the great reform of monasticism was
really begun at Cluny in France, whose first abbot, St. Berno,
died in 927; the second and third, SS. Odo and Majolus
(d. 942, 994) developed this work till the Cluniac influence
radiated everywhere from England to Italy. And around the
year 1000 a whole army of men-Saints stand massively forth.
But this book is about women-Saints, and these are not
known of in such great numbers as rather later on. And
if the years 500-1000 can with some justification be called
the Monastic Age, those from 1000 to 1500 assuredly
witnessed the dawn and possibly the noontide of the Age of
Mysticism.

For our purposes only, I shall mean by "mysticism" the
endeavour to reach a knowledge of and union with God
which are direct and, in a sense, "experimental". By this, in
its turn, I mean that the "mystic" will normally progress by
way of the renunciation of his senses, and of the "images"
of God that they offer him, for the imagination cannot be
good enough as a method of reaching Him, noble and sublime
as its images may be. The "mystic" will further renounce
even the truest human ideas that his intelligence offers him
about God, for, they *are* not God. If he has had the vocation
to advance by this "negative" road, and have persevered in
it, he may, or may not—according to the free gift that God
makes to him—achieve a "direct and experimental" awareness of God which may even fall short only of the Beatific
Vision. This process was not a monopoly of Christianity;
many pagan speculations were concerned with this very
topic.   With some of these the ill-known character
"Dionysius" was at least well-acquainted, and his book,
On the Divine Names and other writings exercised an almost
illimitable influence throughout the "dark" or "earlier" or
"later" Middle Ages. But the "mystics" of whom I hope to

write have quite different qualifications which have hitherto been latent even among the Saints or at any rate were never characteristic of an epoch.

One phenomenon far more prevalent than ever before consists in those abnormal psychic states which culminate in ecstasy—to sum them up in a single word. The "mystic" who endures ecstasy is as a rule quite unaware of anything save the Divine presence and is unable to control his own thoughts or actions. Such states do not prove the existence of sanctity, indeed, they involve a certain imperfection— when perfectly united with God, the *whole* personality is fully free. St. Bernard was to say that the Gift of God is absolutely pure and disengaged from any material image (this of course would include ideas, which are spiritual by nature, but still the product of the human reason); but that, to temper this unendurable vision of God or to provide a "teaching" (i.e., when the Saint is meant to communicate his experience to others), images present themselves one knows not whence. (He has the curious theory that these ideas are provided by angels, since that is the special spiritual work that angels are adapted to!) What startles us is the accuracy and even subtlety of self-knowledge which the medieval mystics reveal, at least as a rule. Clearly, when the imagination plays a great rôle in a complex experience the core of which is supernatural, the more are multiplied the chances of human error; and at times a "mystic" puts down to the immediate action of God what was in reality his own contribution to his complex experience. But the authentic "mystics" never erred about the true origin of the substantial gift given to them.

But along with this very stripped, discarnate adhesion of the soul to God goes, in the period we are considering, an ever more passionate love of God and of His Son made flesh, leading up to what became called in mystical language the "Marriage" of the soul with God. Almost a medieval refrain is the sentence: "He shall kiss me with the kisses of His mouth". We are not surprised then to find how steeped these medieval mystics are in the "Canticle", the "Song of Solomon", a drama of human love every part of which was allegorized by the Hebrews themselves, careful as they were not to allow their sons, while young, so much as to read it. But we must remember that "prudery" was unknown in the Middle Ages; no need was felt to camouflage the history of marriage or of birth. Moreover, the whole period was an allegorical one; every detail of a cathedral, or of a painting, was made to "mean" something spiritual; so that it was all the easier to allegorize the "Canticle". True, this might issue into an arbitrary or wire-drawn symbolism; but alas, we have so disaccustomed ourselves to the whole idea of allegory, that it hardly occurs to us that anything *means* anything.

Though the examples that I shall choose will mostly be drawn from convent cloisters, we must insist that the mystical life in no way need conflict with the married, or the most intense intellectual or exteriorly active life, though naturally it is observable chiefly (but not always) in men. St. Anselm (d. 1109) combined profound scholarship with a sublime yet warm love for God and our Lord, and a heroic resistance to, e.g., royal tyranny (William Rufus): this Italian, abbot of Bec in France, makes a link between St. Bede (most lovable of men) and St. Thomas Becket, destined to follow Anselm in the See of Canterbury and to be martyred in his own cathedral. But were this an account of the whole current of medieval mysticism, we ought to spend many pages on St. Bernard (d. 1153) on whose shoulders "the weight of the whole twelfth century was placed". In him too can be seen how an assuredly mystical life can be combined with the fiercest external activities—negotiations with emperors and kings, Popes and anti-Popes, heretics and Saints, crusaders and the destitute; the honey of his eloquence is poured into intellectual forms as firmly constructed as the honeycomb. But here my point would be that no one yet had worked out the successive stages of the purification of love, love beginning maybe with the love of Christ Incarnate and ascending to pure act of love of God in Himself and for His own sake.[1]

Even now, before reaching our women-Saints, I would like just to mention the earliest document, I think, that has reached us—the history of Othloh, a Bavarian born about 1000; he died between 1075 and 1080. In 1032 he became a monk at St. Emmeran at Ratisbon and directed its school for forty years. He wrote a very full "spiritual diary" and it is this amount of introspection followed by self-expression that seems to me new though I do not forget the *Confessions* of St. Augustine. He experienced an intense repugnance to give himself "wholly" to God despite the vehemence of the divine call: then, in consequence of this, he was tempted to despair, disbelief in the Scriptures and finally in God Himself. Then, "from my lips as from my heart, concentrating all the forces of my mind", he prayed this very modern prayer: "Oh God, if Thou art someone, and if Thou art everywhere, as I have read so often in so many books—now, I pray Thee, show me who Thou art and what Thou canst do. . . . I cannot bear this strife any longer." Through the blackest of black nights, lasting for years, he gradually emerged into the consciousness of the presence, power and love of God, who became to him more "real" than he was to his own self. Probably all the Saints of whom we shall think go through some such "tunnel", knowing in the bottom of their heart that God has not abandoned them; they do not despair nor disbelieve; and their writings are worlds apart in their sincerity, unselfishness, intensity and accuracy of self-knowledge from the diaries of modern pessimists who either boast, or fret and fume, whine and whimper, and in reality rather enjoy the miseries for which they pity themselves;

[1] We cannot here explain how the soul, in no stage of its ascent, loses anything that it ever had possessed. True, when perfect love is reached, we shall not be loving our Lord nor His eternal Father because of the joys that become ours through doing so, but because *God's* will is fulfilled by our salvation; we shall not be *able* to be unaware of Christ Incarnate, since we ourselves will be part of His mystical body, and if our full life is in Him, so does He too find His fulfilment in ourselves. We live already, though we hardly experience it, "in the power of His Resurrection" (Phil. iii, 10).

they do not want to get well lest they should have nothing left to talk—or be talked—about any more.

The short life of St. Elizabeth of Schönau (1130-1164) fell entirely within that of St. Hildegard and helps us towards understanding it. She was put into a monastery when aged eleven, and was twenty-two when she began to experience "abnormal" states of consciousness, of which some seem in no way spiritual, e.g., clairvoyance. Thus, sitting in the chapter-house, where the sky was not visible, she "saw" there was a rainbow. She prayed naïvely in her heart: "O Lord, let me see with my bodily eyes what I am now seeing with my mind." The sisters then began to come out of the chapel and stood looking at something. "What", said Elizabeth's companion, "can it be?" "I expect", said she, "that it is a rainbow I have seen in my mind." They went out to look, and it was. This of course has nothing to do with "mysticism". She distinguishes clearly between the origins of her experiences—when for example their cause was purely physical, or partly so and partly psychological, as when she might loathe prayer, or throw away her psalter, having read but a single verse; but if, e.g., temptation to suicide occurred, here right and wrong entered in; she would pray, and be delivered. Her imagination, too, was extremely active. Thus she "saw" the whole of our Lord's life, or that of some Saint, in every detail; but while she may well have been in genuine contact with a spiritual *and* historical fact, should she wish to describe it (even to herself) she must needs do it by means of what her actual experience, or contemporary art, or hereditary symbolism had accustomed her to. Thus the symbols used by St. John in his Apocalypse were rapidly understood by men deeply versed in the Old Testament prophets, and also, familiar with Asiatic art-forms; he *could* not have drawn his symbols from what is familiar to *us*, e.g., electricity, the radio, machinery in general; and it would have been even more impossible for a contemporary to understand him if, by "revelation", he used such material.

Thus we discriminate carefully between the Gift as given and the way in which it is described by the recipient, especially if the "colouring-matter", so to say, is offered as historical; here, Elizabeth may often have failed to grasp what was historical and what was due to her own imagination, as when she quite innocently embroidered the story of St. Ursula (and her eleven thousand companions) till the foundation in history has entirely disappeared if ever there was one. She knew quite well, however, when she had really been in ecstasy; she required to "draw breath" after an ecstasy and could remember nothing that she had experienced during it; it was different when she had been "near", "on this side of", ecstasy; then she would say what she could, using such symbols as she knew and liked, and indeed her "visions" were described by her in moral and allegorical rather than mystical terms.

Like most medieval mystics, Elizabeth was very practical and downright. As she lay dying, literally everyone was admitted to her cell. To soldiers, she said it was their business to protect the poor, not to rob them; not to tear their clothes or hit them; not to sin against chastity, and so forth. Her brother Eckhardt left an account of her dying. She nearly complained to God that cough and sickness prevented her receiving Communion; an angel told her that, for her deeper purification, she had to suffer a "great smallness" in her life. Pathetic phrase, suggesting that the more vast were the outlook and desires of these Saints, the more they felt the "restriction" of their actual achievement—they had done *nothing* for God or His Church; they *were* nothing. Here is the heart of the mystical life—the *self*, as such, is nothing; it needs to be wholly filled and activated by God.

St. Hildegard, born 1098, died in 1179, aged eighty-one, despite continual illnesses, mental strain and great bodily activity. She too was undoubtedly clairvoyant—to begin at the lowest. One example only. When she was five, she was walking with her governess and saw a cow. "Look", she cried, "how pretty the calf is! White, with marks on its forehead; and its feet and its back are all coloured!" And in a few days, the calf was indeed born, just like that. . . . She was a tenth child and, at eight, was offered as a "tithe" to God in the ancient monastery of St. Disibod (Disenberg). In 1141 she was divinely told to write down her visions. The idea was torture to her (as it was, too, to Elizabeth of Schönau), but the abbot Conon, superior of the women's monastery as of his own, ordered her under obedience to do so. If she resisted, she fell sick; when she obeyed, she recovered. It is unnecessary to discuss the possibly psychopathic element in this. One or two of her manuscripts were sent to the Archbishop of Mainz who appointed a commission to examine them. She then embarked on her big book, *Scivias* (*Si scires vias Domini*: "If but you knew the ways of the Lord") which took her ten years to finish. Meanwhile, against much opposition, she transferred herself to Bingen, overlooking the Rhine. I may say, incidentally, that the drainage system and water supply she planned for her future monastery excited universal applause; she was as practical as learned, and was, I think, familiar with all knowledge then accessible. She knew not only much theology and much of the Scriptures, but also astronomy, botany and medicine; the physiology of marriage; she also wrote music, hymns, and little plays and moral discourses for her nuns, and also invented a sort of Esperanto full of the unusual letter Z which provided a mild and innocent amusement for these ladies. Convents were in fact hives of industrious nuns—more studious maybe than the men's monasteries, though we could quote examples of even brothers of Emperors acting as examiners and even lecturers —though their wives and daughters might do the same.

In 1147, Pope Eugenius III was at Trèves, with a suite of eighteen Cardinals, and innumerable bishops and abbots, among them St. Bernard, and Hildegard's "case" was put before them. The Pope appointed another commission which visited her and returned with part of *Scivias*. She had written to ask St. Bernard to do what he could for her. He answered that he would try but was very busy. . . . The Pope caused to be read—possibly himself read aloud—portions of her manuscript. They were enthusiastically received. The Pope wrote her a brief but fatherly letter thanking God for the gift of His Spirit to her, telling her to remain humble and to speak only with prudence. He also gave her permission to go to her new monastery of St. Rupert—she had, we confess, placidly anticipated this permission and had already gone there—and insisting that the enclosure should be properly observed and St. Benedict's rule adhered to.

Hereupon her correspondence became colossal; the most warlike bishops travelled to visit her; prelates and kings apologized for not yet having done so. She on her side, in her clumsy coach, by roads that were no roads, voyaged this way and that. Barbarossa sent for her and said, afterwards, that all she had foretold to him came true—yet he could omit nothing that might make for the honour of his realm. This can but have meant his campaign against the Pope. In return, she promised him no brief reign but a troubled one; he must remember that he is *given* the sceptre only that he might rule righteously; she utters the most fearful threats in the name of Him who Is, and ends: "Remember this, O King, if thou wouldst live—else shall My sword strike thee!" She wrote with equal severity to Eleanor, mother of Henry II of England, destined murderer of Becket; and to Henry she said: "You have gifts able to win heaven; but see! a Black Bird comes from the North[1] and says to you: 'You can act as you please—can do anything! Off with you, then! Why trouble about Justice? If you obeyed its laws, you would be a slave, not a king'." Her zeal for justice, for the well-being of the common people, is quite characteristic of the times. She wrote to no less than four Popes quite as vigorously. Anastasius IV, when nearly a hundred, begged to hear from

---

[1] The psychological elements that construct this "diabolic" symbolism are at best conjectural: I quote the passage only to show the *style* of her rebukes.

her as his predecessors did. Part of the answer he received was this: "O man, you care nothing for Justice, that king's daughter . . . you leave that princess lying prostrate on the earth stripped of crown and dress by the brutality of your officers. . . ."

Lest you should hazard the rationalist guess that half-savage soldiers and luxurious and venal clerics were still no less superstitious and able to be terrorized by so dominant a personality as Hildegard's, it is well to examine her writings with patient care. At first they will seem chaotic; she forbids herself no digression; her mind was incredibly active and enquiring; she never rests on the surface—she makes a statement, and instantly asks, "How so?" "Why?" For example, writing to the ecclesiastical authority who had put Mainz under an interdict so that no singing in its churches could any more be heard, she launches into an exquisite digression upon music. . . . Man's soul, nay, all creation, is meant to be like a harp on which the loveliest harmonies should be played. Sin has broken the instrument; only a vague consciousness of the powers that dream within it remains to man, like visions that fade into the night. It is for man to restore the instrument, his soul, that God may once again play upon it His perfect music. She then suddenly remembers her subject and says that those who force the churches to be silent do not deserve to hear the angels sing in heaven. In her books on medicine (which really means natural history from the point of view of healing) she certainly sees that the whole world, and man in it, are meant to be in harmony within themselves, and with God. Sin having made the great *discord*, every part of the universe is discordant. Hence wars; hence illnesses! She is then quite logical when she considers that if a plant fulfils its rôle by healing a man, it is very good for the *plant*; *it* enters into a richer harmony. She, like Aristotle, saw that things are improved by fulfilling their function. She regards despondency about one's own times as a very serious fault—for, apparently, the despondent fulfil *no* function. And she sees

Christ standing, His feet in the abyss, His head in heaven, turning to the extremes of east and west, and uttering a trumpet-cry which contains all sounds. (Compare our Lord as the "Alpha and Omega" of existence.) Thereupon the whole interwoven movement—I had almost said dance—of human desires and ideas begins to evolve. In Christ, and only in Him, will the perfect rhythm of the whole of the universe be attained.

We must remember that Hildegard knows well that she sees none of this with her bodily eyes, yet that she is not asleep or just "mooning"—letting her imagination run riot. Her preternatural life in no way interferes with her practical active life. From childhood, she had been conscious of something that she called a "light" within her mind which was not, and did not spring from her mind itself. By a bold paradox she called this "the Shadow of the Living Light". It is not difficult for us to associate the idea of "light" with the mind. We speak of the light of reason. "I'm all in the dark; please throw some light on the subject". God is the Origin and Destiny of all things and is the Absolute Light, for only in the light of God can the world or anything else be understood. And our Lord, says the Creed, is "Light *from* Light"; the Christian will not understand anything properly save "in the light of" Christ. Now all the "mystics" have, as we saw, believed that God "enlightens" them in a way which is essentially superior to man's normal way of reaching knowledge; He bestows—not yet the Beatific Vision, but a direct perception of Himself which is ineffably on the way towards it. (Cf. St. Paul in II Cor. xii. 2, 3, and St. John, Apoc., e.g., iv. 2.) Hildegard, then, was conscious of a light shining within her mind which, compared with her intelligence, was indeed light, but which, compared with the Divine Light itself, was but shadow. But it is clear that no one can express what is above the intelligence otherwise than in symbol, so she (or any other "mystic") is bound to draw her imagery from her own stock-in-trade, so to say—clouds, mountains, castles, roads, composite figures of all kinds. She knows quite well that none of this represents the reality as such—she, like St. John, constantly says: "as if . . .". But next, often enough she draws out her symbols into a long allegory, and here the "vision" is over; her artistic and inventive faculty has free play; finally, she is apt to moralize her account and apply it to actual circumstances. Not that she would have admitted that any of this came solely from herself. So sure was she of the primacy and pervasiveness of the divine action, that when this action made itself felt at all, the whole universe and she within it would stir in response. Hence it was truer to say: "God told me—showed me . . ." than "I thought, I imagined". I feel as though I had been watching in her the very beginnings of creation, when at first nothing was discernible save the watery chaos, "without form and empty", and then gradually one detects in it motion, currents, the taking of shapes and order, due to the very spirit of God.

From now on the field is thronged by a multitude of holy women, living lives of ever increasing penances, fasting, prolonged ecstasies and, after the death of St. Francis, being marked in one way or another with the stigmata. Along with this goes, as I suggested, a more "human" and passionate love for our Lord; we can watch the almost "apocalyptic" Christ of St. Hildegard changing into the Bridegroom of the Canticles. I may mention the Blessed Marie d'Oignies, born near Namur about 1177 and who died in 1213. Married at fourteen, she finally induced her young husband to live with her as celibates; they turned their house into a leper hospital. Ultimately, she resided in a cell near the church. Another such Saint was Liutgard of Tongres (d. 1246). She became, first, a Benedictine, then, athirst for austerity, a Cistercian. She could not rest, she declared, upon angels or Saints, or even upon our Lady, but only on the flowery couch of her Beloved. Asked how she saw the face of Christ, she replied: "In a flash there appears to me an indescribable splendour, and swift as lightning I see the unspeakable

beauty of His glory; at this sight, I could not have remained
in this life had it not instantly passed from my view. A
splendour remains within my mind; but when I seek in
that for what I had seen—though but for an instant—I do
not find it." This is a good instance of how the "mystic"
can describe in the most concrete (or poetic) language what
he knows to lie wholly outside of words.

Margaret of Cortona (1247-1297) was only seven when
her mother died; her stepmother treated the high-spirited
child, destined to great beauty, with chill aloofness. The son
of a local lord seduced her; she lived with him for nine
years, certainly loved him, kept begging him to marry her,
tried to compensate for her sin by infinite goodness to the
poor and by prayer. Legend, it is thought, has dramatized
the death of her lover; it is certain that when he died,
probably by violence, she was evicted from his castle, gave
back all his gifts, and returned home only to find the door
shut there too against her. Utterly destitute, she felt she
could not see her small son starve and was tempted to sell
her beauty that he at least might survive. But two ladies
rescued her; she became a Franciscan Tertiary, devoted
her life to nursing the sick, and even persuaded Cortona to
open a hospital for the sick poor. She created an association
of women to act as nurses, and of men, to ensure its finances.
Her ecstatic life began in 1277. Our Lord said: "What do
you wish, *poverella*—poor little thing?" She said: "Nothing
save Thyself". During her long purification of soul He spoke
always to her as "poverella", but afterwards as "My child".
He said: "I have made thee a mirror for sinners; from thee
shall the most hardened sinner learn how ready I am to be
merciful. . . . I have set thee as a new star in the world, to
bring light to the blind, to lead home those who are astray,
to set upright them whose sins have broken them down."
Her influence became amazing. People flocked from great
distances to her, she sent them on to her confessor who
complained roughly that they were too numerous. "Your
confessor", said our Lord, "has told you he cannot clean

out so many stalls each day. Tell him from Me that when he hears confessions he is cleaning out no stalls, but is preparing, in human hearts, a home for Me." Her body is still preserved and a very old wax mask. She is haggard and her eyes are exhausted; but the eyebrows are wonderfully calm; the mouth, certainly, is sensuous, but the nose most delicate and aquiline.

I am distracted, owing to my desire to depict even with the fewest strokes the saintly women who give sweetness to this century of tension and new birth, and because I find it impossible to do even that. Yet who would have the courage to omit mention of St. Clare of Assisi (1193-1255)? Strangely enough there is but little to be said of her, especially from the angle of the mystical life; this makes her profound and enduring influence all the more marvellous. And certainly there is an atmosphere of fragrant simplicity to be breathed in the convents of Poor Clares as, maybe, nowhere else. There were, too, her sister Agnes (d. 1253) and St. Agnes of Bohemia, daughter of King Ottokar I, niece of the King of Hungary, and betrothed to one royalty after another till at twenty-eight, with the help of Pope Gregory IX, she became a Poor Clare in her own convent at Prague; she died in 1282. St. Jadwiga of Poland (1174-1243: not the same as Blessed Jadwiga who was accepted as Queen of Poland at the age of thirteen and by marrying Jagiello of Lithuania practically brought the whole of his people into the Church). She was not an ecstatic, but a most competent ruler of that land, and aunt of St. Elizabeth of Hungary (1207-1231), who was only twenty-four when she died—but what had she not been through! Married at fourteen to Ludwig IV of Thuringia, she had three children whom, like him, she worshipped. In 1227 he went on a crusade and died. Her grief was piteous. She felt that in him the whole world and any joy that it held was dead. Her husband's relatives treated her with extreme barbarity—they wanted the estates he had left to her. She went to the Wartburg, and there saw "heaven opened, and that sweet Jesus, my Lord, stooping down to me and consoling

E

me. When I saw Him, my face flushed and I laughed;
but when He turned as though to go away, I cried and
became pale [the original text is not quite clear here].
Pitying me He turned His calm face to me a second time and
said: 'If thou wishest to be with Me, I wish to be with thee!' "
She answered: "Lord, I wish to be with Thee and never to be
separated from Thee." She became a Franciscan Tertiary
and led a life of such sweet abnegation and charity to the
very poor, that no wonder her name is still held in bene-
diction, and that she is always known as "our dear St.
Elizabeth". Let us recall too another St. Elizabeth, Queen of
Portugal (1271-1336), famed for her twice making peace
between her native Aragon and her husband's land. She
organized an admirable system of ambulances and "first aid"
and further treatment for the wounded of either army, and
was the predecessor of St. Camillus, as he was, in a true sense,
of the Red Cross. She too became a Poor Clare Tertiary.
With these two Queens we commemorate the little servant
girl Zita (d. 1278), devoted for forty-eight years to the
household of a Lucca merchant; and also the poor little sick
girl Seraphina, lovingly abbreviated in Tuscany to Santa
Fina. She had no one to look after her save one friend, as she
lay, always happy, on her bed of torture. She died, quite
young, in 1253. Grander, maybe, among ecstatics is, first,
the Blessed Angela of Foligno (d. 1309). She was married
and had several sons and had been frankly self-indulgent,
though it is hard to make sure whether these Saints, when
they so bitterly accuse themselves, had been really sinful.
Her conversion was sudden; she became a Franciscan Tertiary, and after the death of her husband she somehow became
the leader of all Franciscan Tertiaries, men as well as
women. Her visions have a certain calm sublimity which is
the stranger as when in ecstasy she spoke very fast, and the
priest who tried to note her words down was often in difficulties. But that is not the whole story. When he read aloud
to her what he had written, she would exclaim almost
petulantly: "It wasn't in the least like that!" There is, of

course, the danger that even a stenographer will not accurately reproduce what is said; but also, the certainty that words, in such a matter, can never truly express what was seen. St. Paul boldly says that he heard "words that cannot be spoken" in the hour of his greatest ecstasy. Two Saints go hand in hand—Juliana of Mont-Cornillon near Liège (1193-1258) and Juliana Falconieri (1270-1341), niece of one of the first Servites. She herself founded the Third Order of the Servites and devoted her life to the sick. When she was dying, she could not receive Communion; the corporal was spread upon her breast and the Blessed Sacrament laid upon it. It vanished; and afterwards the mark of the Host was found upon her breast. St. Juliana of Cornillon, equally devoted to the service of the sick, consecrated her efforts to the establishment of the Feast of Corpus Christi. She underwent incredible suffering at the hands of the ecclesiastical superior of her convent, but died in peace. Her friend Eva obtained sanction for the Feast; in 1312 it became obligatory in Western Christendom; it retains its liturgical glory because of the hymns of St. Thomas Aquinas—the *Pange Lingua*; the *Verbum Supernum*; the *Adoro Te* and the *Sacris Solemniis*. This meagre selection of names from among so very many may serve at least to suggest how varied were the lives led by women who were in the closest union with our Lord, and in the practice of grave penances, and as a rule experienced preternatural gifts of the highest sort.

Returning to the north, no woman "mystic" is historically more important than St. Gertrude the Greater and, with her, St. Mechtild of Magdeburg.[1] It must first be remembered that there were two Gertrudes and two Mechtilds who have often been confused. Gertrude of Hackeborn (1232-1292) was a noblewoman, became head of a Cistercian convent

[1] It is remarkable that St. Gertrude seems never to have been canonized and her writing attracted no attention till about 1505; her popularity was largely due to the Benedictine Lanspergius (1536), and indeed to the Jesuits who preached St. Gertrude almost side by side with St. Margaret Mary. It is remarkable how all the symbolism used by the latter is to be found in St. Gertrude: it was in their temperament and vocation that they differed.

at nineteen, and finally settled in the castle of Helfta given
to her by her brothers, was a first-rate abbess, but wrote
nothing and was not canonized even informally. St. Gertrude
the Great (1256-1301 or 1302) died in that same convent;
nothing is known of her family. The intellectual level of the
convent was very high—I like to think that this spirit, in
Germany, was inherited from St. Lioba (b. perhaps 710 and
d. 779) who came with other English nuns from Wimborne
to help St. Boniface. The abbess appointed her sister,
Mechtild of Hackeborn, as "mistress of novices", and it was
she who had charge of Gertrude, who entered the convent
school aged five. Gertrude insists that she concentrated too
much on secular studies till she was twenty-six; then somehow she was "converted", "passing from innocence to
holiness". It was thus that her life of ecstasy began. We
possess of hers a book called *The Herald of Divine Love*, for
(like all these Saints who "published" their experiences) she
was constantly told that nothing was granted to her for her
own sake only. It consists of five parts; she herself wrote only
the second. The first is a biography by a contemporary;
the fifth contains her revelations about the departed (the
abbess and St. Mechtild both died during her lifetime); and
the other two, further revelations written down by those who
knew her best. She wrote, too, her "Exercises", intended to
educate others in the divine paths. It is excellent, and less
known, apparently, than the "Herald"; it is concerned with
the renewal of baptismal vows; with spiritual conversion;
the vows of religion; love, praise, gratitude to God, reparation
for our sins and preparation for death. Mechtild too composed a *Book of Special Grace*, though it was Gertrude and her
companions who actually wrote it down. Mechtild corrected
the script; it became very popular, was translated into
Italian and is mentioned by Boccaccio, and it seems assured
that Mechtild is the "Matelda" of Dante's Twenty-Eighth
Canto and maybe inspired the whole structure of his
Purgatorio. I have said how strangely this mass of medieval
literature sank beneath the surface; when it reappeared,

writers had lost the sense of the liturgical in which the medievals were steeped and also, I feel, that sense of joyousness that pervaded them.

All these medievals saw the world in an ascending series—what was sub-human (I doubt if they were clearly aware of what was human but sub-Christian); then, the virtuous life of the Christian; then, the collective spiritual life expressed in the Liturgy; then, the heavenly and more real enactment of this Liturgy—Christ sings His own High Mass in heaven. Perhaps Gertrude makes so much of music because of her close association with St. Mechtild, her choir-mistress, possessed of a lovely voice—our Lord calls her His "nightingale"—can we imagine that, in the somewhat intimidated mysticism (French, at any rate) of three hundred years later? Then, all this may be expressed in long-drawn allegories, cumbrous enough to our taste, as when Gertrude is shown her heart as a bridge, buttressed at one end by our Lord's divinity, at the other end, by His humanity. "Bridge"! Another example of the medieval's putting a meaning into everything, even if he could not find one ready-made. (As for us, we profess that the purity of art is spoilt if it endeavours to "tell a story". True, no non-Christian now has much of a story to tell; and when, in music, drama or painting—or modernization of the Scriptures—he professes to offer his "version" of the inviolable history, how poor, how insipid, how utterly "un-helpful" it appears!) Gertrude loves colour—and the most delicate colours; rose and gold, for example, shining into one another. She is *afraid* of none of the senses, though (like all her compeers) she is a most "penitential" Saint. When she is conscious of the praise given by the angelical choir, she "sees" the most exquisite tints in their robes and in their wings; every feather softly stirs in the breeze of their thought and of their love, and *all* is making melody to God.

Read especially Book Three: "While I was standing in the convent after washing my hands as usual before dinner [n.b., critics of the "dirty" Middle Ages—"as usual"!] and

was rejoicing in the hot sunlight", she began to wonder how
it was that the Lord, "at whose beauty sun and moon do
marvel, should so often visit my soul" and yet she herself be
often cold of heart, without feeling, and so perverse in her
association with her fellow-humans. "And suddenly Thou,
whose word was then the sweeter the more my vacillating
heart stood in need of it, [didst say]: 'In what would
my Almightiness be exalted . . . if not by making Myself felt
more, showing Myself, according to what befits time and
place and person? For from the beginning of Creation . . .
and in the whole work of the Redemption, I have employed
rather the Wisdom of Goodness than the Power of Majesty.
The goodness of this Wisdom shines forth best in My suffering
the imperfect till I guide them through their own free will
into the path of perfection'." Here are alike her occasional
obscurity, her sublimity, and her simplicity. She, like
St. Hildegard, is conscious of the whole Church, nay, of all
creation, vitally responding to anything that happens within
her. This explains sentences like these: "Every time you bow,
in choir, the Angels sing Gloria in Excelsis." "Whenever
you venerate the Cross, the trees of Paradise utter their
Alleluia." This begins from the quite scientific truth that
in a vital organism any shock will produce its reverberation
throughout it. And it leads up to the crowning truth, that is,
the Real Presence of Christ in the Church and in the soul.
Christ is the unitive vital bond; it is He who catches up all
these good things and gives them their real self in *His* Self;
in Him they "come alive". And He does this lovingly; we
are His joy as truly as He is ours. Hence when Gertrude was
ill and had grapes beside her, she ate them, trusting that our
Lord within her would like their sweetness, and He let her
know that he did so. . . .

Her writings are full of "local colour". She goes out one
morning before Prime into the court—it was between Easter
and the Ascension—and sat down and thought what a dear
place this was—the water ran so brightly, the trees were so
green, and the birds (especially the doves) flew about in

such full freedom; and above all she took pleasure in the trusted restfulness of this hidden place. And "God flowed in upon her gratitude". Her soul takes in God as the air does the sunlight; it changes into the same "colour" as the Child Jesus, "if one can call colour what will not suffer itself to be portrayed by any visible thing". This is why she sees the inestimable value of the tiniest grain of dust, which she feels herself to be, since God picks it up from the very street and chooses it for Himself. This is why, in short, this childlike soul is so happy in her humility, has such a charm, is (if I may express my own feeling) so sweetly amusing and gay (despite her frequent grave illnesses), so personal and spontaneous, that I am more "at home" with her than with much that belongs to, say, the seventeenth and even the later sixteenth centuries when even spiritual things had to be expressed so formally.

Mechtild of Magdeburg was so called because she undertook a life of mendicancy and penance in that town from 1230 to 1270 when she entered the Helfta monastery. Here she died in 1277 aged almost seventy. Were it not that the other Mechtild and St. Gertrude admired and loved her, I might feel almost nervous about the quality of her spiritual love. This may be because she was a poet and uses many of the current phrases of courtly love, invokes divine love as "Lady Love", personifies not only the Virtues but the Senses and has the strangest dialogues with them, when they invoke her to rest somewhere short of her Beloved—nay, not even in His childhood may she repose; her own heart is adult and so is He. "Image of My Divinity", says He to her, "ennobled by My Manhood, adorned by My Holy Spirit, how is thy treasure called?" "Lord, it is called my heart's desire; I have withdrawn it from the world, withheld it from myself— I can carry it no farther; where shall I lay it?" "Nowhere else than in My divine Heart and on my human breast. There only wilt thou be kissed by My Spirit." "I come to My Beloved", the Lord, "like dew upon the flowers." He looks upon her, and behold: "His Heart in my heart; His soul in my soul, embraced and untroubled." Mechtild's book, which she wrote on small scraps of paper, was named "Light of My Divinity flowing into every Heart that lives without Falsity" but is usually called: "The Flowing Light of the Godhead." I cannot deny that if it costs me a considerable effort to adapt my lungs so far as I can, and, if I may so put it, to the Spanish atmosphere of a St. John of the Cross, three hundred years later, with what a gasp does one try to breathe in the air of this Mechtild in which the other Mechtild and St. Gertrude are so perfectly at home! The fact is, that one period is closing and another about to begin.[1] The transition may perhaps be seen in St. Birgitta of Sweden (1304-1373) and St. Catherine of Siena (1347-1380). Both of them were deeply involved in the frightful politics of their period, and with these I can have nothing to do. Enough first to disentangle, if I can, some elements of Catherine's unparalleled career in which her sanctity is more manifest.

* * * *

St. Catherine of Siena lived when the break-up of Christendom was very nearly accomplished, and she was destined to see the beginning of the Great Schism when, quite apart from conflicting loyalties to kings, men were often quite unable to tell who was Head of Christ's Church. We have to remember the difficulty of communication before there was any system like our own; and the extreme improbability of obtaining an accurate version of events when even the election of a Pope might be surrounded with incredible violence and lies were circulated such as might "deceive the very elect". We wish then in this section to concentrate somewhat on St. Catherine of Siena and to end it with St. Catherine of Genoa (1447-1510), and really, these two together might suffice to present us with a vision of Purgatory endured in this life, and in the next.

Catherine Benincasa was born on March 25, 1347. Her home was built on a steeply sloping hill, so that one entrance,

[1] Note: St. Clare of Montefalco, d. 1308.

on "Dyers' Street", was on the ground-floor, but the other
was in reality a basement where her father Giacomo's dye-
works were. He was a gentle man, but adamant on two
points—no harsh judgments in *his* house, and no lewd talk.
His wife, Lapa, vivacious, hardworking, sharp-tongued and
incapable of telling or tolerating a lie, had twenty-three
children, lived to be over eighty, and energetically affirmed
to the last that her soul had been stuck cross-ways in her
body and could not be unstuck. Catherine became a lively,
energetic child and so strong that she could carry a load of
hay upstairs "as if she were a mule". When she, aged six,
and her brother Stefano were coming home, she saw above
the Dominican church on the hill opposite, our Lord, arrayed
like a Pope, along with St. Peter, St. Paul and St. John the
Evangelist. He looked steadily at her, smiled, and blessed
her "as bishops do" with a triple sign of the Cross. She
stood, paralysed, in the evening traffic; Stefano, who had
gone ahead, yelled at her, returned and tugged at her: "Oh!
if you had seen what I have, you wouldn't have disturbed
me!" Henceforward, the child was "different"; indeed, she
was no more a child.

She started (as afterwards little St. Teresa) to seek for a
spiritual life. She hid; she prayed; she began a hermit's
life (when she ran away to do so, in a neighbouring cave,
she had to come back after one day . . .); she "espoused
herself" to Christ; she began to eat only bread and salad.
When she was twelve, they began to discuss a marriage for
her. Her sister Bonaventura persuaded her to "come out",
as we used to say; she rouged; she bleached her fair hair still
paler—even Lapa told her to! But in 1362 Bonaventura
died suddenly; her "brother" Tommaso, adopted when his
parents died of the plague celebrated by Boccaccio (1349)
and now a Dominican, persuaded her to retrieve her
apostacy by cutting her hair off. Her family, furious,
resolved she should have no time for her prayer-life. She
was made servant to the whole of the household. But she
knew for certain she must join the Dominican Order in one

way or another. In a dream she saw the founders of many Orders, but St. Dominic in fact gave her a black and white habit which already the "Mantellate", women associated with this Order, wore. Her mind was made up. She was fifteen; she assured the assembled family that they could melt a stone rather than her. Her father yielded, lovingly. She was no more to be interfered with. She was given a small room whence, all the same, Lapa took her to some hot springs for her health—she put herself beneath the hottest spring and, thinking of hell and purgatory, scalded herself cruelly. She was, by then, living only on salad, and slept (her hardest penance) scarcely half an hour in any two days. She persuaded Lapa that she wanted to join the "Mantellate". The Prioress said (untruthfully, but to please Lapa) that they accepted only widows. Catherine fell ill—of chickenpox. She said she would recover if she might join. . . . The Prioress said she could if she was not "too pretty". . . . Lapa asked her to come and see . . . but Catherine was "peeling". . . . The Prioress succumbed and the day of Catherine's admission was fixed. And, forthwith, her "key-conversion", so to say. The whole of her womanhood awoke; nerves, imagination, intelligence, all surged up from *within* her. Exhausted after triumph, she asked our Lord where He had been during her hour of vain and sexual instinct. "In the very middle of thy heart."

During these three years, the foundation of the whole of her spiritual life was laid. In a sentence, it was: "Thou art she who is not; I am, who *am*." This is a double vision—indeed, triple. For, it shows, first, the absolute death of self-love, self-worship—"Thou art she who *is not*"; then, the sole Absolute Being, *God*; yet, thirdly, that Creation *does* exist, after its fashion; the world exists, and in it, Catherine. But why? For no imaginable reason save that God loves it and loves her. Catherine, seeing this so clearly, could not understand why anyone else failed to do so. To say that such blindness was due to sin, led her back to the forever unanswerable question: "Why does anyone ever make a wrong choice?" She felt that at any rate she was called to make good something of the world's idolatries; she felt herself so riveted to Christ upon His Cross that during the uproarious Carnival of 1367 she became conscious that she was "betrothed" to Christ; He and she were never more to be separated, in love or work. She was now allowed to "come out" from her three years' seclusion. She did the work of the house—baking; laundry. She visited hospitals, both the Scala, which still exists, and the leper hospital; her ecstasies began to be noticed and talked about. She acquired such an ascendancy in Siena that she could escort two of her brothers intact through that town when it was full of bloodthirsty fighting. Practically every city was then torn by savage feuds between families insanely jealous of one another, or with other towns, or involved in quarrels between Pope and Emperor, or just between the nobility and rich merchants or between both of these and the very poor. I have wondered if it was not the constant sight of bloodshed that turned her mind so definitely towards the thought of Christ's own saving Blood. Her father died; she had no proper home; she felt herself fixed to the divine Wounds and that our Lord took away her heart and put His own in its place. Her will and His were as though identified. She fell sick and was thought to be dying, if not dead; half Siena flocked to her room. But she came back to life realizing that it was altogether for the apostolate that she was henceforward to exist.

And it is from now on that we read of the astounding conversions due to her; of old gnarled blasphemous soldiers; furiously vital youths like Giacomo of the fierce Tolomei family; of bitterly sarcastic and argumentative clerics; of inquisitives who came merely to stare at her; of gossips and critics who (this may seem odd to us) apparently were exasperated by her eating nothing—in fact, by now she did no more than chew and swallow the juices of a little lettuce, and even what she swallowed she could not retain.[1] Add

---

[1] The evidence is very full and disagreeable; the fact is not without many parallels.

the numerous ecclesiastics who came to examine and test her, or to receive advice, or indeed rebuke. One of these was the Englishman, William Flete, a Cambridge B.A., who lived a melancholic introverted life in a wood near Lecceto. He adored Catherine but could be obstinate, and when she tried to "externalize" him a little and told him to come and work in Rome, he annoyed her by staying just where he was. . . . However, a sort of group—*Caterinati*, "Catherinized" men and women—did form itself and followed her about.

It is now that we begin to hear about her correspondence, which she dictated—two or even four letters at a time—to bewildered "secretaries". Sometimes it was not clear who should write what, so they all wrote everything; yet it was found that the sentence always "fitted into" each of the letters concerned. This surprises me the less because her letters are—not incoherent—but usually a rapturous out-pouring of mystically fervent exclamations; hence it was not so hard to make these "fit together". Since, moreover, many of the recipients were men of violent passions or wealthy and worldly prelates, we have constantly to recall that they genuinely possessed the Faith and were swept off their feet by the sanctity which they recognized, even if the difference it made to them was but momentary.

It may astound us that Catherine's surviving corre-spondence practically opens with a very long letter to Pierre de l'Estaing, the new papal legate to Italy. Impossible to tell how far or in what shape her reputation had reached. She was no letter-writing maniac; but when she saw it would be to the point to write to anyone, she did so whoever he was, and the dyer's daughter was listened to more, I think, than her contemporary, St. Birgitta, who went royally around hedged with nobles and with a cohort of bishops, and whose invective was even more violent than that of St. Margaret of Cortona, St. Angela of Foligno or Catherine's herself. What provoked such vehemence? For a hundred and fifty years before Catherine's time, the Popes had chiefly resided not in

Rome, or even Italy, but in France. And no wonder! Italy and Rome especially were in a deplorable condition. Birgitta, in Rome for the jubilee of 1350, talked of priests going around with swords and coats of mail under their short cassocks; lamented the non-administration of the Sacraments even at the hour of death; simony so rampant that there was a mock-litany of our Lady of Simony; described convents as brothels and the desecration of basilicas—St. John Lateran was indeed burnt down in 1361—and much more that it would be idle and unseemly to relate. The Popes, in short, helpless to control the savage rivalry of the great Roman families, were probably safer elsewhere. All the same, Catherine was determined to get the Pope back to Rome; he had become established at Avignon and the papacy, under the heavy threats of the French kings and Cardinals and with the Pope himself too often French, was beginning to seem a nationalist French institution. Moreover, the insane luxury of the papal court (even when the Popes personally were correct morally and tried to check abuses) was such that Catherine declared she could not endure the reek of Avignon's vices; as for the Cardinals and papal kinsfolk, she wrote: "Drive out those evil shepherds, those wolves and devils incarnate, who think of nothing but gourmandizing, palaces and fine horses . . . alas that what Christ earned upon the Cross should be wasted on harlots." She was much more tender with horrible lay tyrants—even a Bernabo Visconti of Milan—than with clerical scandals; in St. Francis's own friary at Assisi the friars fought with knives. . . . Still, she sighed: "Corruption must work its way down to the very roots before all can be well again."

It was now that she was called to the General Chapter of the Dominicans at Florence to be examined as to what she said and did. She was approved of, and it was probably now that she was given Raymond of Capua as a sort of supervisor. They returned to Siena only to find it plague-stricken. Even in ordinary conditions, "St. Antony's pigs" alone were deputed to be street-scavengers. A brother and sister of

Catherine's had died and eight of her nephews and nieces. Catherine and all her friends devoted themselves with heroic self-sacrifice to the sick and all of them fell ill. They recovered and went to Montepulciano where Raymond of Capua already was. He was still puzzled as to the genuineness of Catherine's preternatural experiences. It was now that he himself received an experience which should reveal Catherine's interior life. Looking down at her, he saw beneath her veil, not her face, but our Lord's. "Who art thou?" he asked, terrified. The answer was: "He who is." And it was in Pisa (April 1, 1375) that Catherine received the Stigmata though, as she prayed, they remained invisible; yet she felt their pain such that she thought to die of it; but in their strength she embarked on the last, brief but most apostolic part of her life.

Meanwhile she was writing to every potentate about the new Crusade she was urging, but we can omit this topic, since not only the Crusade never eventuated, but she was wrong in imagining that in the violently disunited Europe a common effort *could* be made, especially as city after city, party after party, was breaking away from the secular papal sovereignty. The butchery was such that one wonders any Italians were left alive. But Catherine told her friends to save their tears—this was milk and honey compared with the future, when not laymen would be the rebels, but the clergy. Details about this too I omit. There came a point when the Pope, Gregory XI, said he would return to Rome but meanwhile laid Florence under an interdict, adding conditions for its removal such that it was out of the question that they should be fulfilled; though if they were not, all Christian princes were invoked to make war upon the wretched town. This would have meant its extermination. Catherine offered to go herself to Avignon to intercede for the Florentines; the miserable citizens agreed to anything and she started in May, 1376.

Two days after arrival, she saw the Pope. He did not understand her Tuscan; Raymond translated it into Latin.

The Pope said he left the matter in her hands, only let her not forget the dignity of the Church. She wrote joyously to Florence; but no envoys came, and the Florentines seized the moment for heavily taxing the clergy. The Pope said: "They are mocking you and me. They will send no envoys, or, only envoys without powers." Finally, envoys came, but the government had changed; they said they had no powers to treat through Catherine. Everyone seemed to be cutting his neighbour's throat and his own. Catherine was infuriating papal Avignon by her denunciation of its sins; it became an entertainment to see her fall into ecstasy at Communion, and to stick pins into her. The Pope continued to vacillate as to his return. Florence was a poisoned thorn in her side—it now begged the Emperor, Hungary, Venice, Genoa to join in preventing the Pope's return to Rome. The Inquisition summoned her, and opened the examination by calling her a vile slut; the Pope told her to shut the door in their faces if they returned. . . . However, they became her friends. Meanwhile the French Cardinals persuaded a holy man to tell the Pope he would incur frightful disasters— even poison—if he went to Rome. Catherine said there was quite as much poison in Avignon as in Rome; he must act as a man, not a boy, and take the bitter for the sweet. He did in fact leave for Rome on September 13, the French Cardinals bursting into tears, and his father throwing himself flat on the threshold to prevent departure. At Genoa, the Pope again vacillated; he visited Catherine at night, in disguise— Rome itself was in revolt; but at long long last he reached Ostia on January 13, 1377; Rome yielded; he landed at St. Paul's-Outside-the-Walls; Rome was illuminated with unheard-of splendour; the Pope endowed Catherine with three confessors who might absolve all whom her words had touched, and a portable altar so that she could have Mass anywhere. Yet incredible local massacres continued: Catherine wrote the letter containing a sentence for ever famous. "It is as though the devil had captured the world. . . . I can say no more. I die, and yet I cannot die." Enough to say that Florence was again defying the Pope and Catherine was sent to negotiate.

But on March 27, 1378, Gregory died suddenly, and amid fearful tumults Urban VI was elected. He was as fierce in his attacks on luxury and simony as ever Catherine had been; so it was declared that Urban had been elected only by Cardinals afraid of death; they excommunicated him. After many tempestuous episodes, in one of which, at Florence, Catherine was sought for to be burnt as a witch, the climax came when in 1378 the Great Schism began— the anti-Urbanites elected the Cardinal of Geneva as "Pope" and named him Clement VII. Catherine wrote a letter of hard logic to the three Italian Cardinals who had joined in this—"you were present when devils elected a devil—an anti-pope!" Urban sent for her to Rome. He received her surrounded with his Cardinals. "This little lady (*donniciuola*)", he said, "has put us all to shame." He wanted her to go to Joanna, Queen of Naples, to consolidate her loyalty, taking with her Karin, daughter of Birgitta of Sweden. But this was really too much; Karin remembered all too well the fate of her brother Karl, on whom that "Harlot on the Throne" had set her eyes (see p. 77). The visit was postponed; Catherine confined herself to letters, though very candid ones. She resolved to create a band of men devoted to holiness and prayer in Rome itself; *this* should be her "crusade". She wrote to friends—Flete included, but he would not leave his thickets. Still it is said that his pamphlets helped to keep England Urbanist. Charles V of France died in schism; the King of Spain too went "Clementine" and imprisoned Urban's envoys, so Raymond, who had shirked going to France, now refused to go to Spain. Catherine wrote him a scorching letter; but later the breach was healed and her last letter was to him. Clement asked Joanna for protection; she gave him the Castello del Ovo to live in; but there was a riot; he fled back to Avignon; Joanna ended by being suffocated in bed.

Things continued to go badly. Even in Rome, 1380, the

people threatened the Pope with death. Catherine, by now almost a moving skeleton, unable to swallow even water, dragged herself daily to St. Peter's, and, under Giotto's mosaic, still in today's basilica, felt that the whole weight of the Ship of the Church reposed on her. Yet she went daily from the Minerva to the Apostle's Tomb to pray. As Lent approached, she wrote for the last time to the Pope, begging him to be firm as to the evil government of the Church but gentle in his methods. He disregarded this; relentlessness became almost a mania with him; in 1389 he died, hated and forsaken. For the last eight weeks of her life the Saint remained in bed—that is, on a board fenced with four other boards, as though already in her coffin, and indeed they kept thinking she was dying. An ecclesiastic came to ask her to make a "testament". She dictated her customary thoughts about complete self-abdication, and then, a vigorous declaration that one must *never* judge the consciences of others, even when their acts and motives seem obviously sinful. For such, one must have sincere compassion and then offer them to God, as she herself did—for life and work and pain, or death and peace. She lingered till the Sunday before Ascension Day, her face calm and sweet as ever, but her body paralyzed from the waist down. She appeared to ask for, and was given, the Last Sacraments but then to struggle, it seemed, with demons. She kept saying—some sixty times—lifting her right arm and letting it fall heavily on the bed: "I have sinned, O Lord; have mercy on me!"; then, but lying still: "O Holy God, have mercy on me." Then, often: "No—never my own glory, but God's." After three hours, she became radiant with peace—a true transfiguration. She implored yet again the papal blessing, and again advised each of those present about their future. By an exquisite act of Providence, her aged mother Lapa was there, and Lapa's blessing too she again and again implored, and all wept to see how Lapa recommended herself to Catherine's prayers, that she might have God's grace and not even in her grief offend Him. Catherine prayed again for the Church, for

F

Urban the true Pope, and for each who had been entrusted to her, begging them to remain united in love. Finally, she made the sign of the Cross, blessed them, and said: "Thou callest me, O Lord, and I come. Not by my merits but through Thy mercy alone which I beg in virtue of Thy Blood." She cried out the last word several times, and then said quietly: "Father, into Thy hands . . .", and so died, at noon on April 29, 1380, aged thirty-three.

I have asked myself whether I ought to have said anything about St. Catherine since inevitably I would have to say so much too little. Nor do I exactly wish, in these sketches, to show chiefly the "ordinary", "approachable", "human" element in the Saints that we are studying, though it has always been a pleasure to encounter it and to feel that there is no "great gulf fixed" between them and ourselves. Yet in Catherine there is nothing that is "ordinary", or what there is, is swallowed up by the preternatural. To live, even immobilized, e.g., in a state of extreme sickness, without food or sleep, would be strange enough, but so to live when in a state of continual physical and cerebral activity of the intensest at once puts such a personage apart. Yet this is the least marvellous element in her life. While there are a thousand little "human", indeed tender, touches in her work and writings, they may seem submerged in her life of constant ecstasy; her cruel and continuous suffering was, so to say, the price she had to pay for her most intimate union with our Lord while she was not yet in heaven. If we seek for what is "imitable" in a Saint, we find little enough in her, not even any account of extraordinary self-inflicted penances such as we read of in the life, e.g., of St. Rosa of Lima and very many others. It is true that she was called to the "Apostolate of the individual" in the sense that she completely enthralled innumerable men and women (I should surmise, chiefly men)—they were "en-Catherined"; but, given the extreme variety of people who were so, we cannot suggest that she was a sort of "specialist" in souls; impossible to exaggerate the difference in character of those whom she directly met and swayed. No king—no tyrant—of today personally meets and spiritually influences—for good or ill— such a number or variety of contemporaries, to say nothing of the devotion Catherine inspires in multitudes ever since her time. But I do not think that this was what she would have regarded as her supreme vocation. And with many, from Queen Joanna downwards, of course she failed.

One main ideal of hers was another Crusade. And in this she had not even the beginning of success. One may suppose that her view of those she was dealing with was quite mistaken. Few, from the Popes to prelates or possible lay-leaders, really cared more about the Holy Sepulchre than our own rulers do today. I cannot see that her attempt at reforming the papal court had any success. We may thank God that that reform has come about; if anything, our ecclesiastics are much harder put to it to survive at all, than desirous of living in luxury. It may be worth suggesting that despite her invective it was not *she* who swerved into violence or even heterodoxy as many another then did, especially that small yet important percentage of Franciscans whose indignant attacks, and prophecies, led them only to the stake. Her "reform" of the Cardinals did not succeed. But her supreme desire, on the part-human plane, was to bring the Popes back to Rome. Yet she was not the only force that did so bring them back, and little satisfaction could she draw even from a Gregory or an Urban when they did return. In fact, one would say that the presence of Urban in Rome went far to render inevitable the Great Schism, since nationalism not only survived but increased; and the existence of anti-popes (at one time three!) did more to confuse the faithful about the very nature of the One Church than even the indignity of the higher clergy did, which assuredly disguised the Church's Holiness.

We have, then, to look elsewhere for the transcendence of Catherine. In her writings? These consist of her "book" (about which I have said nothing) but much more, I think, of her letters. Now I hold that it is practically impossible to convey, by a translation, the *flavour* of any late fourteenth-century writer into a northern tongue. We, on the whole, like terseness and a certain "dryness", whereas Catherine dictated the torrential emotions of her heart; was constantly using adjectives like *dolce* (and it is hard to avoid "sweet" as a translation of that, and we get a sense of cloyingness), and she used a number of metaphors, and elaborated them (especially those connected with the Blood and Death of the Lamb of God)—which to us may be even repulsive. Again, we like a certain reticence, even in spiritual affairs, whereas her letters almost always begin at the highest pitch of mystical fervour and I do not know what even those who received them, and genuinely held the Faith despite their crimes, would have made of them. As I said above, they may well have been frightened of Catherine, as the Huns and their followers were of SS. Peter and Paul, and yet not have amended their ways. It is right to recall that Catherine had her very practical side; she was an excellent cook and nurse, and could be quite caustic in her talk, as when she was discoursing rapturously about heaven and the poor Raymond of Capua went to sleep (remember Eutyches and St. Paul!). She said: "I don't intend to stay talking to the wall! It would do you no harm to attend!"

Perhaps it is best to go right back to Catherine's original lesson—"I am He who is; thou art She who is not"—than which indeed she never got any further, so that indeed it was Christ who looked forth from her eyes, and His Heart which beat within her own.

It is good, then, to go back to Siena or any other Italian town of that time; not to romanticize them; to be aware of their stench, of streets slippery with blood, and also of Catherine moving about there, human yet so etherealized as to be almost the very image of the True God and of His Son, Jesus Christ; and I am glad to add myself to the procession which on May 5, 1380, escorted the relic of her head through Siena, flowers falling, tapestries waving, bells crashing their ovation; hundreds of children marched there; all the confraternities; whole phalanxes of friars, hermits, abbots and bishops; and to find myself just behind the canopy, along with Lapa, the "very simple" Lapa, a bent old woman now well over eighty, knowing at least this—that she had been called to be the mother of her God-glorified daughter, Catherine.

All divisions of history into definite "epochs" or periods are inexact though convenient. I am regarding this chapter as concerned practically with persons whose lives fell between 1350 and 1550, though some that we have mentioned have already overlapped into those years and others will continue to live beyond them. But they lived during the over-ripe and indeed decaying Middle Ages, or the joyous exuberant youth and over-rapid development of the Renaissance, and witnessed the recurrent ending of a world which forthwith is reborn differently. All these periods contained much that was horrible; but also, marvellous examples of holiness which are always disregarded by the historian even when he passes judgment upon morality. We have spoken of St. Catherine of Siena (b. 1347), and proceed to speak of St. Catherine of Genoa (d. 1510), and then, very briefly, of other holy women, who are to be read of during those two hundred years; and while I cannot so much as name a tenth of the Saints or Beatae who might be written of, I have chosen a few who have seemed to me "important" in the annals of sanctity, or perhaps, who have merely caught my imagination by some special charm, or even oddity, of their story.

St. Catherine of Genoa was born at Genoa in 1447. Her family, the Fieschi, was extremely illustrious; two of its members in the thirteenth century had been Popes. By the fifteenth century it had reached the zenith of its glory, and Jacopo Fieschi was Viceroy of Naples. Her mother, Francesca di Negro, was also of noble descent. When Catherine was thirteen, she asked, through her sister's chaplain, to become a nun, but was refused by the convent as too young. At sixteen she was in fact married to Juliano Adorno, of an ancient but impoverished Ghibelline family, whereas her own was Guelf. It was hoped that thus the Adorni would be replaced in honour as of old. That this did not happen was due to Julian's character; he was unfaithful, violent-tempered and reckless in money-matters. For five years Catherine tried to be true to her religious ideals, but became melancholic, which can hardly have propitiated her husband. She then attempted, during the next five years, to lead the ordinary gay "society" life of her time, though not, presumably, yielding to grave sin. None the less, her melancholy was in no way alleviated, and on the eve of St. Benedict's feast, 1473, she made the strange prayer: "St. Benedict, pray to God that He make me stay three months sick in bed!" This apparently did not happen; but two days later she went to the chaplain of her sister's convent and asked his blessing before confession. But she was so overwhelmed by the sense of the love of God and her own unworthiness that she could but repeat, interiorly, over and over again: "No more world! no more sins!" It is possible that the confessor was called away for a while; but at any rate, that day Catherine found herself unable to do more than mutter that she could not then make her confession. Soon enough, however, a vision of our Lord carrying His cross made her ready to do so publicly if need be, but she made it in the normal way, received Holy Communion on the feast of the Annunciation and soon thereafter did so daily, exciting adverse comment, for the practice hardly existed at that time. About now, her husband had nearly ruined himself; and his heart was changed; so they left their palace for a very small house and devoted themselves to the care of the sick in the hospital of Pammatone. In 1479 they went and lived in the hospital itself, and so capable did Catherine prove herself that eleven years later she was appointed its matron or manager-general and after a while also treasurer. These positions she had to resign in 1496 when her health finally broke down; perhaps she had never fully recovered from the plague which she caught while nursing its victims in 1493 (four out of five of the residents in the city are said to have died); but she must, too, have been much weakened by her fasts and penances and, to my mind, still more by the terribly exhausting spiritual experiences which were hers. For the body cannot but pay heavily for graces given to the soul. In 1497 her husband died, "a man of rather wayward disposition", she said gently; but her beloved Lord had assured her of his salvation. She for her part continued to live in the hospital.

For over twenty years Catherine had found no priest able to understand her, and had seldom gone to confession, simply because she did not know what to say. About 1499 a priest, Don Cattaneo Marabotto, became rector of the hospital, and they, at last, understood one another. Catherine said: "I do not know where I am, either in soul or body. I should like to confess, but I am not conscious of any sin." He himself made the curious remark: "As for the sins she mentioned, she was not allowed to see them *as* sins thought or said or done by herself. She was like some small boy who has committed a trivial offence in ignorance, and if someone tells him he has done wrong, he starts and blushes though not because even now he has experimental knowledge of evil." Catherine's mind was both logical and independent, so that in what did not concern dogma she sometimes reached practical conclusions that are unexpected. She did not scorn indulgences, but seldom if ever made use of them—she *wished* her "selfish self" to be punished. Similarly, we are told, she seldom asked others to pray for her or invoked the Saints, nor did she join any Third Order—let alone enter a convent—though her husband after his conversion became a Franciscan Tertiary. I say nothing of the appalling sufferings she went through (preternatural, assuredly, whatever their psychic or physical coefficients may have been) which never interfered with her practical sense, so that her accounts, which involved all the affairs of the hospital, were never a penny wrong; as for her own property, she made four wills, as circumstances changed, and duly added codicils.

Catherine wrote two treatises: *Dialogues of the Soul and the Body*, and the treatise on Purgatory. The doctrine of the latter is of high importance, especially as so little has been defined about Purgatory—in fact, only, I think, that it exists, and that the souls there are helped by our suffrages and especially by the Holy Sacrifice of the Mass. The usual way of describing what happens to them there is to say that they are being made to suffer in order to pay off the remaining temporal debt of punishment for forgiven sin. But since the "place" where they are is called "*most aptly Purgatorium*" and not *Expiatorium* or some such word, it seems clear that no mere extrinsic debt is being paid off but a real change is taking place in the soul that God is purifying. St. Catherine does not see a list, as it were, of unexpiated sins for which the debt is gradually being remitted after due punishment; she does not consider the soul remembers past sins at all; all that the soul has sufficiently "seen" is God, and it is thereupon conscious of being unlike Him and is in pain for that very reason. So does it love God that any sense of unlikeness to Him is agony to it. But the very fact of this pain implies purification; for to suffer because one is not perfectly what God wants one to be is no barren suffering, but a suffering due to love; the soul certainly longs to be finished with its pain, not because pain is agony to *it*, but because pain shows that it is not yet perfectly "according to *God*". One may say that exactly in proportion as its pain increases, so do its purification and its joy, for no joy can equal the knowledge that it is becoming more like to God and exactly what God wishes it to be. "This process of purification to which I see the souls in Purgatory subjected", she wrote, "I feel proceeding within myself". That is, the prayer so often all too lightly uttered: "Give me here my Purgatory", was granted in her own person. In a sense, she offers us more than St. Catherine of Siena at first sight does. The Sienese Saint seemed to base herself wholly on her non-being —"Thou art she who is not"—and her union with Christ might seem to have been an identification with Him—it was

His face that looked out from beneath her wimple. (Of course, *no* human words can properly express divine mysteries, such as our incorporation into Christ and our being truly part of His mystical Body. So I am speaking of emphasis only, not of exact and exhaustive propositions.) The Genoese Catherine, however, emphasizes the terrible riddance of accumulated "rust" which covers and corrodes the *real self* which is "according to Christ Jesus", and yet we see how that self suffers, not because it does not fulfil its own ideal of purity, but because it so much loves the God who does not wish it to remain another moment or in any degree unlike Himself.

The last three years of her life were spent in great suffering with which no doctor could cope; but on September 15, 1510, she died in perfect tranquillity at dawn.

* * * *

Links chiefly within this chain of sanctity are supplied by St. Birgitta of Sweden (about 1303-1373) and her daughter Catherine (d. 1381). Birgitta was not yet fifteen when she was married to Ulf Gudmarsson, the prince of Nierck, himself only eighteen; their marriage lasted happily for twenty-eight years and they had eight children. About 1335 Birgitta was summoned to be the chief lady at the court of King Magnus Eriksson who had married Blanche of Namur, and in that pleasure-loving court she found it her duty to try to correct the lives of the Queen and her husband, without success however, despite the visions she was already receiving, which became matter for mockery in the court—"What was she dreaming about last night?" At last she obtained leave to go with her husband to Compostela and half the rest of her life was spent in pilgrimages. On the way home, Ulf fell ill, and recovered only when Birgitta had promised that he would enter a monastery. He did in fact enter the Cistercian house at Alvastra where he died in 1344. She herself founded a monastery at Vadstena of which the buildings alone exist today.[1] She continued more than ever to have visions, and to denounce wrong-doing, excluding neither royalty nor the nobles nor the hierarchy. Indeed she wrote vehemently to Pope Clement VI urging him to leave Avignon for Rome. She herself went to Rome with a vast retinue for the Jubilee of 1350 though there was no Pope there. Her departure must have been a relief for the Swedish court, but the people had loved her for her tireless beneficence and it was amid the weeping poor that she embarked from Stralsund.

In Rome she lived in great personal poverty and austerity, but devoted herself as before to the humblest service of the sick and needy. After a while, she asked her daughter Catherine to visit her. Catherine had been married to a young man who agreed that the marriage should remain nominal. She further persuaded her brother Charles's wife, much to Charles's annoyance, to abandon the elaborate toilettes in use in the society of that day. He also forbade his sister to go to Rome; however, she went, only to find her mother was absent, admonishing the "very worldly" abbot of Farfa; and only after a week of searching did Birgitta's director discover Catherine praying in St. Peter's. Birgitta, though with difficulty, persuaded Catherine to remain with her in Italy, though the poor girl longed for home and husband. She was about nineteen, very tall and fair, and since Rome was in a desperate state of chaos, she was not allowed to accompany her mother who was constantly touring churches. Left to herself for long-drawn hours, she began to pine: "I lead a miserable life, like an animal in a cage, while the others go and nourish their souls. My brothers and sisters in Sweden can serve God in peace." But after about a year her husband died, and henceforward her life became identified with her mother's and she shared in the obloquy that Birgitta's fierce denunciations periodically brought down upon her. Birgitta did not however cease her pilgrimages and

[1] However, the Bridgettines in Devonshire descend in an unbroken line from the pre-Reformation community, and this cannot be said of any other religious community here.

was for visiting the Holy Land along with Catherine, two of her sons and others. One of these sons was Charles, and at Naples the wanton Queen Joanna I, fascinated by the tall blond northerner, determined to marry him though his third wife was still alive; it is said that Charles was not reluctant. However, at the last moment, he fell sick and died in his mother's arms. She proceeded to the Holy Land with Catherine, returned to Rome (having vainly exhorted the Cypriotes and Neapolitans to a better life) and died on July 23, 1373. To Catherine it fell to bring her mother home. They went from Ancona to Trieste, through Austria and Poland to Danzig and then by sea to Sweden and finally to Vadstena where Birgitta was buried in July 1374. As for Catherine, she became a nun and then Superior there; but the King and every Swedish notable implored her to go to Rome to get Birgitta canonized. Since after five years the affair was not yet concluded, Catherine returned to Vadstena and died there on March 22, 1381. Her mother was canonized just ten years later.

Naturally holiness is found chiefly among those not handicapped by wealth or exalted station; still, it is good to find that it exists also there; Savoy seems to have been specially favoured, to mention only the Blessed Louise of Savoy, born 1461, daughter of the Blessed Amadeus IX, Duke of Savoy, and related to almost every royal house. She married Hugh of Chalon when she was eighteen, and the marriage was as holy as it was happy. After her husband's death she with two maids-of-honour became Poor Clares, and one of these young ladies wrote of her that she was "so sweet and generous, debonair and gracious, giving affection to all, charming to all". That is high praise for one who was also, personally, austere. She died in 1503, aged only forty-two. She was the cousin of the poor mis-shapen, unwanted little princess Jeanne de Valois (daughter of Louis XI) who was forced into marrying the Duke of Orleans, and he, when he became King Louis XII, obtained a decree of nullity from Rome and left her free for a life of prayer and charity,

though making her life-long "Governor" of the Province of
Bern.   She founded an order of nuns—the Annonciades—
in honour of the Annunciation; and it is characteristic of her
humble spirit that its superior was to be called simply
Ancelle—the "handmaid" of the Lord. Though Rome thought
there were enough religious Orders of women—there was
already a military (!) order of the Annunciation in Piedmont
—none became more loved than she. Her life fulfilled itself.
She was canonized in 1950, after four and a half centuries.

St. Elizabeth of Hungary seemed to repeat herself, on a
smaller scale, in Blessed Jeanne de Maillé (1332-1414). Her
father was Baron Hardouin VI of Maillé in the Touraine,
and it was arranged that she should marry a boy called
Robert de Sille whom, by her prayers, she had saved when
he had fallen into a pond. But her grandfather, who had
settled this, died on the actual wedding day, and the two
decided to follow their real wish which was to live celibate.
However, they adopted and brought up three orphans.
Robert, alas, was all but fatally wounded and made prisoner
at Poitiers, and Jeanne sold her last jewels and her horses
to pay his ransom. Their gratitude for his return expressed
itself in generous alms for prisoners, and when Robert died
in 1362 his family took remorseless revenge for the im-
poverishment of his estate owing to these charities and even
seized her dowry and drove her from her home. Jeanne lived
first with an old servant who treated the destitute lady with
contempt; and then with her mother, where she learnt,
indeed, a good deal of simple medicine, but was so pestered
by offers of marriage that she found a small house at Tours
and there remained, caring for the sick and especially for
lepers and for prostitutes. She became a Franciscan Tertiary
and renounced her very last belongings, which alienated her
few surviving friends.   Henceforward she moved about,
begging her food, and actually having to sleep in pigstyes or
kennels, till finally she settled into one little room at Tours
and, strangely enough, became so known for sanctity that
royalties chose her to be godmother to their children or kept

her (feeling so out of place!) at their court. Meanwhile, all children adored her; the small street-boys of Tours surrounded her, calling out, "Blessed be God and our Lord Jesus Christ", which she had taught to them—as indeed she had to a magpie which she caught and tamed. But her dearest devotion remained the care of prisoners. She died in her tiny room, dressed as a Poor Clare.

But probably the most marked personality of this period is St. Frances of Rome (1384-1440). Like many pious little girls, she begged to be a nun, but her father insisted on her marrying an equally noble and wealthy youth, Lorenzo Ponziano, with whom in fact she lived for forty years with never a quarrel. None the less, she longed for the "religious" life and found that Vannozza, wife of Pontiano's brother, had cherished the same hopes. The two young women devoted both time and money to the service of the sick, their husbands never interfering, but Frances's confessor insisting that she must not "clash" with her own home. And indeed she was always perfect in its management, and in the education of her three children, for whom she had earnestly prayed. When plague devastated Italy and Rome, she and Vannozza spent their whole time serving them, and at last she received leave from her father-in-law to sell her jewels and to wear none but the plainest dresses. But worse: in 1408 Ladislas of Naples, ally of the then anti-Pope, appointed a count Troia as governor of Rome. Lorenzo was stabbed— the Ponziani had always been loyal to the true Pope—but Frances nursed him back to health; however, Troia, having to fly, resolved first to revenge himself on Rome, and among other cruelties took the elder boy Battista as hostage, but, by a seeming miracle, restored him while Frances was still praying for him in the Ara Coeli. Ladislas, furious, sacked Rome, pillaged the Ponziano possessions and re-took Battista, who however escaped and joined his father. Frances, Vannozza and the two little girls, Evangelista and Agnese, lived in a corner of the half-ruined palace, serving those who were poorer still than they; but three years later

Evangelista died in another onset of pestilence. A year later, she appeared to her mother and said that Agnese too would die (she did, aged sixteen) but that Frances would thenceforward always be conscious of the presence of her guardian-angel. In 1414 peace returned; the Ponziani regained some of their property; Lorenzo came back, a dying man, from exile, and found that his wife was known throughout Rome for her power to heal sicknesses and reconcile disputes. She then planned a "union" of women living in the world, bound by no vows, but offering themselves—as "Oblates"—to God for the service of the poor. After seven years they acquired a building called Tor de' Specchi, a name which has adhered to the community. After the death of Lorenzo and Vannozza, she finally left home and lived with the congregation of which she never would allow herself to be called the foundress. For a brief time she was its superior; but sorrow, work and penances had sapped her vitality and she died on March 9, 1440; her last words were: "The Angel has finished his task; he calls me to follow him." Her relics now lie in the church of Sta. Francesca Romana, on the site of the old temple of Venus and Rome, on the left of the far end of the Forum, near the Colosseum.

The story of St. Joan of Arc (d. 1431) is too well known for us to need even to summarise it; St. Rita of Cascia (1381-1457) has a romantic legend and still inspires great devotion, but her biography seems to have been written first in 1600 and its sources are unknown. It relates that she was married against her will to a brutal and violent man in whose steps their two sons walked all too closely. One day her husband was touched by her patience and implored her pardon; but very soon afterwards was brought home wounded to death. Her sons vowed to avenge him, but Rita prayed that they might die rather than commit murder, and in fact they fell sick of the same fever and died. Rita then entered a convent under Augustinian rule in 1413 and died there in 1457 after all those years spent in remorseless austerity and charity.

Passing into the realm of purely mystical sanctity and

suffering, we mention first Blessed Lydwina of Schiedam
(1380-1433), the child of simple labourers. In the winter of
1395-6 she went with friends to skate on the frozen Dutch
canals; there was a collision; she fell and broke two ribs.
Complications set in; at first she resented this and longed for
the free life of youth; a priest, Father Pot, gradually taught
her to meditate on the Passion, and after three years she
perceived that she was to be a victim of expiation. The
description of her sufferings and disfigurements would be
insupportable to the casual reader's nerves; she passed moreover into the almost "normal" condition of the great
ecstatics and could neither eat nor drink nor sleep, and she
developed powers of healing, prophecy and clairvoyance.
On Easter Tuesday, 1433, she got abruptly worse; her little
brother ran for a priest, but she died, as she had wished, alone.

Lydwina had nothing to do but to suffer, though she had
looked forward to activity; Colette (Nicolette), the daughter
of very humble parents in Picardy, seemed vowed by nature
to self-effacement yet became involved in half the tumults of
her time (1380-1447). She was quite young when her
parents died, and she shut herself up for years as an
anchoress, having joined the Third Order of St. Francis. The
Poor Clares, she perceived, no more observed the primitive
rule. Under obedience, she left her cell to reform this, but
found she could do nothing without supreme authority; and
for one living in France none could seem Pope save Pedro
de Luna under the name Benedict XIII. She so impressed
him that he constituted her Superior of the whole Order of
St. Clare. She began then to travel through France, Savoy,
Flanders, Germany, suffering rebuffs of all sorts but succeed-
ing best in Savoy, whence her reform travelled back actually
as far as Spain. Incredible as it may seem, she actually
wrote (along with the Dominican St. Vincent Ferrer) to the
Council of Constance begging the Fathers there to depose
Benedict XIII, who alone of the three claimants to the
Papacy was refusing to accept the result of a new election.
Benedict, to whom humanly speaking she owed everything,

was in fact deposed and Martin V elected. Here then we see how a life of extreme activity can be allied to a mystical existence as wonderful as any.

Three more very notable ecstatics belong to this period—first, St. Catherine of Bologna (d. 1463) was maid of honour to the little Margaret d'Este at Ferrara (this terrifying family produced at least two Beatae; it was not till 1501 that Lucrezia Borgia married the heir to the then Marquis), but when Margaret married Malatesta of Rimini, Catherine became a Franciscan Tertiary and afterwards the whole community joined the strict observance of the Poor Clares and, as ever new houses had to be opened, she was finally made Superior of that in Bologna. It was here that she died, and you still may see her, seated, grandly dressed but blackened by time. It is strange to think that those tiny hands, so perfectly preserved, painted the exquisite minia-tures and illuminations that you may see in various towns, for she was a true artist.

The Blessed Osanna Andreasi (1449-1505) was born at Mantua and was a relative of the Gonzagas. I whole-heartedly accept the affirmation of a singularly "pure" revelation she received when aged five. She heard a "voice" saying: "Child, life and death consist in loving God." Thereupon, "led by an angel into Paradise", she saw all creatures praising God after their fashion, was told that this praise would be our chief function in eternity, and that it should be our chief work and happiness in this life too. Save for difference in phraseology, this is a perfect echo of St. Hildegard and St. Gertrude, indeed of St. John and St. Paul. She was allowed to join the Third Order of St. Dominic though she was not *professed* as a Tertiary for thirty-seven years. This may have been because her parents died early and she had to look after all her brothers and then *their* children. It has rightly been pointed out as among the anomalies of this period that the fiercest tyrants would not only pay devout homage to ecstatic saints, but implore their advice and even follow it save (one would think) in what concerned morality. Anyhow, Frederico Gonzaga, third Marquis of Mantua, off to the wars, committed not only his wife and six children to her care, but also, all but the complete management of his marquisate. On his return, he was always consulting her. His son Francesco was married to Isabella d'Este and continued to be Osanna's most intimate friend and was present at her death, and exempted for her sake the Andreasi family from taxes for the next twenty years.[1] It is quite impossible to relate in detail her agonizing distress about the state of the Church at that time. Her close friend and biographer, the Olietan Fra Girolamo, suppresses many of her more outspoken declarations. However, he records that she prayed thrice for the salvation of the Pope, that is, Alexander VI. Twice did God seem ready to show mercy to him, but the third time He remained silent. She turned to our Lady and the Saints, but "God ever remained motionless with aspect and countenance of wrath, and gave no reply to anyone that prayed—not to the Madonna, nor to the Apostles, nor to my soul."[2] It is pleasant to know that this very sublime mystic gave a "party" on the occasion of a nephew of hers singing his first Mass, and invited the Marquis of Mantua to it. . . . I can but mention St. Catherine de' Ricci, a Florentine (1522-1590), who early became a Dominicaness at Prato. Her mystical life provides all the usual (if I dare so speak) material for psychological examination, especially in what concerns the ring with which our Lord espoused her, a phenomenon witnessed to by so many people in so many different ways. What is unusual is this—she kept up a correspondence with St. Philip Neri, though she never left her convent; Philip— the most cautious of men when giving evidence—insisted

---

[1] If any readers want to know what the Gonzagas and Estes were like then, I venture to refer them to my *Vocation of Aloysius Gonzaga*, pp. 8-13.

[2] The Thurston-Leeson revision of Butler's *Lives* mentions (June 20, p. 261) a "privately printed" essay of the late E. Gardner, "A Mystic of the Renaissance—Osanna Andreasi of Mantua". I sincerely trust that this may be made public; Prof. Gardner's material is invaluable and known to few, though his deductions are not always indisputable, any more than, e.g., Baron F. von Hügel's about St. Catherine of Genoa.

that she came and talked with him in Rome. But we do not propose here to discuss the question of "bilocation", though, to me, some instances of it seem solidly evidenced. Catherine was one of the Saints who not only saw but *enacted* the various episodes of our Lord's Passion. As connected with the d'Este, I mention here the Blessed Lucia de Narni (1476-1544). She was an Umbrian and the eldest of eleven children. She resolved to remain unmarried, and after a purely nominal alliance which lasted three years, she went home and then to a Roman convent and then to one at Viterbo, having become a Tertiary of St. Dominic. It was at Viterbo that she received the stigmata and participated in the sufferings of our Lord's Passion. The loss of blood was so extreme that this could not be hid; she was examined by doctors, bishops, inquisitors, a Franciscan prelate (the Majorcan Franciscans did their best to suppress a picture of her bearing the sacred wounds, on the grounds that a decree of the Franciscan Sixtus IV had forbidden, under pain of excommunication, that any one save St. Francis should be represented as having the stigmata); nay, she was examined by the Sovereign Pontiff, Alexander VI himself. Ercole I, Duke of Ferrara, wanted to found a Dominican convent there, and smuggled Lucia out of Viterbo in a clothes-basket fastened to a mule. But she was only twenty-three, and Ercole wished his convent to contain a hundred Sisters, so he invited—of all people—his daughter-in-law Lucrezia Borgia to collect novices for him. She collected indeed an amazing crowd, and Lucia was quite unable to remain Prioress. Anyhow, in 1505 the Duke died, and she disappeared for thirty-nine years from the eyes of men. She was allowed to speak only to her confessor; a Sister acted as constant wardress; Lucrezia, the new Prioress, and the Dominican Master-General treated her with real savagery, and when in 1544 she died, the populace was amazed; people thought this had happened long ago. The reaction was immediate. She was acclaimed a Saint, and her cultus was approved in 1710.

I conclude this period on a lowlier level (which does not

mean "less prayer" or "less penance"!) by naming the Blessed Lodovica Albertoni (1437-1523), who, after her noble and wealthy husband's death, devoted her life to long hours of prayer (she nearly lost her sight by weeping over the Passion) and charitable work ... she used to give out loaves, inserting coins into them, and praying that the most needy would get the largest coins. ... Add the Blessed Paola Gambara-Costa (1473-1515), married when aged twelve with such splendour that the very wheels of the coaches were gilded. The Blessed Angelo da Chiavasso, a Franciscan, not only decided that she was called to be married, but gave her an extremely rigorous rule of married life, including the injunction: "I will always obey my husband and take a favourable view of his failings and try to prevent anyone else's knowing about them." The oddest incident in her life is that out of charity she harboured in their castle a young woman who, in her innocence, she did not realize was, or soon would become, her husband's mistress and was to take command of the whole place. This girl after a while fell sick, was nursed with extreme devotion by Paola, was genuinely converted, and died. Whereupon the illness having ended rapidly and the body being swollen, Paola was accused of poisoning her, and indeed, it was the Borgia period.[1] So, while I remember with gratitude the Blessed Seraphina Sforza (1432-1478) who was married to a widower, the Grand Constable of Sicily and brother of the Duke of Milan, a horrible man who, to justify his alliance with a local doctor's daughter, accused Serafina of adultery; after unthinkable humiliations she became a Poor Clare among those who had given her refuge —while I remember this, I like to end with the Blessed Helen Duglioli (1472-1520), a girl from Bologna, who married when about twenty a Benedict dal' Oglio with whom she lived very happily for thirty years. She died almost immediately after he did. Everyone knew, without other evidence,

[1] We should insist that at certain times, even at the beginning of the Christian era, "poisoning" became a sort of monomaniac complex in the popular imagination. Thus anything said *by Italians* against the Borgias must be heavily discounted because of their hatred of Spaniards.

and went on doing so, that she was a Saint, and her cultus was confirmed by Leo XII in 1828. Thus we return to "ordinary people" about whose sanctity other "ordinary people" are seldom at fault, provided the notion of "sanctity" has not altogether faded out of their minds. There are those who speak easily of a "holy" priest or nun because they know that such a vocation has somehow set them "apart" and that they have an additional obligation of living up to a high standard—not that the mere fact of a man's being a priest makes him spiritually holy, or that a layman is excluded from being so. But I fear that too often what "holiness" really means—the perfect adhesion of our will to God's—is forgotten because our understanding of what God is, is itself so much weakened; and again, our recognition of the Life and Passion of our Lord is so dimmed; so the most that "good" people aim at is a reasonable ethical behaviour in reasonably comfortable conditions. It is good, then, that both "extremes", so to say, should be recalled. The great mystics remind us that after all we are habitually conscious only of the outermost fringe of creation and are not directly perceptive of God at all; the vision of infinity and "real Reality" awaits us, if we be but faithful. And the preternatural sufferings of many a Saint, and even their penances, reveal to us a little—a very little—of what the Passion really was, and what purification must be ours here or hereafter. But, as we keep recalling, for the few who are "placarded", there must surely be very many who remain unknown, or known only to those who (as we hope soon to show) have made them the subject of their laborious research. The ordinary historian will not of course do this; nor will he recognize sanctity even of the more obvious sort when he sees it, but will regard it as fanaticism or an instance of psychological aberration, judging that the possibilities of human life are exhausted by what he normally sees of it. Yet we, as Christians, ought to see life primarily as transfused throughout by the Spirit of God, and therefore, with Sanctity, either achieved, or not yet made perfect.

CHAPTER V

THE BREAK-UP OF
CHRISTENDOM

SANCTITY SEEMS, at times, to disappear from the life of this or that nation and to drift elsewhere, though this may be due to the lack of research and sheer documentation. Still, if we take France as from the death of Henri II (1559) and study what is known of the wonderful flowering forth of holiness both among men and women, including very simple people who are not likely ever to adorn our altars, it is with stupefaction that we read even the ordinary histories, which quite omit the *fact* or *force* of sanctity in a nation, let alone the hysterically partisan pages of a Michelet, who was once supposed to know more about France than anyone else.[1]

As background to the spiritual chaos of the time, we must see the breaking-up of Christendom itself. When Charles V became not only King of Spain (1516) but Emperor (1519), France felt that she must fight for her very survival and looked to the German Lutherans for help and then to the Mohammedan East—the Sultan. At first Francis I was favourable to the Lutherans but then began to fear they would plot against him, and persecuted them. When

[1] In what follows I have freely helped myself by the late H. Bremond's *Histoire littéraire du sentiment religieux en France*: if something equally monumental existed about other countries, it may well be that the efflorescence of sanctity during this period—betokening the existence of seeds or roots present for a long time though invisible—might be exhibited. I think it certainly could be, were this book about men Saints: but, as I have said, holy women were apt to remain encloistered and their record is found with difficulty. And anyhow, in the many revolutions an enormous mass of conventual literature has perished. Of course, I never use the word "holy" or similar words save in complete docility to any decision of the Holy See.

Calvinism, a little later, became widespread, Henri II attacked it even more fiercely, but by then the "Religion" was definitely a savage political and military force though no doubt many of its simpler adherents were peaceable; it remains that when in 1560 the Protestant leaders determined to kidnap the king, a series of wars began which were waged with the utmost brutality. The Queen-Mother Catherine de' Medici turned for help to Spain, and the Protestants to Elizabeth of England, and indeed offered her the port of Le Havre as bribe. Since I do not propose to relate, even in outline, the history of France or even of the ruinous wars of religion, it is enough to say that the House of Guise created the "League" to defend the Catholic Faith and also hoped to find one of its members on the throne in succession to Henri III, though Henri of Navarre was the proper heir. He was however a Calvinist, and the Pope had assured him that if he remained so, he never would be king, but that if he abjured and was absolved by the Pope himself he would receive the throne also. Henri in fact abjured (July 25, 1593) and the chances of Protestantism in France, and the utility of the League, were alike made an end of. The situation was not immediately clear. It was nationalism that had broken up Christendom and France was very nationalist. Its kings mostly tended to think of themselves as nationally the equals of the Popes; its bishops, to subordinate the Pope to a Council. So, since the Council of Trent consolidated the papal position, its decrees were never officially promulgated in France. Henri, indeed, sought his absolution not from the Pope but from the French bishops, which was a true victory for Gallicanism, especially as the absolution was sure to be ratified in Rome. In fact St. Philip Neri sent his friend Baronius, the Pope's confessor, to tell him he could himself not be absolved if he refused the ratification. This act of the Saint shows that he believed in the sincerity of Henri's conversion, and I hold that all the history of the king's conscience, which was directed by the admirable and meanly calumniated Père Coton, proves it too. But if, in the forefront of French social history existed these quarrels, alternately fierce and squalid, they must not be permitted to blind us to the far deeper tale of sanctity that could be related.

Fascinating is the tale of Antoinette—history never got so far as her surname. She was a widowed peasant, a Provençale, who gave up field-work for prayer and austerity. She heard of a young César de Bus, born in 1544 at Cavaillon, who went to Court and returned the perfect young libertine. Now a certain hatter called Guyon had made his shop a regular focus of piety; he used to march men off by the score to confession in Avignon. . . . Antoinette came to Cavaillon and established herself just opposite the de Bus. She moved freely about and began to be talked of as a Saint. César used to stop and stare at and then laugh at her. She begged him to reform—he laughed the more. She went to Guyon who suggested this: she could not read; let her therefore take with her the *Lives of the Saints* and ask César to read a few lines of them to her. . . . (Strange *equality* and liberty, after all, in times when "classes" were in some ways so sharply differentiated!) He laughed still more, till suddenly, one day, he yielded. He offered himself to Guyon and Antoinette for "direction" and went on to the Avignon Jesuits. In 1576, he definitely "gave his heart to God"; by 1582 he was a priest. He had a cousin, Jean-Baptiste Romillon, born in 1533. His father, falsely accused of heresy and despoiled of his wealth, in desperation thought he had better become a genuine heretic, did so, and brought up his son as a fierce Calvinist, which did not prevent the youth from becoming a reckless debauchee. But the memory of his mother haunted him; some Calvinist sermons disgusted him; in deep melancholy he visited some relatives, the Châteauneufs. M. de Châteauneuf had brought from Paris as a present for his wife Luis de Granada's "Treatise on Prayer". She lent it to Romillon who compared it, page by page, with Calvin's "Institutes". In 1579, grace overwhelming him, he abjured his heresy; over forty, he went to school with children and finally was ordained, leading a life as austere as his cousin's had become.

It would be pleasant to write about the rebirth of the Dominicanesses and the Ursulines in the South and the sisterly mingling of servant girls and aristocratic maidens within their walls; but I prefer to recall Nicolas and Dauphine Rampalle, two middle-aged folk of humble estate, converted, about 1580, by a mission preached in their town of St-Rémy. They decided they had "no time to lose" and transferred themselves to the "beautiful and devout city of Avignon" to be near their son at school there and to educate their daughters. Their house too became a "focus of devotion"—and "devotion" meant a *great deal* of prayer, of spiritual reading, of austerity and of active charity— Nicolas, "wherever he thought he could render some service to God, thither carried he his feet, his hands and his heart". Two of his daughters and two of his nieces went off to Arles and founded an Ursuline convent; one of them indeed founded altogether six. The son became a priest. We ought not to regret the disappearance thus of a whole family; for after all, these priests were widely "apostolic" and most of the nuns kept some sort of school and "instructed many unto righteousness" and shine like stars (almost invisible to ourselves) unto eternity.

One more example drawn from these hidden layers of society. Marie Teyssonnier was born at Valence about 1575 and died in 1648. Her parents were small commercial folk, had become Calvinists, had her baptized as a Calvinist and married her off to a Calvinist notary living in an almost wholly Calvinist village. She was thirteen, but they allowed her to remain at home two years more. Meanwhile they had re-become Catholics of a sort, but all that Marie knew was that she should kneel while praying whereas the others sat. She could not read or write, but longed to *possess* a book of the Gospels and got one, and during an illness kept it under her head, and at all times near her. Her husband

Pouchelon was devoted to her but had an appalling temper
and scared her half to death when he pulled out his knife. . . .
She developed a craving for Mass; he let her go to it, but
himself went to the wars; he returned after two years to find
her a convinced Catholic, was instructed, and died con-
tentedly about 1595. Marie lived in a tiny house of her own,
but was destitute. Yet she kept with her a close friend,
Marguerite Chambaud, and her confessor was the friar
Louis de la Rivière. Somehow she penetrated to the heart
of the mystical life and when Père Coton, confessor of
Henri IV, happened to pass by there, he found her uni-
versally venerated though there was nothing sensational or
extraordinary about her. Indeed she had a very sober
common sense. She liked sermons, but not preachers who
dragged in the Scriptures "by the scruff of the neck" (*par
le poil*) or interlarded their discourses with "fables and
worldly stories". At that time there was an amazingly
prevalent devotion to St. Mary Magdalen, now, alas,
evaporated. Marie de Valence (who of course identified
the Magdalen with the sister of St. Martha) was very clear
that the centre of this devotion was not merely repentance
for those sins which offered such chances to rhetoric, but the
"better part", the love that made her adhere so close to
Jesus. Père Coton[1] retained a sort of "higher command"
over her spiritual life and wanted to have her in Paris to
supervise her preternatural experiences more closely.
Duchesses and princesses were mobilized to bring her
thither—after all, it was she who had long ago predicted
that he would be royal confessor. She did not want to do so,
and her bishop, who valued her presence, forbade her to go;
but royal curiosity was aroused. . . . Marie de' Medici,
awaiting her son Louis XIII, at Lyons, sent Richelieu
himself—Richelieu, though not yet cardinal—to summon
Marie to an interview. She was extremely reticent with
the statesman; she did not *want* to go. "It is not an affair

---

[1] His delicate, rather sad, aquiline and bearded features are known to us
by a good engraving: so too is Marie's small, neat, smiling face.

of want, madame", said he, "but must." She went. What she said to that strange Queen, who knows? But when over sixty she met M. Olier, then only thirty, and was as open with him as she had been reserved with Richelieu; Olier on his side felt overwhelmed with her holiness, though, he keeps insisting, it was impossible to keep pace with the tide of high holiness then sweeping through the Church.

Marie provides the most charming after-glow of the Middle Ages; you feel back in the company of Hildegard. She sees everything in symbol—our Lady is a lovely orchard. Complementarily, she looks at everything but instantly sees a divine truth *in* it and enjoys it as St. Gertrude would have done. The Duchess of Nevers took her to see a famous garden. It was very hot and they gave her a parasol. She did not open it but forthwith saw in ecstasy the care of God sheltering her soul. They came to one of those fantastic Renaissance fountains which worked mechanical dolls and even a hermit who rang a bell. At once she saw our Lord, a fountain of living limpid water. Another fountain sent up a perfect vase of water within which a candle burned . . . but for her, this was the soul in which charity was triumphant— the waters of grace; the fire of divine love. "Tell me, water", she once said, "tell me the path towards my Beloved. Should I not stream gently back, by selfless love, towards the place of my beginning?"[1] Yet as her life drew to its close, all this imagery faded away and she was left with that mysterious consciousness of God which is at the summit of prayer. It is sad that after her death she should have been criticized and the naïf book about her by Fr. de la Rivière have been episcopally condemned, though not only St. Francis de Sales, St. Vincent de Paul, the French Oratorians vied with one another in devotion to her, and though the Jesuits had rigorously censored the book. We have to see in this one of many symptoms of that Jansenist fear of "mysticism", and also, hate for anything connected with the Jesuits, which progressively disfigured this period and were so alien to the

[1] Cf. Post-Communion, 1st Sunday in Advent'

innumerable simple stories that could be quoted, like that of the ignorant peasant woman who kept cows in some mountain and whom a very devout nun undertook to instruct in the elements of Faith—only to find that the poor creature never could finish the Our Father which she kept beginning while at her work, because the very first two words so enthralled her that she remained all day, weeping happily, upon that single thought. It is almost with regret that we say goodbye to these "little people" and the red earth, the rocks, the dry scent of the rosemary, the wild lavender, the pine trees of Provence and pass to quite a different world—that of great priories and abbeys.

It is a pity that the word "Reformation" has become so closely attached to the Protestant revolutions that it has grown tainted for our hearing, and that we tend to forget that the Church's children need always to be "reforming" themselves, and that when, as sometimes happens, this new spiritual revitalization happens on a wide scale, one can speak of the monastic life, indeed of the very Church, as reforming themselves. When we speak of the "reformation" of the great French monasteries at this time, we do not usually mean more than that they had been, so to say, hibernating; had become quiet homes for elderly ladies living a respectably devout life more or less in community. The annals of such houses are full of charm; of dignity, courtesy and even of humour. (Imagine the friendly smile of the nun who wrote of a certain abbess grown enormously fat, yet never passing a Saint's statue without a genuflection. She slept on a plank; but when she was dying they insisted on giving her a feather-bed. She sank into it as into a fathomless abyss, could not move, but made no complaint . . . she never did. "Do not be frightened, dear daughters", she said to the bewildered nuns, "but slide me to the floor." They did so, and there she remained.) But during the Wars of Religion the "observance" in such great monasteries had collapsed. There was practically no enclosure; the habit itself might be left aside; nuns could have their meals privately; yet in one abbey, most sonorously denounced, we discover that "not the least" of the "crimes" of its inhabitants was the "affectation" of wanting "fine furniture". We briefly recall that the level of culture in such institutions might be very high—we know this from the sort of book that so often was read there, and the languages freely spoken; and after all, this is not astonishing, since so many of the Sisters came from very elegant families, and from these, in France, were *expected* habits of dignity and authority, *savoir faire*, and often charm, often wit.

Two points about the "reform" may indeed surprise us. First, the youth of so many of the "reforming" Sisters, and again, the way in which all ecclesiastical groups co-operated to this end—Capuchins, Oratorians, Jesuits. Opposition came chiefly, I think, from without—from parents who wished to force some daughter into a great convent as its abbess whether or no she had a true vocation; also relatives, accustomed to visit nuns freely in the parlours, resented the introduction of grilles, the enclosure, veils. If some of the clergy disapproved of the reform, was it because they felt themselves rebuked? On the whole these elderly ladies adapted themselves astonishingly well to a mode of life they never had foreseen; here and there sarcastic things were said —e.g., to the young Margaret of Kircaldy who had come from Scotland to the abbey of St. Peter at Rheims but went on, however, being called *la belle Ecossaise*; it was often not what we might have expected that occasioned most resistance —a uniform diet was without great difficulty accepted, both by the more dainty Sisters because their daintiness made them feel ashamed, and by others who found that their digestions did not really suffer—but many a die-hard nun found it a true sorrow to exchange their white habits for the Benédictine black—not but at the other extreme, at Beauvais, hot-headed "reformists" wanted also to wear black surplices.

One must remember that the position of these abbesses was extremely dignified and was sanctioned by papal bulls which, as we said, some powerful member of a girl's family might obtain over her head. Now a certain Marie de Beauvilliers somehow focused on herself the praises of the period. She was so lovely that even Queen Louise, widow of Henri III, called to see her. She entered a convent ruled by an aunt in a dignified but sober fashion. This aunt wished to be succeeded by her and was furious when a relative obtained for Marie the control of the Montmartre abbey; she said that Montmartre was a scandalous place and so worked on the poor girl's confessor that for three months he refused Marie absolution if she insisted on accepting what after all she was not free to refuse. Her bulls arrived from Rome and in 1598 she left for Montmartre, with one country girl in love with prayer, instead of the companions she had hoped for and whom her aunt denied to her. There is of course an instinct which makes those who describe a "reformer" blacken what preceded him or her; so I cannot take too seriously the tales told fifty years later of how the Montmartre nuns tried to poison their young abbess. . . .[1] The situation was saved by that strange Englishman now known as Fr. de Canfield, whose method of "reform" was, not to denounce abuses but to improve what was good. He determined to make a Saint of Marie, and was followed by St. Francis de Sales and others. Marie died in 1657, having been a little too aristocratic perhaps, a little too "Old Testament" (as was said of another nun), more august and less attractive maybe than Ste. Chantal. Yet the "reform" was accomplished by her within three years and the monastery became a real centre of the mystical life in its various forms. Thus Marie Granger (like others) about 1630 saw in vision the Sacred Heart and drew a picture representing it as thorn-wreathed and nail-pierced (St. Margaret Mary did not enter her convent till 1671); another Montmartre nun,

---

[1] There was, it is said, a sturdy old nun who looked after the material side of the house and who would taste, first, any dish that was set before Marie. Now since she, at any rate, adored her young Superior, I think it quite possible that she tasted the dishes to see if they were properly cooked, and that on this was based a legend that she did so lest they were poisoned.

Charlotte Le Sergent, could not endure the discipline put by St. Ignatius's "Exercises" into prayer; it seemed sheer hell to her to plot out her spiritual anatomy and mark her faults on paper; "points for meditation", when read out, were no better than Arabic; but also, she hated the Office in choir and wished to be a lay-sister to escape it. But not *that* way lay freedom. She passed by way of a very tender love for the Humanity of our Lord to the purest prayer; became mistress of novices and prioress and dear even to those who had most misunderstood her. Yet her "conversion" had begun long ago. When she went to church she had the habit of "distracting herself" by watching other people, and expected to get much fun from a very grimy charcoal-burner kneeling before a crucifix. But suddenly she saw that his eyes were full of tears. She was touched (as we are) to the heart, and it was then, really, that her sublimer prayer began, which she, like others, so long misinterpreted.

One more only of these "reforming" nuns, Marguerite d'Arbouze (1580-1626). She was seen almost from the outset as a reincarnation of St. Gertrude; I myself cannot understand that. Anyhow, she "went to the sources" in her desire to restore the original spirit of Benedictinism; and if, as we saw, every kind of religious Order (to say nothing of the arrival into France of the Teresian Carmelites; see p. 104) helped in the matter of the reform without any endeavour to tug in their special direction, maybe there *was* a certain infusion of discipline which the logical French spirit needed into the somewhat indeterminate life as ordered by St. Benedict. Meanwhile she soaked herself in the Scriptures and more than most, I think, studied St. Thomas, the Areopagite, Blosius, St. Bernard, Origen (!), St. Bonaventura. It remains that her literary as well as spiritual ancestors were Benedictine. She is truly "Gregorian"—solid, free, sublime.

She was at first in a "mitigated" monastery, but obtained leave to transfer herself to Montmartre—Mère de Beauvillier's sister had been her abbess so far. But in 1613 the Princesse de Longueville and her sister offered the priory of Notre Dame de Grâce which they had founded to Marie de Beauvilliers. She took a "colony" there and left Marguerite behind as prioress and novice-mistress when she herself returned. Six months later she came back, and found the prioress in intimate touch with the whole of Paris from the Queen and the future Queens of Spain and of England downwards. Was Marie jealous? Did she fear lest Marguerite was going too fast, especially in the matter of building? A chill was felt between them; but Marie generously yielded when the Val-de-Grâce petitioned for a still stricter rule than she herself had introduced to Montmartre. Gossip began to say that Marguerite was aiming at being abbess, and it seems certain that she wrote to the Cardinal de Retz begging him to prevent her return to Montmartre. But Marie did not open his reply till she had practically kidnapped the poor Marguerite and put her back there. It is quaint to read that no one could prevent great ladies from enquiring, or sending their pages to enquire, how she was—she always answered "quite well"; and meanwhile had to nurse Marie herself through a grave illness and was over a fortnight without going to bed. . . . Finally, in 1618, the irrepressible Queen obtained that she should be abbess of Val-de-Grâce, which so upset Marie that Marguerite fled to an Augustinian house till the papal bulls should come. The Queen was present when she was blessed as abbess, took her in her own carriage to Val-de-Grâce, terrifying her all the way by saying that the King was hunting there and would certainly want to see her and she would have to lift her veil. . . .[1]

[1] One must remember that in any such episode the facts (of which we probably have but a small percentage) are matter for history: the *motives* for actions are often supplied by the biographer's trend of opinion (in this case, he simply worshipped Marguerite). I think the *fact* that Marie kept her as sole nurse through a grave illness proves her esteem; also, that she really thought the incredible popularity obtained in a moment by Marguerite might be bad for her, and that she was, in her inexperience, going too fast with her building. All the same, there may have been just a touch of jealousy in her action; it is quite idle to suppose that really holy people have no faults at all; and in any case I find the story very entertaining.

The new abbess, on arriving, was astounded to be met by nuns in surplices cascading with lace; they had prepared her abbatial rooms with lovely tapestries and embroideries, all of which she made a clean sweep of that same night. (This certainly suggests to me that she may have been precipitate ... the poor nuns after all had *meant* to please her! But what had become of the "stricter rule" they had petitioned for?) Unluckily the adoration that Anne of Austria had conceived for her and her twice-weekly visits drew throngs to the monastery; but among these were many first-rate men of whose advice Marguerite made full use though never forgetting her essential Benedictinism; she simply could not understand jealousy or smallness of spirit. And she possessed such a catalogue of talents—architecture, carpentry, music— that she was unlikely to make a mistake of a practical sort, especially as she was no sentimentalist. She noticed that in the Mass for Our Lady of Compassion came the words, *lacerans vultus et pectora*—tearing face and breast. The Church as such had not sanctioned this Mass, so it must not be sung, for our Lady did no such thing. She stayed here about five years, and then astounded everyone by resigning. What is more, to please her, Louis XIII had given up his right to appoint the abbesses of Val-de-Grâce, and she caused to be appointed a nun who did not belong to her own family, thus breaking a long tradition of nepotism and much to the annoyance of an aunt who regarded her own election as a foregone conclusion.[1]

Had she resigned because she already felt too ill to govern her house properly? And she refused to found several other monasteries! All the more surprising is it that she yielded to the entreaties of Charité-sur-Loire and set off with a small company, having borrowed a clock to make sure of the proper

[1] "Nepotism" as such need not have been a bad thing—the career of St. Charles Borromeo proves that. A Pope or any other ecclesiastical personage might know his own family better than he knew others, and might perceive that some one member of it would be eminently fitted to hold such or such a post. Still, it had not on the whole worked out well, and Marguerite required courage as well as clear sight to break with the system.

hour for saying Office, and a little bell to ring when the time came. A charming voyage! "The nightingales", says the priest who went with them and wrote her life, "seemed to invite them to sing hymns." At fixed times they all got out of the carriage and made naïve little conferences under the trees where the very flowers which they picked for her were clothed with the beauty of God. But at Charité her sober unimaginative devoutness displayed itself. The nuns had based their piety on "enslavement" to our Lady, wore little chains, and even made a vow about it. The "devotion" was not strictly speaking new, but it had not yet the popularity it won from the propaganda of St. John Eudes, Grignion de Montfort and M. Olier. The abbess however abolished it in favour of a purer Benedictinism. But the abbess of Charenton implored a visit. Her nuns were at loggerheads, for or against the "reform". Marguerite insisted on going there. It poured with rain; the horses were exhausted by the appalling roads; the carriage stuck between two stones and was smashed by a fallen bough. They couldn't even get a fresh egg for dinner. Marguerite became despondent. She spoilt everything; better that she should die. After three weeks at Charenton she started back, really ill, with limbs much swollen. They had to halt at a country house where despite the best doctors and many prayers she died on August 16, in the Octave of the Assumption, as she had foretold. She pronounced the name of Jesus, and "her soul followed the sigh with which she had spoken it".

As a transition to the next two heroic figures of whom I speak, I merely mention the Blessed Jeanne de Lestonnac (1556-1640). Her father was a prominent Bordeaux Catholic; but her mother, a sister of the famous essayist Montaigne, had become deeply "Calvinized", and, with a Calvinist sister-in-law, did all she could to seduce Jeanne from her faith. Whatever else has to be said about Montaigne, he was indignant at this, and to him, and to the fervent arguments of a younger brother, Jeanne's perseverance, under God, is due. In 1573 she married Gaston de

H

Montferrand, Baron de Guienne; but alas, in 1595 her father died; in 1597, her husband, and then her eldest son. She resolved to become a religious and entered a convent for which her health proved inadequate. Thus she found her real vocation, which was to open Catholic schools for girls both of the richer and the working-class; the two sorts of school operated side by side. She wished to found a "Society of Mary" parallel to the Society of Jesus (cf. pp. 129), but this idea was never realized; nor is it easy to see how her Notre Dame Sisters (not to be confused with those founded by St. Julie Billart and others) differ from other teaching congregations. Her personal life, however, experienced the recurrent test of enmity within her own foundation. A very jealous nun won the ear of the Cardinal Protector of the Congregation, and Jeanne was treated and spoken to in ways which seem incredible to those who expect to see some measure of decency retained among Religious. She was reduced to complete silence and immobility for three years and even threatened with expulsion. She accepted this terrible experience most perfectly; her reputation was better than restored; she died in extreme peace and surrounded by love.

Bewilderment has often been expressed that Mme. Acarie (Blessed Mary of the Incarnation: 1566-1618), who coped with kings and queens, soldiers and lawyers, Saints and moral outcasts and who, we shall see, influenced the whole of the religious future of France, could become practically unknown. Barbe Avrillot was a Parisian, but her parents were so severe that you would be told, nowadays, that she would be victim of the perfect inferiority complex. At school she wanted to be a nun and serve in a hospital, but the sick, they said, were so numerous that their reek was intolerable. Appalled, her mother threw her into a whirl of gaiety and married her off at sixteen-and-a-half to Pierre Acarie, very prominent in the League. He was a good man, but excitable, unstable, desperately improvident, and unconsciously bullied his wife badly. They had six children, all very healthy and happy and devoted to their mother, who so soon as possible made it clear that whether or no they were to be nuns they must have the best possible education for great-ladyship—their backs must be as straight as their consciences. If they were naughty she waited till they acknowledged it themselves, and then got the birch. . . . One day M. Acarie found his wife reading romances. He disapproved, rushed out and bought some pious books superbly bound, and then some more. One sentence sufficed to shatter the whole of her perspective: "*Trop avare est celuy—A qui Dieu ne suffit*". The Spirit so invaded her that she could not control herself—she would scrub her hands, play the spinet, *not* to be rapt into ecstasy, as St. John of the Cross knocked his knuckles on the wall lest he should suffer such a "Dislocation". She uttered loud cries which alarmed the neighbours. Relays of doctors bled her—she did but put on weight and her complexion grew more brilliant (and, I say at once, these "beginnings" were very soon controlled). For a while it was the expatriate Fr. Canfield who pacified her; Pierre Acarie produced the *Revelations of Blessed Angela of Foligno*, but his wife wanted no more books. Back he swung; he had her denounced from the pulpit and caused her to be passed over at Communion; said that she neglected the servants (with whom, in fact, he himself was somewhat too familiar), whereas, during the Siege of Paris, she had managed the rationing of half the city and had taken a very strong line against buying up and hoarding food. Then, the crash. Henri of Navarre became a Catholic; the League collapsed, and Acarie was exiled from Paris.

He left mountains of debts. Insane largesses to the League had ruined his father too. Relatives rounded on Mme. Acarie and told her to send her children to learn cobbling. (But she found good schools for all of them.) Creditors invaded her and took the very plate off which she was eating. And this woman of ecstatic prayer tackled the chaos single-handed; sat up all night composing legal documents so accurately that no lawyer had to correct them; disregarded every insult (some are shocking to read about), and put the family on its feet again. But alas, one day her horse stumbled; her thigh was broken in several places; she was dragged and then jolted in a cart twenty miles to Paris. The doctor who was setting the bone cried: "But I must be hurting you horribly! Are you alive or dead?" She just said: "Finish what you are doing." But in 1597 she slipped and broke it again, and yet again; she could never now walk without a stick. Finally she made friends with the King, and at last brought her husband home.

Her house became always full of laughter and gaiety, a "social centre"; she was careful that her daughters should be as prettily dressed as ever, though she herself longed that her dresses could be "all of one piece" and not need scores of hooks and tapes. But also, the house radiated charitable work—the visiting of the sick and poor,[1] and was a centre to which everyone, royalists or ex-Leagueists, trooped for spiritual advice. St. Francis de Sales came there every other day despite, said he, the mud "of which there is always such a lot in the Paris streets". . . . (Here speaks the Savoyard!) But he stood in such awe of Mme. Acarie that he refused to be her director though he was her confessor for some months —a good example of the distinction between the two positions. It is worth remembering, when we see how men of all ranks and callings came to profit by her counsel, her spirituality and her very presence, that the French spirit is realist and very critical, and that the official theologians of the time were intensely jealous of their prerogatives, especially if belonging to the Sorbonne as M. Duval, her biographer, did. Yet here was she, a married woman, at the head of the "reform" of innumerable convents and even "orders" throughout France, and of groups of "dedicated" women devoted not least to education. She has been called the "conscience of France".

---

[1] A film recently admired, *Monsieur Vincent*, was, for the sake of dramatic simplification, misleading. St. Vincent was emphatically *not* the only organizer of charitable work in Paris, let alone in the Court, or in France.

But in 1601 the French translation of St. Teresa's *Life* was published (she died in 1582). Mme. Acarie did not like it— nor the Saint. However, Teresa appeared to her and told her to introduce the Carmelite Reform into France. The thing seemed impossible, but Teresa repeated her visit. More discussions, in which St. Francis de Sales took part. Two Orleans princesses approached the King, who flatly disapproved—there were enough religious orders already; convents took up room and interfered with trade and traffic— why go to Spain for Superiors? At last he gave reluctant consent. St. Francis wrote to the Pope. The King veered round and became enthusiastic. A house began to be reconditioned; Mme. Acarie hobbled round supervising each detail—the bricklayers worshipped her. She then formed a group of possible Carmelites, seeing accurately into their minds: "*She* avoids faults by prudence and tact, not grace. *She* will advance by her falls, and renewed falls. *She* will make progress in virtue but not in the interior life." She did not always have this sort of intuition, nor always the sense of God's presence, but she *was* normally aware of the direct guidance of God in her intensely active life and would even stop short in the middle of a sentence if she did not perceive that God was telling her what to say. This must be partly why she, so gay, so versatile, so charming, none the less inspired that mysterious "awe".

Meanwhile the epic journey of some of her friends into Spain to fetch the Carmelites had begun. It was composed of some gentlemen for safety's sake and some ladies who would form the immediate contacts. M. de Bérulle, after- wards founder of the French Oratory and Cardinal, followed them. The most entertaining difficulties could surely be foreseen, the clash, for example, between two etiquettes each developed to the extreme; between the white-hot pride of the Spaniard and the lucid individualism of the French; the austere grandeur of the southern tradition and dainty Parisian elegances which neither the splendours of Versailles nor the puritanism of a Pascal were going to supersede. And at first the Spanish friars insisted that the nuns must be exclusively under *their* direction and that they must come too, an exclusivism quite contrary to St. Teresa's spirit and corrected only by papal authority.   The return journey began, complete with six very apprehensive Spanish nuns, among whom were Anne of Jesus and the charming lay-sister (afterwards choir-nun) Blessed Anne of St. Bartholomew, of whom the latter especially had been intimate with St. Teresa.   Anne of Jesus was too rigid and detested everything French—she was convinced that France was almost wholly heretic and hardly Christian at all; she afterwards left for Flanders along with others of the "foundress-nuns".   At Paris a tremendous and even royal welcome awaited them; the first convent was inaugurated, little Andrée Levoix, Mme. Acarie's faithful servant, being given precedence over noble and opulent novices, being god-mothered by the two Orleans princesses.   Unmoved by criticisms or compliments, Mme. Acarie now meant to efface herself.

Impossible.   Carmels were asked for everywhere; despite her torturing leg she had to tour around for consultations. Her three daughters all became Carmelites[1]—the second, Marguerite, was a vivacious girl of a most sanctified all-but impertinence. . . . Her mother once asked her for advice; her candid reply almost shocked bystanders.   "Well", said she, "why else did she ask for it? She knows perfectly well I haven't any tact. I say what comes into my head."   Indeed, she did.   Anne of Austria, for example, liked to visit these convents with a tumultuous retinue.   She asked Marguerite why she kept so much in the background.   "Your Majesty— if Your Majesty only knew how long it takes us to recover from your visits, you would, ever so kindly, leave us to our solitude!"   Mme. Acarie had always begged confessors not to mention "vocation" to these three girls, so abhorrent to her was the idea of "coaxing" anyone to be a nun; indeed,

[1] Of the three sons, one tried to be a Jesuit but became a soldier: the eldest married and held honourable posts: the second became a priest and left his vast collection of books to Rouen cathedral on condition that the library should be open to the public.

she diverted most of the girls she had trained away from Carmel—mostly towards the teaching congregation of Ursulines which, with her cousin, Mme. de Sainte-Beuve, she brought to France.

She nursed her husband through his last illness; he died in 1613.

Long ago, St. Teresa had "told" her she must enter Carmel as a lay-sister. But how could she? Neither to sing the Office, nor, with her broken thigh, to do hard work? Above all, after thirty-one years of married life, spent almost all of it in inventing, in creating, in governing, to obey the minutiae of a Rule administered, maybe, by those whom she herself had trained? Yes, enter she did, at Amiens, and after a while was "under" her daughter Marguerite, now sub-prioress. Yet her life, despite constant interruptions from irresistible personages come to beg her advice, was happy; she was free, at least, to pray. But she had, twice more, cause for suffering. M. de Bérulle had composed some "devotions" that seemed contrary to the spirit of Carmel: too abstract; too subtle. She, with two priests who were "directors" in the convent, resolutely opposed the intro-duction of those prayers. Bérulle, despite his genuine virtues, lost his head and exclaimed: "You are small-minded and deluded, and have done nothing but harm in anything you have mixed yourself up in." "What words!" exclaimed M. Duval, "what violence!" It hurt the elderly and now sick woman cruelly; in her humility, she thought it must be true—her life had been a delusion; she had done only harm. This was needed, perhaps, for her final purifica-tion and radical detachment from her own vast work. On February 7, 1618, being then at Pontoise, she caught cold and began to suffer terribly. She who had never complained was unable now to prevent herself from asking God to have mercy. "My God", she once cried out, "I can no more! *Can* for me!" How else translate: "*Je n'en peux plus: pouvez pour moi!*" At long last, on Easter Wednesday, as the priest was about to anoint her eyes, she closed them of her own accord and opened them no more. She was beatified in 1791.

Mme. Acarie must not be confused with Mme. Martin (*née* Guyard), who was born at Tours, October 28, 1599, and was also called Mary of the Incarnation. She married a silk-merchant and had one son who became a Benedictine and wrote her life. Left a widow after two years and having educated the boy, she joined the Ursulines (see above), felt called to the native missions of Canada, and in fact arrived in Quebec in July, 1639. Her monastery (founded where the Ursuline monastery still stands) was burnt down in 1650. She stood firm against the threats of the Iroquois, rebuilt her monastery, and died after thirty-three years of unremitting work in Canada. I say no more about her here, because of the pages about "missionary nuns" below.

Jeanne Frémyot was born at Dijon on January 23, 1572, of good Burgundian stock. Her grandfather, informed (he felt) by God when he should die, went on a family tour to say goodbye. He was too weak to mount his mule, so this considerate beast spread its legs out till it was almost flat, and he got on it. "It only shows how unreasoning animals submit themselves to man when reasoning man submits himself to God. . . ." His son, Bénigne Frémyot, held very high office though most of the Burgundians were Leaguists; he almost ruined himself by raising a force of his own and fighting for the King throughout the civil wars. His only son was kidnapped and the Leaguists sent to say that if Bénigne did not change sides they would send him the boy's head. He declared he would sooner his son died innocent than himself sully his soul with treachery. But they thought that ransom would be worth more to them than a headless boy; so Frémyot became both poorer and happier. When Henri III was killed, the shock to Frémyot was such that all the hair of one side of his head turned white in a single night. But he went on raising troops till Henri IV became Catholic

and King and arrived at Dijon ready to heap favours on a
man proved to be so faithful. Frémyot said bluffly: "If Your
Majesty had not said so heartily: '*Vive* the Roman Church!'
I never would have cried: '*Vive* Henri IV!' " The King,
delighted, gave him the "archbishopric of Bourges and the
great abbey of St-Etienne", for the old man wanted to
devote his last years to God. But since he had married again
he made over the see of Bourges to his son André, who lived
there but was not so much as ordained priest for nearly ten
years. Frémyot lived at St-Etienne, occupying the whole of
the abbot's house. Here Jeanne was brought up, very happy,
and *fille à toute folie*, as she recalled when a nun. From
fifteen to twenty she lived with her elder sister and was
constantly asked in marriage; an old lady kept begging her
to use powder and paint to attract these gentlemen, but she
liked neither the end nor the means. One anecdote survives.
The Poitou had been savagely devastated by the Huguenots.
Impossible to ride abroad without coming across profaned
churches. This made her cry, so that she dared not take off
the mask that noblewomen wore in public, for people noticed
her red eyes and wondered what was worrying her in her
brother-in-law's castle.

Now a very rough old Baron, Guy de Rabutin de Chantal,
had, like his fellow loyalist Frémyot, ruined himself, though
most probably by extravagance, and his son Christopher
was apparently not less extravagant; so the two old gentlemen decided their son and daughter had better marry. This
occurred with incredible splendour on December 29, 1592.
Jeanne was twenty-one; her husband, a little older. Happily
they had fallen wildly in love with one another, for Jeanne
found that a whole estate had to be put right—debts, repairs,
rents, discipline among the staff—she seemed to become
responsible for everything, though she had not even learnt
to keep accounts. She resented the end thus put to her liberty;
but Christopher explained that it was his own mother's
tact that had saved the family from total ruin, and Jeanne
resolved to emulate her. Soon, the servants adored her.

During her eight years of married life and nine of widowhood, she almost never had to change them. Even then, this was considered a miracle. . . . Debts were paid off, the estate prospered and the granaries "burst with wheat"; she was always at the service of the sick tenantry even when they were so disgusting that their own parentage turned away. Still, in a famine year, the destitute kept applying at the "big house" for help, and Jeanne caused a second door to be opened so that the applicants could enter by the one, and file out in due order by the other. Naturally, there were those who ran rapidly round and came back to the first door to get a second dole. Jeanne, perfectly aware of this, reminded herself with a smile that she herself had had to ask God for mercy over and over again.

St. Jeanne afterwards related with much good humour to her friend and fellow-Visitandine Mère de Chaugy the various tricks she used to get rid of importunate gallants when her husband was away at court, or fighting, or hunting, and Mère de Chaugy wrote it all down with the demure amusement proper to her generation which had not yet grown prudish. Jeanne felt that she ought to be "more devout" but practically all her prayers "simply ended with requests that her husband might be brought home safe". He came, and the round of parties, dancing, hunting began again, and many prayers were allowed to slide. But she always got up early, to see to household affairs; and if Christopher obstinately went on sleeping and kept the chaplain waiting too long for Mass, she would draw the curtains back with much rattling, and if that failed, lit a candle and put it under the poor man's nose. Anyhow, he had left court for good. But one day he went out shooting with a M. d'Anlezy, one of his best friends. Exactly what happened, no one knows. His friend's arquebus went off and the Baron fell. "I am dying, my cousin, my friend", he said, "I forgive you with all my heart, it was an accident." He sent four servants to find a priest, and another to the Baroness. "Tell her only that I am wounded." She was in

bed, her youngest daughter having been born only a fortnight before. She hurried to the cottage where they had
taken him. He said, "My love, God's decree is just; we must
love it: I must die." She insisted he must recover. He saw his
friend some way off, walking to and fro as if off his head.
"Cousin, my dear friend—the blow reached me from heaven
before it came from you. Do not sin by hating yourself for
that which was no sin. Remember you are a Christian!"
The doctors came; Jeanne, distraught, cried that they *must*
cure him. When they saw that the wound was fatal, she
would not accept it. She went out and asked God to take
everything—her father, her children, but not him. After
nine days he died (1601) and her world seemed finished for
her. Yet she was gay with her children; solicitous for the
sick, only she would not go out to parties and none but the
servants knew that she kept going to a little wood to cry
there. But she began to long for a "spiritual director",
though in spite of her upbringing having been "good and
honourable, I had never heard a word about spiritual
directors or anything like that." One day, when riding
through the fields and praying about this, she saw at
the foot of a hill a bishop. Much later she recognized
in him St. Francis de Sales. He on his side, by a lake in
Savoy, had seen a woman in widow's dress. But for a while
this celestial telepathy had no issue, and indeed all went
wrong.

Her father called her to Dijon and devout friends urged
her to a priest who specialized in "direction"—of the most
ill-judged sort. He made her vow to obey him—never to
take anyone else for director—never to repeat what he said—
never to discuss her soul with anyone else. And on to the
tormented woman he piled all sorts of "devotions", so that
when at last St. Francis did "direct" her, the servants said:
"My Lady's first director made her pray thrice a day and
the whole staff was driven crazy; now, Monseigneur of
Geneva makes her pray all day and it interferes with no
one." But next, it was her gruff old father-in-law who

summoned her and her children to live with him at Monthelon—else he would marry again and disinherit them. She went and found (you might have expected it!) that the Baron was utterly under the thumb of a housekeeper who had installed herself there with her five children, and had no intention of abdicating. With infinite tact Jeanne not only got the house into real order, but won the heart of the truculent old barbarian who wept like a baby when after eight years of penance she left. She even took charge of the housekeeper's children and even combed their hair. . . . One day in early 1604 her father told her that the Lent was being preached at Dijon by a good preacher—the young Bishop of Geneva (Francis was thirty-seven; Jeanne, thirty-two). The moment she saw him she felt sure it was he who would help her. She had her chair put just before the pulpit to see and hear him better. He on his side asked André Frémyot, the Archbishop, who the young widow was with bright brown hair—*claire-brune*—who was so attentive? "My sister!" They all dined together, Francis being puzzled by this gay elusive lady in elegant half-mourning. "Elusive", for after all, not only she had her vows, but her director had actually put one of his flock to keep an eye on her in Dijon. . . . She did, however, see Francis on and off; he—with less perhaps than his usual shyness—hinted that she might keep her crowd of suitors rather more at arm's length. Impulsively, she cut off her hair and burnt it; and also learnt that her director had no right to extort those vows from her. On Wednesday in Holy Week the Archbishop (who was to say his first Mass next day) arranged an interview, and after long hesitations the Bishop with his mother and sister and Jeanne with two friends met half-way between Dijon and Savoy; she spoke freely, but that evening he said nothing. Next day he said: "Madame, let us sit down. I am very tired and could not sleep. My mind was at work all night over your affairs." Then he begged pardon for his delays, and said he now felt sure that God wished him to guide her.

It is clearly impossible to describe even in outline the linked spiritual history of these two Saints. Francis was still a strange mixture of hesitations and decisiveness. Thus he kept insisting on "liberty"; anything that he said to her must be treated *grosso modo*, not too meticulously . . . yet he watched details—she was dainty about olives and fried snails . . . but since they were not bad for her, let her eat them! And since she had resolved not to marry, let her be done with half-measures in regard of suitors. "Scissors, knife, for such knots! Your nails are too short to disentangle them!" One incident was characteristic of both. She feared that she gave too much talk, too many sighs, to the memory of her husband; but she fiercely repelled any hint that she should so much as see M. d'Anlezy again. Francis agreed that she need not seek him out; but *if*, if, she met him, let her be gentle, kindly. . . . Meet him she did; and, hearing that he had recently become a father, she forthwith offered to be the small boy's godmother. The tentative steps of the Savoyard —the impulsive leap forward of the Burgundian *grande dame*! So with prayer. She still loved vocal prayer, especially the Psalms, of which she had a metrical version on her saddle, so that she could sing them while riding about the estate. But the Dijon Carmelites tried to dissuade her from using imagination or reflection. . . . She consulted Francis. He said that so sublime a prayer might be well for those already high up the mountain of perfection, "but for the rest of us, who are still in the valleys, I *think* it is better for us to use all the means at our disposal" (*pièces*; like chessmen). Once or twice he had found himself in the presence of God without any "preparation" and was much at his ease there; but "I would never dare to step off the high road and make that a normal method." "All the same, I don't imagine I know such a lot as to be other than very content, I say, extremely very content—to abdicate my view and follow those who have every reason for knowing much more than I about the matter." Later, he was to write that at this time he still had "much to learn".

He simply refused to talk about Jeanne's vocation. "Give me a year", he said; then another year. Finally, at Pentecost, 1607, she went to Annecy and said she would do what he told her. She knelt: "You must join the Poor Clares." "So be it!" "No, you are not strong enough. . . . You must be a nurse in the hospital at Beaune. . . . Or perhaps a Carmelite after all." At last he outlined the Visitation Order as her destiny— though saying it could not be begun for six or seven years.[1] But accomplishment was nearer than that! She was still at Annecy for Corpus Christi. After the procession she was tired and resolved to lie down till Francis de Sales, who had carried the monstrance, should have dressed for dinner. She approached the staircase; several noblemen precipitated themselves to help her up it. . . . She laughed, and took the arm of the little Baron de Thorens, St. Francis's brother, saying: "This is the one I choose for partner!" Instantly everyone assumed that she meant to marry one of her daughters to him. But the de Sales were poor; both Frémyot and Rabutin were planning much more splendid alliances for their granddaughters. Jeanne would say nothing definite, though the Bishop's mother was enchanted. But, on October 8, St. Francis's little sister, whom Jeanne was bringing up with her own children, died suddenly. Impetuously, forgetting all those plans, Jeanne vowed she would give the de Sales one of her own daughters to compensate. Then she recalled that if indeed Marie-Aimée, the child in question, married a Savoyard, it would be all the easier for her to live in Savoy near her daughter and also near St. Francis. (The children were in fact married in 1609.) Jeanne must have been rather taken aback on finding that her father had brusquely settled her affairs on his own account. Marie-Aimée was "arranged for"; it was time the other two little girls should go to school at the Ursulines; the boy, Celse-Bénigne, had also been "arranged

---

[1] Mère de Chaugy gives as sole reason for the distant date, Francis's resolve that all Jeanne's children should be well established before she began her career.

for".[1] Jeanne asked, therefore, if he would not allow her to take
the vows of religion. The day after Marie-Aimée's marriage,
Frémyot agreed. Alas, early in 1610 one of the other little
girls, Charlotte, died; on March 19 of that year Jeanne said
goodbye to her home. I may say at once that her separation
from her children should not be too dramatized. Marie-
Aimée was constantly in and out of the convent where her
mother was to live; the other little girl, Françoise, actually
lived there so long as she was small; she was radiantly happy
and could, like her mother, tame squirrels and birds, though
the laces and ribbons they gave her made her rather shy of
the Bishop. The day came when she too had to be
"established". The Comte de Toulongeon was settled on and
in 1620 Jeanne wrote to Françoise that her fiancé was
coming to see her. She hopes the girl will not find him *trop
noir*, too grave, if not dour. "Most certainly I am very glad
that it is your relatives and I who have settled this marriage
for you, and without you. . . . It is true that M. de Toulongeon
is fifteen years older than you are, but, my dear, you will be
much happier with him than with some young idiot, brain-
less, immoral, like the young men of today. Your husband . . .
does not gamble; he has spent his life honourably at court

---

[1] Briefly, Celse-Bénigne got on very well at court and as an officer—too
well to please Richelieu who chilled down the liking that Louis XIII had for
the young man by saying that Chantal "snapped his fingers at everyone".
Duelling was then forbidden under pain of death: the young man never
fought on his own account but often as a second. He was leaving a church
where he had just made his Easter duties when he was told his friend
Bouteville needed him. He went off, just as he was, "in black velvet slippers"
and fought "with his usual courage and success". He then fled to a brother-
in-law's. Bouteville was duly executed, and Chantal returned to court as
though nothing had happened. *Il se moquait de tout le monde.* . . . Jeanne had
been convinced he would be beheaded and prepared to go and help him to
die well. In 1617 she was feeling he was "already half lost"; but in 1623 he
married Marie de Coulanges though even she could not keep him from
duelling. In 1627 he was fighting against the English: on July 22 he went to
confession and communion, had three horses killed under him and then fell
himself. Only six years later, his young widow died—no blow had hitherto
been so grievous to Jeanne. And "his poor little orphan daughter!" she
cried. At one time, Jeanne foresaw a religious vocation for this child, but in
1644 she married the Marquis de Sévigné and became the very famous
woman, a household word among thousands who probably have never heard
of Mme. de Sévigné's grandmother.

and in the army . . . you would not have the good sense that I believe to be yours if you did not welcome him with cordiality and candour." So perfectly seventeenth century was this Saint! I do not know what perspective will be that of men living three hundred years ahead of us, as we are of the Baroness![1]

There has been much dispute as to what, exactly, Francis meant the Visitation to be. Yet it seems to me clear. It should be an Order—not for the sick, but for those who frankly could not survive the austerities of Carmel or the Poor Clares. But his nuns must be nuns who *prayed*, and, God granting it, with a prayer higher than the ordinary. But he certainly meant them to spend "a good part of the day" visiting the sick or doing other good external works. But the powerful Cardinal of Lyons thought that such virtue could not survive save behind grilles; so the Visitation became cloistered. Francis often said: "I have not accomplished what I meant to." I think it is clear that he "meant" very gently to effect that evolution in the "religious" life of women which St. Vincent de Paul, for example, almost *without* meaning to brought about; as for men, the Friars and then the Jesuits had largely accomplished that evolution.

Jeanne never regarded herself as foundress of the Visitation, nor its Mother General (the houses were to be independent) nor was she always re-elected Superior in her own. Despite this she used to be thought of as the supreme authoritarian— possibly in contrast to St. Francis de Sales who was regarded as affected, a Saint of "drawing-room piety", by those who stopped short at the literary mannerisms imposed by the seventeenth century and gave no heed to his utterly

[1] We have to confess that Françoise and Celse-Bénigne came to be at cross purposes as to which should inherit the fortune of their uncle the Archbishop. Celse-Bénigne begged Jeanne to intercede for *him*. She said that the Archbishop detested being hustled; that anyhow he was reserving benefices which should produce 6,000 *livres* annually for any son that Celse-Bénigne might beget; and so, let him remain content with what "God and Monseigneur your uncle" have already provided. In a slightly naïf postscript she advises him to write to his uncle as often as he can. She was always delighted, grieved or terrified by his adventures and concerned about his finances. Yes; a perspective both heavenly and seventeenth century.

uncompromising doctrine. She was, and needed to be, courageous, and her portrait certainly shows a vigorous Burgundian head full of "character". She *disliked* "managing" things, especially details, and wrote (1627) to tell St. Vincent de Paul so—he had even more to do, but at least his work was varied, hers monotonous. Even when her impetuosity was under control (perhaps it never was, quite!), she detested wasting time or words. When the question of beatifying Francis arose in Rome, she said: "The dilly-dallying of that place is sheer death—and here too!" Probably when she had to force herself to be firm, she may have *seemed* a little autocratic; and among her nuns were yet greater aristocrats than she, who could not divest themselves of court manners, who liked to use scent or wear high heels, or sweep great curtseys even in the refectory (it is pleasant to recall that once everything slipped off the dish that was being handed . . .). She knew too how different things sound when read and when spoken, and annotated letters she had dictated lest they should seem too stiff. Such a temperament—which may have to rebuke yet hates to cause pain—may have to be on guard equally against imperiousness and softness. She did not like being written about to other convents, and once she had to rebuke a Sister sharply for having done so. The Sister melted into floods of tears. "But you're crying!" said Jeanne, patted her, told her stories till she laughed, succumbed and said: "Oh—write anything about me you like, I don't mind!" She then went to the kitchen and cooked a nice little supper for the Sister "and", says the chronicler, off to the opposite extreme of conventionalism, "actually extended her kindness to such lengths as herself to pass the dishes out to her through the serving-hatch." She knew she was much criticized, even within the Visitation convents, but: "I really don't do so much harm as they say", she wrote. I think it possible that her cult of simplicity and distrust of religious emotions made her seem bleak. She preferred the blunt Savoyard French to "French-French" (it is said that her own French was twenty years ahead of that

I

of St. Francis); she pruned letters from all exaggerated phrases. If she was clear-headed as to herself, so was she as regards others. To Sisters who would not say they felt ill but wanted the Superior to be the first to notice it and sympathize, she quoted the preacher who said he would not denounce a notorious sinner by name, "but I will throw my breviary at his head". But she too had her inconsistencies. During the plague, many towns (and their convents) were "isolated" by order. Thus she was forbidden to come within a mile of Autun. A Sister came out to a field to cry out, from afar, how her convent was faring. Jeanne could not bear this, but made the sign of the cross, embraced the Sister, and put her into the carriage which had held not only herself but her daughter Mme. de Toulongeon and her granddaughter, Gabrielle, aged six. "If", said the poor Countess, "I were not convinced that my mother is a Saint, I should be shuddering with fright." Still, cats were supposed to carry the infection; she had them all killed, though she could not exclude the poor Francis from the parlour, though he came from the most infectious part of all.

But during his last few years, he very seldom saw her, seldom wrote, wished that the Visitation should stand on its own feet. Certainly he had more and more work of his own to exhaust him, but she had to beg him, even so, to write once or twice a year to convents or even Sisters who had need of a little consolation. At last, in December 1622, she managed to meet him at Lyons. "Which of us shall begin first?" he said. "I", she urged, "my heart badly needs to be 'reviewed' by you!" He said, "But do you still want things so urgently—and want to choose? We will talk about ourselves at Annecy; at present let us settle the affairs of the Institute." She put away the notes of what she had wanted to say and took out the list of business matters. After four hours' discussion, Francis told her to go to Grenoble. She went, and on December 28, he died. So they never met at Annecy.

I have said little that might indicate Jeanne's sanctity, but have, as it were, spent time in describing the wire which, divinely electrified, radiated light and heat. It must be enough to say that during her remaining years she still disguised her ever-increasing exhaustion under her alert demeanour and rapid walk. She lived entirely on faith. She remained in darkness about herself and could not *feel* the truth of anything she said. She actually longed for death and "wasted time" looking up how long her relatives had lived and trusting she would not live longer than her father who had died at sixty-three. The truths of religion brought her no consolation but, rather, exasperated her. Even the "spiritual reading" during meals seemed torture to her. She lived, then, in absolute trust, not allowing any reflection on her state or on anything else, to ruffle her. In the summer of 1641 she left Annecy for a tour through the Visitation monasteries of France; she was even sent for to Paris by the Queen; her life seemed more thronged than ever. But on her way home she caught cold and became rapidly worse. On December 11, at Moulins, she received Viaticum. Next day, she sat up, dictated a letter of goodbye to all her houses and signed it, and then lay down, her sense of duty satisfied. During the night she caused St. Jerome's epitaph on St. Paula to be read, and cried that we, alas, are but "atoms" compared with those heroic women. Then she had the death of Francis de Sales read to her and part of his Treatise on the Love of God, and the death of St. Monica related by her son Augustine. When she heard that Monica did not "mind" dying away from her country, "That is for us", she said. In the evening of Friday she asked for the Commendation of the Soul to be read, which it was, several times over, "for her agony lasted long", and she listened attentively. She was asked if she did not hope to be met by St. Francis. "Yes, I trust to that", she said, "he promised me that he would. . . ." About six o'clock she took her crucifix and a blessed candle in her right and left hands, and when the priest reminded her that her great pain was the herald of the approach of her Beloved, she said: "Yes, Father, I am going." Then she said "Jesus" three times and three times sighed gently, and so left this life. She was beatified in 1751 and canonized only sixteen years later.[1]

If I have spent so long over French women, this is due not only to my love for France dating from childhood, but to my ignorance of what documentation of a similar sort exists about other countries—anyhow, it did not seem accessible—and possibly because there *were* more women in France who trod the flatlands upon which we too tread and yet became Saints or saintly, without being cloistered upon earth but habitually inhabiting the skies of ecstasy and enduring abnormal preternatural vocations. Thus it may seem less strange that there is here no chapter about St. Teresa of Avila (1515-1582); but though her life was very colourful and eventful, her doctrine is so overwhelmingly important that it might not have suited this book.[2]

Something similar might be said of St. Margaret Mary Alacoque (1647-1690), if only because her rôle in the development of the devotion to the Sacred Heart of our Lord

[1] It is with real regret that I relegate thus to a note the Congregation of La Sagesse (in America, the "Daughters of Wisdom"). It was in reality founded by St. Grignion de Montfort who was chaplain to a hospital at Poitiers. Perhaps he could have done little without the help of Marie-Louise Trichet (the founder's name was Louis-Marie) who became a kind of matron in the hospital. She was only nineteen when he gave her the habit of a small group of nurses—the habit, unlike any others that we know of, being simply that of the peasants of Poitou. When he died in 1716 there were only four members of his Congregation; but when Marie-Louise died, there were altogether forty houses. Strangely enough she died (1759) on the same date, at the same hour and in the same house as St. Grignion de Montfort had died. One feels almost desperate at being unable to relate even in outline the history of this heroic Congregation, especially during the great Revolution when the guillotine seemed permanently installed. There is a good account in *Les Filles de la Sagesse*, by M.-T. Le Moign-Klipffel, 1947. Nor can I here try to explain the special devotion of the Founder to the Holy Wisdom of God, or to our Lady, whom he wished to associate always with her Son. The Sisters have gravitated towards teaching, but are faithful to their original work among the sick, in or out of hospital, and do much service among lepers, especially in Africa.

[2] Not to have dwelt on St. Teresa must be a proof that I could not, e.g., dissociate her from St. John of the Cross nor even from her Dominican or Jesuit directors. Dominant as her personality and influence are, they are not *isolated* within the current of Catholic Life.

needs to be defined. She did not originate it; it goes back at least to St. Gertrude; St. Francis de Sales had given the Hearts of Jesus and Mary—which he called "this *one* Heart" —to the Visitation Order as its "device" or crest; St. John Eudes had preached the doctrine of devotion to the Hearts of Jesus and Mary before Margaret Mary's time—on entering the Visitation convent of Paray le Monial she found his Mass in honour of our Lady's Heart already being celebrated there, and the order was steeped in this very symbolism. But while St. John Eudes is spoken of in very strong words in the Breviary as the originator of the liturgical cult of the Sacred Heart, it was certainly St. Margaret Mary who, with the collaboration of the Blessed Claude de la Colombière, "popularized" the devotion. Indeed, she gave a somewhat different "bent" to it. The words spoken to her are famous— "Behold this Heart which has so much loved men!" St. John Eudes's motto might have been: "Behold this Heart which so much loves God!" He concentrated on the inner life of our Lord and His Mother, but especially in so far as it was directed towards God in love and adoration. His writings, too, were somewhat elaborate, if not obscure, and certainly not to be assimilated by the multitude. St. Margaret Mary, on the other hand, displayed the love and suffering of our Lord's Heart precisely in regard of us men; and she herself suffered terribly at the thought of man's ingratitude and emphasized the need of expiation. Her nature was really light-hearted and gay, but her girlhood was repressed and snubbed by her step-mother; and on entering the Visitation convent the young *bourgeoise* found herself in a world of convention and "aristocratic" ideas; many of the nuns were members of the provincial nobility, always inclined to be stiffer than really "grand" personages; and she was, as some think, without natural "charm" and was awkward, though her clumsiness may well have been due to the "abstraction" caused by the spirit of intense interior prayer which was beginning to absorb her. For some time, then, she was treated with an austerity more or less deliberate; it did not help that she felt ordered by our Lord to rebuke the Community, in public, for their shortcomings as to religious spirit and observance. But gradually she was better understood and was made mistress of novices and it was here that she could first explain that love for our Lord's Sacred Humanity which itself was so little understood. In proportion as Jansenism developed its chill and rigorous doctrines, the devotion to the Sacred Heart proved a real antidote, though for long it was attacked also by the orthodox upon theological grounds. It is important, as we said, that this devotion should not be regarded as wholly due to St. Margaret Mary; she played a very great part as its apostle, but it anteceded her, and continued to develop after her.

But looking, if only for a moment, towards Italy, it is impossible not just to mention St. Mary Magdalen de' Pazzi (1566-1607), a noble Florentine who became a Carmelite at sixteen, largely because she could thus receive Holy Communion daily. Like most ecstatic Saints, she had much to occupy her; she was novice-mistress and sub-prioress. Her life seemed a sort of "dialogue" with God, our Lord (especially in His Passion), our Lady and the Saints. Where St. Teresa had prayed either to die or to suffer, she prayed not to die, that she might suffer more. She too underwent the appalling purification that such Saints endure; for five years she suffered complete blackness of soul, and savage temptations to blasphemy, unbelief, impurity and even gluttony. In 1590 she "came to herself", took her superior's hand and said: "The storm is past." Her body did not fall to dust. You see it now, like (so it paradoxically struck me) a noble peasant-woman's, sunburnt, calm and dignified.

Nor can we omit St. Hyacinth Mariscottis (1585-1640), born of a noble family near Viterbo. Her early piety seemed to have quite evaporated into frivolity; she was twenty when, having determined to marry a Marquis Cassizucchi, she found herself disregarded in favour of a younger sister. Piqued by this, and feeling a fool in the eyes of society, she fled to a local convent of St. Bernardine without the slightest intention of keeping the rule; in fact, she equipped for herself a sort of cottage at the foot of the convent garden, which she got her father to furnish luxuriously, had special meals cooked for herself, and wore a very elegant habit. Up to date she had twice, I think, vowed to reform, but after ten years of this existence she again fell ill, confessed her faults publicly, and began a life of extraordinary prayer and penance. During an epidemic she heroically nursed the sick, and founded two confraternities, one for collecting alms for the sick, the poor, and prisoners, and the other for finding homes for the aged. I do not think I know of any exact parallel to this.

And we are glad to recall two Saints who were South Americans, from Peru and Ecuador. Both withdrew from the "world", but their world, though Spanish in great measure, had also a strong admixture of Indian blood in it and was forming a "society" not fully like the European one. St. Rose was born in 1586 and lived in Lima, and died in 1618, the same year, therefore, as Mme. Acarie. She closely copied St. Catherine of Siena and joined the Third Order of St. Dominic. She combined solitude (she had a little "hermitage" in the garden) with much house-work. Out of her short life she experienced no less than twelve years of complete "desolation" and her penances can be regarded only as a sort of cumulative expiation of the sins of her surroundings. The other is St. Anna Maria Paredes (1619-1645); and out of her life—also short, also terribly penitential—only one incident stands out; it shows the spirit that animated St. Teresa, who as a child wanted to seek martyrdom among the Moors. Anna Maria, fired by accounts of the Jesuit martyrs in Japan, ran away from home, but she too was brought back. One pure lily grew up from her grave, and she was called the "Lily of Quito" and thus made fit alliance with the Rose of Lima. The life of St. Veronica Giuliani (1660-1727) overlaps this period, nor will I dwell on her save to say that she was born in the district of Urbino, became a Poor Clare, gradually found her character transformed—her heart had been said to be made of steel; in the end, after a life of ecstasy and suffering, the cross was found deeply marked upon that heart. I like to recall that this mystic *par excellence* was, like nearly all of them, most practical; she installed a system of water-pipes throughout her convent that won universal admiration. . . . As for St. Germaine Cousin (1579-1601), who somehow became a kind of star of sanctity for France, she was a shepherdess near Toulouse, sickly and deformed from childhood, disliked by her father and harshly treated by her step-mother. It cannot have been only the great Revolution that postponed official recognition of her sanctity till the reign of Pius IX.[1]

---

[1] I can but mention Bd. Margaret Pole, Countess of Salisbury; martyred 1541.

CHAPTER VI

THE MODERN WORLD

BY THE "modern world" I do not mean the "contemporary world", but the new world that was born, so to say, with the great French Revolution, though it had been prepared for long before that. Indeed, during the eighteenth century the stream of sanctity seems to have flowed underground. Apart from a few Beatae whose cult was largely local, I can at the moment find only one woman-Saint who overlaps with St. Veronica Giuliani—Mary Frances Gallo or (to use, as seems mostly done, her mother's surname) Basinsin. She was born at Naples in 1715 and died there in 1791. Her father treated her very harshly, and when she became a tertiary of St. Peter of Alcantara she had to suffer at least as much from the rigidity of her directors. But she had chosen to be called Mary Frances of the Five Wounds; and her life of terrible penance and sublime prayer was no doubt needed for that decadent century. It is true that in most parts of Europe there was shocking mis-government at the time; still, it would be false to picture a handful of greedy and cruel nobles, lay or ecclesiastic, at one end and a starving proletariat at the other, with nothing between. As we shall see, the few names, and then the multitude of names, that come to the surface *imply* the existence of innumerable households which were both modestly well-to-do, and virtuous. None the less, there was everywhere a spirit of discontent with the absolute power of princes and the insane luxury of their courts; and above all, what was called the "Enlightenment" was sapping the foundations of all authority and inflaming imaginations with doctrines of equality and liberty which in fact issued into still worse tyrannies, or at least incredible chaos.

During such periods whole institutions may be destroyed; or survive only to die out afterwards; or revive and manifest an amazing vitality, which is just what the Church did. One of our difficulties is, in fact, the multiplicity of heroic characters we now encounter. Nothing on any national scale can be created out of hand; so we find small local groups coming into existence, ministering to local needs. But since local needs are in great measure identical—nursing the sick, teaching children—those who try to serve them, though disconnected, will be very like one another. In proportion as they develop, they will have to adopt much the same sort of life and rules, wear much the same sort of dress, and call themselves by similar (sometimes identical) names—"Poor Servants of . . .", "Sisters of (e.g.) St. Joseph, our Lady". And they will suffer much the same trials, from outside (jealousies; fears that they want to monopolize), and from within (clashes of temperament, personal ambitions, formation of cliques leading to actual schism—it is amazing how far such human frailties may go even among good people). So in course of time, you find a number of "Congregations" which are practically indistinguishable and are doing practically an identical work—for they may find it necessary, in the circumstances, to enlarge the scope of their original work and become still more like one another. If one asks: "Why do they not coalesce and ensure an immense economy of personnel by means of a central government and a few large noviciates instead of scores of tiny ones?" that may be because they feel they have each grown up into a "personality" which they do not want to lose; or again, because the bishop in whose diocese they originated does not want their government to be centralized outside it and able to move its subjects freely about without consulting him. Still, it would be a pity not to say something about some of the holy women who founded these congregations even though un-canonized, because each of them is signalized by some special event or characteristic; yet it is impossible even to summarize fully the life of each, for that would make this book interminable; if I spend much longer over some than others, I can but pray that the children of the latter will not think I slight or disesteem their foundress! And if I omit even to mention certain Congregations, that is partly because I do not even know them all, and because I cannot compose this part of my poor book with a mere dismal catalogue of names.

But I seem to be about to do just what I wanted not to do and was begged not to do—to write only of "Congregations" and their foundresses, and indeed I shall have chiefly to do that! "Do not forget", I have been urgently asked, "the humble mothers of families—perhaps the mothers of those very foundresses—or the simple women who spend their life in drudgery and *also* prayer! Try to find Saints among *those*!" It is in fact, sometimes, rather cynically suggested that members of Orders have an unfair handicap, for their "cause" can be backed by the wealth or "power" of such Orders. We can safely say that no amount of wealth or power could get anyone canonized as a Saint who was not a Saint; on the other hand, Orders are able to circulate information about their members who seem to them to be holy and win them publicity and cause them to be invoked for miracles. But in our Chapter V, i, we saw how it was once the habit to look out for and recognize holiness wherever it was to be found and even to write about it. This is no more so in England. Perhaps Latin countries still have the "instinct for sanctity" more than northerners;[1] but then, Italy, and especially Spain and Portugal, have been definitely inclined to keep their women out of any limelight. Anticipating, I will mention the Blessed Vicenta Maria Lopez y Vicuña (1847-1890, beatified 1950), foundress of the Daughters of Mary Immaculate for Domestic Service—the scope of her Institute has widened; but it still concentrates on young girls who may be doing, or preparing for domestic or other work. When she said she wanted to be a nun, her

---

[1] Thus in *The Month* (e.g. May 1947) I was able to quote from an immense number of Italian brochures about modern young laymen who were truly remarkable for virtue.

father was quite horrified because she did not propose to remain behind a grille. The wide smile of the Saint, when a nun, contrasted with the very demure photos of her girlhood, suggests an almost impish glee at having got her way (which was also God's) and *no* grilles. But not only she was photographed! You can see, too, her mother and her aunt Eulalia, responsible for so much of her upbringing. And you see, there, the maximum of *character*—a truly Spanish individuality combined with faith in an honourable tradition; a deep power of loving together with unswerving loyalty to duty; in short, a Spanish pride all the purer because of a paramountcy of the Spirit. I mention too the Blessed Maria Soledad Torres Acosta (1826-1887; *Soledad* means "solitude" and is applied to our Lady after the Crucifixion), because she too was Spanish and beatified in 1950, and because of the immense influence upon her of her parents and grandparents, with whom, alternately, she shared her youth. Born in a very poor quarter of Madrid, baptized two days later, she was confirmed when hardly more than one year old—perhaps because so frail. Even as a child she had an amazing instinct for helping the sick, like the "green" fingers of a born gardener. But not till she was twenty-five did she meet a Don Michele Martinez who planned to form an organization for helping the sick in their own homes. He chose her with six others as its nucleus; but he was not the man to provide a real religious—or medical—formation or even a "rule"; two of the seven died; the others left; other recruits came but the priest was busy and could not attend much to them; they were in extreme poverty; anti-clericalism attacked these "Servants of Mary"—they must leave off their religious dress which "made a bad effect in the streets of Madrid"; the original house might remain as it was but any new ones must submit to "modifications" imposed by the Government. However, the Governor himself was attacked by cholera and forthwith demanded to be nursed by *two* of these Sisters. The storm passed for the hour. But others loomed up. Don Michele suddenly sailed for the foreign missions and took some of the Sisters with him; Maria Soledad was left, alone indeed, to support the whole enterprise. Then, a recurrent feature in such histories (see pp. 151, 158), a brilliant, "dynamic" Sister, Maddelena Balledor, possessing apparently all the qualities that the self-effacing Foundress had not, succeeded in ousting her from her superiority and even from Madrid. But her dynamism soon seemed likely to explode the whole organization. Maria Soledad was called back; a more prudent "director" was substituted for the impulsive young priest who had been dazzled by Sister Maddelena. Tenacity joined with humility had conquered. The Handmaids of Mary Immaculate continued their development, and communities of Maria Soledad as of Vicenta Vicuna are at work in London.

i

At least from the earlier Middle Ages education had been available for girls, though wholly (I think) within convents where the children were as cloistered as the nuns. St. Angela Merici (1474-1540) is regarded as the pioneer of girls' schools, even though she and her associates began by teaching in their own homes. In 1525 she went to Rome; Clement VII asked her to stay there and open schools, but she was shy and went back to Brescia and not till 1535 did she found her order of Ursulines which spread rapidly, though all the houses remained independent and gradually differed widely in their customs. In 1900 Leo XIII convened a Congress of Ursulines from all over the world; thus the Roman Union of Ursulines was formed; not all communities agreed with the papal plan, but retained their separate independence. The Venerable Anne de Xainctonge (1597-1612) founded in France another "Ursula" Congregation; to avoid confusion its members are sometimes called "Ursules" and in 1902 "of the Blessed Virgin" was added to their name. They made what seems to me the tactical mistake, as others did, of saying they wished to be as like the

Jesuits as possible and therefore to have no enclosure. Hence grave difficulties arose (see p. 129); but the positive ideal has survived.

Slightly later than St. Angela, the Blessed Alix Le Clerc (1576-1622)[1] was from Lorraine; she was passionately fond of dancing and the elegant life, but felt drawn to change it and called on St. Peter Fourier, then parish priest at Mattaincourt. He, famed for his accessibility, said he was too busy to see her. Though piqued by this snub, she made her life more ascetic and finally he became her director. At long last, in 1597 he allowed her to form a small group to which after a while a powerful lady gave a house, and the Congregation of Notre Dame was begun, slightly before that of Jeanne de Lestonnac (p. 99) or the introduction of the Ursulines into France by Mme. de Sainte-Beuve (p. 105). Fourier is said to have initiated teaching by means of "classes" instead of individual tuition; I find it hard to see exactly what is meant by this; classes certainly pre-existed him. No matter. In the matter of "enclosure" he compromised. He obtained that it *should* exist, for the Sisters, but that the children should be admitted within it, which seemed an audacious innovation. He became, however, singularly aloof from Alix, maybe because of a clash of temperament. He, calm-headed, may have thought she was too much of a visionary; and though (as often happens) her more abnormal experiences diminished as she grew older and enjoyed a more tranquil union with God, he never let her think of herself as "Foundress", nor, apparently, was she ever Superior of any convent. She was in fact set aside in favour of an early companion, Mère Gante, who differed radically from her in that she wished each house to be independent and have its own noviciate. But after three hundred years it was Mère Alix's ideal that was decided on by Rome. She was beatified in 1947.

Mary Ward (1585-1645) was a true heroine, though her

[1] See a brief "life" of her, very vividly sketched by Mrs. M. West (D. Organ, London).

career presents problems largely because many documents are still inaccessible. But her ecclesiastical difficulties were equalled, if not surpassed, by many a Foundress who came after her. Of an ancient Yorkshire family, she was sent at five to her grandmother who had been in prison for the Faith. In due course she went to the Jesuits at St. Omer and, ill-advised, joined the Poor Clares as an "extern", and even opened a Poor Clare monastery for Englishwomen at Gravelines. In 1609 she returned to the perilous life of England, earning thus a reputation for instability. Still, she collected a little group wishing to be as like the Jesuits as possible, if only because "enclosed" life was *not* possible in England. Through her friend, Thomas Sackville, she put a Memorial before Paul V asking that her associates should be indeed "Religious" but wear no special habit nor be "enclosed". The Pope did not commit himself, but wrote to the Bishop of Namur asking him to look after her. Already she met with opposition, not only because of her proposed "innovations" but (I think) because of her advertised but ill-considered (so it seems to me) desire to be "like the Jesuits". But one remark made by a Roman priest got (if I may risk the slang) under her skin. He spoke of "first fervours", and said: "After all, they are only women." She often recurred to this. "I must and for ever will stand for this truth, that women may be perfect, and that fervour need not decay because we are women!" Four times in two years she crossed to England and her personality could not lie hid. The Archbishop of Canterbury said she did more "harm" than many priests and that he would rather have six or seven Jesuits than her, and that he only wished he could see her. . . . So she *called* on him. . . . He was out, but she scratched her name with a diamond on a window and went home. . . . She was caught, imprisoned, but neither executed nor kept in gaol; why, no one so far is sure.

But she had not been so much as seen in the various educational Houses that had been asked from her. Hence, disaffection among some of her own Sisters such as to make

her visit Gregory XV (who had succeeded Paul V) to get her
Institute "confirmed".[1] This amazing group—Mary, four
companions, a priest, a maid and Mr. Wright—covered the
1,500 miles to Rome in two months, walking as much as
thirty-five miles a day. She obtained her audience with
Gregory, old and ill, within four days; she prepared a new
Memorial and presented it to the appointed Cardinals. Its
rejection was, I think, inevitable because it demanded point-
blank that her Institute should be as like the Jesuits' Society
as possible, and, directly under the Pope, not the bishops.
She had heard in prayer the words: "Take the name of
the Society. Fr. General will never permit it. Go to
him." It is hardly now possible to judge of the origin or
even the exact bearing of these sentences. The General, in
fact, was consistently kind to Mary, but had already
forbidden his English subjects even to teach catechism in her
schools. Further, the agent in Rome of the English secular
clergy put forward a document full of obloquy of Mary. She
bravely asked if she might stay in Rome that her work might
be observed; this was granted and the success of her poor-
schools was enormous.[2] Yet the situation remained confused.
A school was opened at Naples; the Bishop of Perugia called
her thither; she re-visited the Pope, who at once gave leave
for a chapel in her Roman house and appointed yet four
more Cardinals to examine her proposals. They were
favourable; but a new storm of slander blew up from
England; the Roman schools were closed. She set out for
England itself; both in Italy and over the Alps an almost
royal welcome was given her. The Emperor invited her to

[1] Her cousin, Robert Wright, went too and to his life's end devoted himself
to her and then to her successor Mary Poyntz. He performed every menial
office, seemed "always in prayer", and winter or summer slept always on the
floor. He died at eighty, his very name, or rank, unknown save to his
Superiors. The existence of this sort of man or woman must be *assumed* as the
"background" of all whose names for sanctity have become known.

[2] On January 25, 1623, her sister Barbara died and it is significant that
the Jesuit General recommended her to the prayers of all in the Professed
House; all the Jesuits and all the priests of the English College offered
their Mass for her. A good example of how prudence and charity can
co-exist!

Vienna; she was to go to Prague; a house—the "Paradeiser Haus"—was given her, where her work continued till 1808. But there were still attacks even from within her own houses. I feel that while all depended on her, she had no adequate system for *governing* her houses. She could not be always everywhere! She returned, though desperately ill, to Rome; the Pope, kind as ever, allowed her to plead her cause in person before yet other Cardinals; but, unlike St. Ignatius, she never defended herself nor refuted calumny; she simply set forth yet again her ideals. In 1629 the Naples house was suppressed. The Neapolitans, indignant, petitioned Cardinal Barberini that the "heroic and holy labours" of these English ladies might be restored, astonishingly alleging that where there were so many helps for men, this, the only one for women, might not be abolished. But for a while the calumnies proceeding from a clique of whose inspiration jealousy was the least disreputable part, more than conquered. Mary was grotesquely arrested as "heretic and schismatic" and imprisoned in a convent of Poor Clares who soon recognized the holiness of their guest. She succeeded in writing letters in lemon-juice to her associates, enjoining strict obedience to the Holy See. At Munich the Elector Maximilian I had received secret permission from Pope Urban VIII to preserve the Paradeiser Haus, despite the bull of suppression. Mary, shut up in one room, fell mortally ill but was refused the Sacraments unless she signed a recantation beginning: "*If* I have ever said or done anything contrary to the Faith . . ." She asked if the Pope or the Holy Office had required this and was told no. (Who then, had? I do not know.) She refused to permit this tendentious "if "and wrote directly: "I have never said or done . . ." The Last Sacraments were then administered by a Franciscan, moved to tears. But petitions and protests were reaching the Pope, who said he had been kept ignorant of her arrest, cancelled what was decreed against her, appointed a special Congregation to re-examine her plans and said she should return to Munich. In 1632 she went back to Urban, who said that no one

K

doubted her orthodoxy and that those who wished might stay with her in Rome under his own protection. In fact, seeing that the persecution did not cease, he at last took vigorous action, increased the pension he made her, lent her his own carriage and his doctor and sent her wine from his own cellar—"it would suit her . . ." But she fell ill, received the Last Sacraments again, and the Pope sent her his special blessing by the very Cardinal who, six years before, had signed the brief condemning her as heretic. . . . She recovered, but felt she should visit Spa; Urban wrote recommending her to every Nuncio by whom she would pass as a "great servant of God . . . not only a woman of great prudence and extra-ordinary courage and powers of mind, but what is much more, a holy and great servant of God." She decided to go on to England, where the Pope had given her letters to Queen Henrietta Maria. At once she became a magnet and was asked to undertake the education of girls, but went first to Yorkshire where she was in constant danger owing to the war between Royalists and Parliamentarians raging not least around York. Alas, she became much weaker and on January 1, 1645, received Communion for the last time. On January 26 she died. They had to bribe the minister at Osbaldwick to allow her burial, even though without ceremonies; but a throng of Protestants too attended the funeral, exclaiming: "There never was such a woman—never!" It was in 1686 that a house—the Bar Convent—was opened in York, where it has taught the Faith ever since, despite all interferences. It was tragically injured in the recent war, but has thank God survived. The Rule was approved in 1703 and confirmed. Some confusion may exist owing to the various "branches" of the Institute of Mary, an important one being that initiated in Ireland by Mother Mary Teresa Ball (1794-1861); but they all look back to Mary Ward as their true Foundress and Mother. Enough, then, has been said to show how prompt was the response of women, within the *Catholic* Reformation, to God's vocation, and how quick they were to discern the needs of the new era, and how the future has justified them. For we have also seen the beginnings of what became almost a law of life and death in the new organizations—trials due perhaps chiefly to a desire for central government, and for a freedom from enclosure; but also, interior dissensions, amounting again and again to a veritable crucifixion for the Foundress and sometimes her disgrace and expulsion. This we shall continue to observe.

We can now recall names from the definitely pre-Revolution or Revolution era. Julie Billart (1751-1816) was born at Cuvilly in Picardy. Even as a child she had a genius for explaining the catechism to still smaller children. But one day as she sat by her father, a shot was fired at him through the window, and this gradually incapacitated her nervously. After 1790 a "constitutional" priest was appointed to Cuvilly; she would have nothing to do with him nor allow others to. In grave peril, she was spirited away to Compiègne but became worse and quite unable to speak. When the Terror was over, she was sheltered by friends at Amiens, and under the direction of Fr. Varin, an ex-Jesuit, incredibly active and creative, one of the strongest links between old and new (p. 182), she began the Institute of Notre Dame, whose aim was educational. In 1804 a priest told her to make an act of faith and take one step in honour of the Sacred Heart. She rose, and was completely cured. The Institute then throve—and was tested. A young, inexperienced and headstrong priest succeeded Fr. Varin, attempted to make all sorts of changes within the Institute and even set the Bishop against Julie. She was driven out of Amiens and her work seemed ruined in France. She retired to Namur where the Mother-House still is, and at last died peacefully on April 6, 1816, while reciting the Magnificat; and her Sisters are known from end to end of England and indeed all over the world. St. Marie Madeleine Postel (1756-1846) and Jeanne Antide Thouret (1765-1826) were even more hardly tested. Mère Postel opened a school for the poor in the little Norman port of Barfleur when only eighteen. During the Terror she, like others, carried Communion to the dying. Hostile inquisitors somehow never noticed the door into her own secret chapel. Unhappily, when worship was resumed, the new priest was jealous of her; she had to leave, but opened a new school in Cherbourg and with three others began in 1807 the Institute of the Sisters of the Christian Schools. But her life was much tossed about. Thus after the return of the Sisters of Providence to Cherbourg she courteously retired lest her own Sisters should seem to be encroaching on the field of others; even the priest who originally welcomed them thought they had better disappear. Her obedience was further tested when her Rule, by which the Institute had lived for twenty-eight years, was set aside and that which Rome had sanctioned for the Christian Brothers was substituted. However, at last she was given a ruined abbey at the restoration of which, though she was eighty-two and worn down by penances, she toiled like any labourer. She died aged ninety and was at once venerated as a Saint. As for Jeanne Thouret, she was born near Besançon, was accepted for the Sisters of Charity, but owing to the revolutionary chaos had to fly to Switzerland and Germany, always working for the sick and poor. Recalled to Besançon, she was asked to take charge of the asylum there, but found it contained not only lunatics but beggars, orphans and criminals. A new Institution had to be created, the Daughters of Charity; invited by Joachim Murat to Naples, it throve. In 1818 Pius VII confirmed it, but making each house subject to the local Bishop instead of the Archbishop of Besançon, a Gallican. He was furious and ordered the convents in his diocese to exclude their Foundress should she dare to visit them. Hoping to heal this nascent schism, she called, but the door was shut against her. It is hard to see what else the poor Sisters could have done, if their own convents were not to be closed; still, it is Jeanne who has been beatified, not the prelate. Others I can but name— St. Emélie de Rodat (d. 1852), quite recently canonized,

who *recovered* her "first fervour" and founded the Sisters of the
Holy Family; the Venerable Marie Rivier (d. 1858),
Foundress of the Presentation Sisters; and Marie de Bondy
d'Houet (d. 1858), who, still quite a young widow, nursed
the wounded soldiers of Napoleon's troops and in 1820,
along with Fr. Varin (p. 133) founded the Congregation of
the Faithful Companions of Jesus. That I have not specially
dwelt on the Society of the Sacred Heart is explained below
(p. 182).

Mère Ste-Marie, Henriette Le Forestier d'Osseville
(1803-1858), was born at Rouen, had thought, after a
childhood of perfect innocence and also zeal for foreign
missions, that she was called to the Society of the Sacred
Heart. But events led her away from this to the foundation
of a new Institute for the care of orphans, and this at first
was called the "Congregation of our Lady of Charity for the
Orphans of Mary"; fortunately it has become known by the
less unwieldy title of *Virgo Fidelis*—the total fidelity of our
Lady to her Son was to be its enduring inspiration. Almost
at once their fidelity was tested; by 1832 the plague of
cholera had reached France from Asia; the Sisters devoted
themselves heroically to the sick, and were all of them
preserved from infection. We pass rapidly to an allied subject.
The Crimean War broke out; and without delay France sent
her chaplains and Sisters of Charity to Pera. Scutari had no
one like them, but wished it had. When Florence Nightingale began to seek recruits from the London hospitals,
Protestants of good will asked to go too, to show that they,
"as well as the Roman Catholics", had the spirit of self-
sacrifice. The Government at last said that ten Catholic
Sisters might go. Bishop Grant of Southwark found five
English nuns willing to go; he got at that time no response
from Ireland. In desperation he turned to the religious of
Virgo Fidelis, by then established at Norwood in South
London. All volunteered. He said he would give them a
definite answer before the date of departure, which was
Monday. Not till 9 p.m. on the Sunday did a messenger

inform them they must be at London Bridge at 7 a.m. next day. They sailed, and did a task that was not theirs to the admiration of all. In fact, authorization for the departure of Sisters of Mercy was very soon obtained, and the Norwood nuns returned to their home. The appalling conditions that prevailed in the Crimea can be read about in their due place; it is no bad thing that those accustomed to the discreet decencies of a school should see with their eyes the horrors that the outside world contains. The foundation at Norwood can be regarded as one of the many benefits that England derived from the continental revolutions—in this case, that of 1848. But those who now see the great convent there can hardly imagine the almost comical destitution in which the original foundation was made—to say nothing of the hysterical Protestant outcry against the nuns. There is, alas, no space to write of the Faithful Virgins' mission work in the West Indies; enough to say that it was on April 28, 1858, that Mother Ste-Marie died at Norwood (she was buried in France) almost at the same time as the series of our Lady's apparitions were ending at Lourdes.

From Belgium, we must also quote the Venerable Marie Thérèse Haze of Liège. When the French revolutionaries invaded Belgium this distinguished family had to fly; her father died on the way. Her mother and four sisters survived by means of manual work; with one sister, she opened a small school; it expanded; a Congregation called "The Daughters of the Cross" was formed; it passed over the sea; became well-known here, and was governed by Mother Haze till she died in 1876 aged nearly ninety-four. Here too, almost at the outset the Foundress was all but set aside by an ambitious and more brilliant woman; but this came to nothing. The central activity of the Institute is education, the range of its activities is remarkable—orphanages, prisons for women, schools for "young delinquents" or for domestic training; during the Franco-Prussian war these nuns too and their ambulances won universal homage;

indeed, the Empress Augusta, not a Catholic, sent a long letter to the Superior with the Cross of Merit instituted by her husband to reward the courage of German women in the earlier war. Needless to emphasize the Sisters' devotion during epidemics; the *physical* horrors of not a century ago were almost as ghastly, though on a smaller scale, as those which have gnawed like gangrene into our own history, though we have surpassed them in psychological and moral iniquity.

One of the great dangers run by religious Congregations is the material adherence to the tradition set by their Founder and failure to notice developments happening elsewhere, so that their standard of teaching or nursing does not rise correspondingly. This danger is largely obviated today by schools electing to remain "free" and yet accepting official inspection. But Eugénie Milleret de Bron (afterward Mother Marie-Eugénie de Jésus, 1817-1898) was among the first to realize that the level of Catholic girls' education was too low. She was herself not only remarkably intelligent, but determined to raise that level higher, which was in part her reason for calling the Congregation she founded in 1839 the Sisters of the "Assumption". It was her wish that, to compensate for any extra "elegance" her children might acquire, they should visit the very poor in their homes (perhaps this proved difficult to persevere with) and be competent keepers of accounts! Her "life" is well worth reading also for the sake of her quite extraordinary "director", the Abbé Combalot, a man of the most explosive personality. This Congregation must not be confused with that of the "Little Sisters of the Assumption", founded in 1865 by Fr. E. Pernet and Marie Antoinette Tage (1824-1883) who became its first Superior. Its main work is the nursing of the sick poor in their homes (cf. p. 139).

One of the earliest in "modern" Italy to devote herself to education was the Venerable Maddalena of Canossa. Born in 1774 at Verona, she lived with her uncle Jerome, her father having died early, in his castle of Canossa. She felt called to the Carmelites, but returned from their noviciate to manage the whole household and estate. When Napoleon was campaigning in Italy, it was at Canossa that he lodged. During the revolution, she went with her uncle to Venice and there realized her vocation. Returning to Verona she organized the Institute of Daughters of Charity, or "of Canossa" and it is they who have carried so far into modern life that ancient and ominous name. She died in 1835. On a humbler scale at first the work of Mother Antonia Maria Verna (1773-1838), Foundress of the Sisters of Charity of the Immaculate Conception of Ivrea, developed itself first in northern Italy. Her history does not seem to me to have any special colouring save the domestic problems of her Sisters' relationship to the Sisters of Charity of St. Vincent de Paul and conflicting counsels due to this, and even division of her Institute. Nearer our own time come two recently canonized Saints—St. Bartolomea Capitanio (1807-1833), who obtained a secular teacher's certificate that she might the better devote herself to the service of youth. Her work spread so widely that she needed a companion and met St. Catherine (afterwards Vincenza) Gerosa (1784-1847), whose bent had been to nurse the sick—indeed she had already opened a hospital for the poor. But thenceforward both activities were carried on together. They too were advised to affiliate themselves to the Sisters of Charity of St. Vincent de Paul, but north Italy at that time was under Austrian control and no religious house might be opened which depended on authority in a foreign land. But as "Sisters of Charity" they were papally approved. I find an unusual charm in this humble co-operation of an older with a much younger woman and free modification of the plans of each so as to harmonize with those of the other.

With these remember the Blessed Paula Frassinetti, born at Genoa in 1809. Very frail, she was sent to join her brother, parish priest at Quinto. Here she revealed her miraculous insight into the most varied characters, and this together with her tact and unselfishness made her miraculously successful with children. Then began the Institute of Dorothean Sisters which has spread not least to Portugal and Brazil, and to which Lucia, one of the children of Fatima, for a while belonged. And also, Aloysia Borgiotti, born at Turin, 1803, daughter of an important advocate and at first enjoying the frivolities of life. She wished to join the Sisters of Charity, but her mother and brothers were ill and she had to look after the entire household. When they died, she joined a group who tended the sick poor who were too shy to ask for help, and worked devotedly in those wretched homes for thirty-one years. In fact, she was already sixty-two when called to enter the Sisters of Nazareth which a Lazarist priest, Fr. Durando, was organizing! She actually became Superior of this and is known as its co-founder.

A glance at Germany. In a sense, the background is French. For St. Peter Fourier (d. 1640) founded the Canonesses of St. Augustine of Notre Dame to educate girls—he failed in what concerned boys—and his methods were surprisingly original and "modern". But this is a book about women-Saints! In Germany Catholic enterprise had to begin again after the various revolutions and the Napoleonic Wars, and was rudely interrupted by the Kulturkampf (which increased from 1871 to 1877 and faded gradually out from 1878 to 1891). At Stadtamhof in Bavaria Maria Theresia Gerhardinger (1797-1879) began, at the urgent request of her parish priest, to renew the education of poor children, and a new Congregation of the "Poor School Sisters of our Blessed Lady" (the School Sisters of Notre Dame, in the U.S.A.) was formed and "approved" in 1865. Its immense development was due to its being sent for by emigrant Germans to the United States. During the Kulturkampf thirty of its German houses fell victim but rose again. The gap between these Sisters and Fourier, and the changes made locally by ecclesiastical authority, were so considerable as to warrant our regarding this as an original enterprise. But we cannot forget Mother Clare Fey (1815-1894) who founded the Society of the Sisters of the Poor

Child Jesus. Its scope—it intended at first to educate only the very poor—became so much extended that its original characteristics were almost submerged; it has become famous for its exquisite needlework. In the Kulturkampf, the Empress, not a Catholic, obtained at least a delay in the application of the law; none the less, its headquarters are now at Simpleveld in Holland. Mother Fey's spirit was a loving and happy one, like that of the Holy Child Himself, and this is what she wanted to prevail in her houses. But it is precisely a "spirit" which it is impossible to convey by means of a book, let alone half a page! With her name must be linked that of Franziska Schervier (1817-1881) as friend if not direct collaborator; she with four others ultimately founded the "Sisters of the Poor of St. Francis"; and that of Maria Kaspar (1820-1898), whose "Poor Handmaids of Jesus Christ" passed on the whole from the care of the sick to that of schools; and *again* Mother Schervier's devoted friend Maria Bonzel (1830-1905); and possibly above all Pauline von Mallinckrodt (1817-1881), sister of the famous politician, Hermann von Mallinckrodt, co-founder of what became the "Centre Party", of whom Falk himself had to speak in terms of high respect. Pauline began by consecrating herself especially to the care of the blind; could but this book be illustrated, to show to readers the truly "noble" features of this great lady and servant of God! We ought to allude, from among the multitude of holy German women, to Elizabeth Eppinger (1814-1867) who founded the Society of the Holy Redeemer especially for the care of sick and poor in country parts and small towns; and Sister Emilie Schneider (1820-1859), born of a "mixed marriage"; she joined the new society of the Daughters of the Holy Cross, vowed to every kind of merciful work. She was a true "mystic" and her experiences were notably like those of St. Margaret Mary.

Two specially endearing characters come from the United States. Elizabeth Ann Seton was born in New York, August 28, 1774; her parents were non-Catholic—her father,

Dr. Bayley, was the first Professor of Anatomy at Columbia College; her mother, the daughter of an Anglican minister; she died when Elizabeth was three; her father re-married and his convert son, James Roosevelt, became Archbishop of Baltimore. Elizabeth married a Mr. Seton in 1794 and they had five children. There were business troubles; her father-in-law died in 1798; Elizabeth had to look after the large family along with her husband who also was not strong. In 1803 they had to sail to Leghorn, but Mr. Seton died at Pisa in 1803. The family with whom she resided gradually revealed to her the Catholic Faith; she was received in 1805, and there was such a storm among her relatives that she became really poor. One scheme after another had to be abandoned as "proselytizing"; she was threatened with legal expulsion from the States. But in 1808 she at last could open a school in Baltimore and her life became more and more like that of a Religious—even before conversion, she and her sister-in-law Rebecca were known as the "Protestant Sisters of Charity". A Community was formed; its Rule was to be that of the Sisters of Charity of St. Vincent de Paul, and three of those Sisters were to come from France to train the new community, but Napoleon forbade them to leave France. The Rule, however, with modifications, was approved by Archbishop Carroll of Baltimore, and Mother Seton with eighteen Sisters took their vows in 1818. Schools, asylums for orphans, were entrusted to them; but she had grown much weaker, and died in 1821. She was a voluminous writer and translator; and though for doubtless good reasons her community was afterwards divided, part following St. Vincent's Rule accurately, others, with modifications still thought suitable to the States, all look back to her as having been the first to introduce the Sisters of Charity there. I find it difficult to express the tenderness and sweetness of this valiant and suffering soul; the more "old-fashioned" books are perhaps the more sympathetic, e.g., her *Memoirs, Letters and Journal*, by Robert Seton (2 vols., New York, 1869).

Anticipating a little, we mention at once Cornelia Peacock (now known as Mother Connelly (1809-1879)). Born at Philadelphia, her father was of Yorkshire, her mother, of Spanish stock; but Cornelia was always reticent about her home. In 1831 she married a brilliant young clergyman, Pierce Connelly. Both seemed perfectly suited to their position, yet both became convinced of the Catholic Faith. Cornelia was received in 1835; her husband in 1836, in Rome, where they were much fêted by society, lay and ecclesiastical. But funds began to fail; they returned to America and in 1838 Mr. Connelly became English professor in the Jesuit College at Le Coteau in Louisiana; Mrs. Connelly taught music and had the joy of meeting Mère Duchesne (p. 181). But Mr. Connelly, probably feeling his talents somewhat wasted as a lay-master in a religious house, informed his wife on October 13, 1840, that he had resolved to be a priest. The shock was terrible; she clung to her home, and early next year another child was to be born. But she had already offered herself to God. In the January of 1840 she was walking, radiantly happy, with her children, in glorious sunshine. She was impelled to cry: "Oh God, if all this happiness is not to Thy greater glory and for the good of my soul, take it from me. I make the sacrifice." Next day a dog with which her little son, aged two and a half, was playing, pushed him into a sugar-boiling vat. Horribly scalded, the child lingered for forty-three hours and died in his mother's arms. But if Mr. Connelly were to become a priest, long negotiations would be necessary at Rome. He left for England, arranged with Lord Shrewsbury to have his eldest son, Mercer, educated at Stonyhurst, and accepted the post of travelling-tutor to a young Mr. Berkeley, heir to Spetchley Park. This would get him to Rome, and also test his vocation. So Cornelia's home was anyway broken up; she spent a happy yet lonely year in a cottage belonging to the convent of the Sacred Heart. After a while Mr. Connelly fetched her to England and then to Rome and seemed to foresee a great social success for her, and even, for himself, an indefinitely prolonged tutorship of Lord Shrewsbury's heir. However, they presented their petition to the very paternal Gregory XVI; the matter was put through with astonishing rapidity and in 1844 Mr. Connelly received minor orders with the intention of joining the Society of Jesus, while Cornelia became a "postulant" with the nuns of the Sacred Heart, living as before in a cottage with her little son Frank. (It was during this time that she and a companion painted the picture now everywhere known as "Mater Admirabilis".) But the year was one of interior desolation. Happily, St. Madeleine Sophie Barat (p. 181) came to the Trinità and perceived that Cornelia was destined to found an educational Order of her own, but allowed her to remain domiciled in the convent. In July, 1845, Mr. Connelly was in fact ordained priest, but no more intended to be a Jesuit. In the same year the Pope told Cornelia to draft a Rule for a teaching Order, though without announcing that she should be its Foundress, nor that her immediate work would lie in England, not the States. But she was not there long before Bishop Wiseman told her she was to be head of the new Institute and begin work in the Midlands. But a shock: Fr. Connelly suddenly removed her children from her care, despite all promises. The sacrifice was terrible, but it was made. Mother Connelly with three others left therefore for Derby where Dr. Wiseman put a very large convent, built by Pugin but now demolished, at their disposal. This was the cradle of the Society of the Holy Child Jesus.

Unfortunately, Fr. Connelly was, maybe unconsciously, determined to get control of the Society. He sent them as "chaplain" a young Italian, Fr. Asperti, quite ignorant of the English spirit, which he resolved to arouse from its somnolence. He tried to "direct" the Sisters; failing in this, he turned on the unhappy parish and created trouble everywhere. Wiseman had been transferred to London and decided that the Sisters had better leave Derby; he offered them the splendid terrain at St. Leonard's where their convent and school still flourish. They left for this at the end of 1848. But far worse was in store. Pierce Connelly began definitely to try to control not only the community but Mother Connelly in person; he removed the two elder children to Italy; he had a new set of Rules printed; he declared that *he* had created the "Order"; Dr. Asperti himself was disillusioned and became, for Connelly, "that villain Asperti"; he demanded that Mother Connelly should be restored to him as his wife and the mother of his children and finally took the matter to court. A first decision went in his favour; the verdict was afterwards reversed by the Privy Council. Enough has been said to make clear the agonizing time through which Mother Connelly passed; Connelly himself apostatized, and what cut Mother Connelly even deeper than the almost insane anti-Roman pamphlets that he published was that he caused her son, Mercer, who shared his instability, to give up his faith. The two younger children were also led astray; the little girl recovered her faith and lived and died heroically; the boy Frank never returned.

It is not for me to describe the expansion of the Congregation nor the final approbation and confirmation of its Rule, nor even its special methods of education, nor the further trials which awaited the St. Leonard's house—they were on quite a different plane (i.e., financial) from those we have described. But I have wished to indicate once more that the road to sanctity always leads to the Cross. As for the final misunderstandings about the Rule and method of government, they would be far too complicated to be even outlined here and anyhow they are an affair of long ago. At the time, they caused Mother Connelly acute suffering and humiliation—people even thought the whole Institute would be abolished or at least that she would be relegated into complete isolation. But the impression that her life leaves with me, apart from her extreme fortitude, is that of the serenity with which she went through all her trials. The explanation is that she really had at the outset made her sacrifice—the full sacrifice of self—and having laid it on God's altar, she never once robbed that altar. She died on April 18, 1879, and is buried at Mayfield.

Mother Theodore Guerin (d. 1856) was not an American, but she became the first Superior General of the Sisters of Providence there—an "athlete", said Cardinal Gibbons, "who made great conquests for Christ and His Church". She was in fact a woman of the highest endowments, culture and charm, and also holiness, tried by much suffering.

Evidence of sanctity could be found in Africa, India, China, Japan, but the material is at present inaccessible; strangely enough, I think it would display a "mystical" way of life rather than what we would call creative or organizational. Yet after all, given the psychological history of the Orient, it may not be so unexpected. I must however mention Mary McKillop, Mother Mary of the Cross, Foundress of the (Australian) Sisters of St. Joseph (1842-1909); see her *Life* by G. O'Neill, S.J. (Pellegrini, Sydney). She was of Scottish Highland descent; her ever-faithful family had provided eight bishops. Her father married a kinswoman, Flora Macdonald, both families having emigrated to Australia. We have written, so far, of countries different among themselves, but all of them, even Canada, even the U.S.A., "old". Australia, a hundred years ago, was all of it new and a continent, not a country. I think that the most constructive elements imported into it were Scottish and Irish. Hence Mary's tenacity and imagination; she "very nearly" had second sight; she felt she must teach, and become a "religious". An aged Portuguese doctor, whom some thought mad, others a prophet, said he saw her at the head of numbers of virgins in brown. She met a Fr. Julian Tenison Woods, the cause (so I think) alike of her tragedies and her glories. Impossible even to outline their history properly here. Remember that Australia was soon in the fever of gold rushes; Bishop Ullathorne had not yet convinced the world of its atrocious treatment of "convicts"; bishops themselves seem to have been temperamental in the extreme, enduring problems declared themselves—should Mary's associates (approved at first by the Bishop of Adelaide), scattered all over an enormous territory, have a central "government", a central noviciate? Should they—a terribly acute question—accept Government grants, and therefore, Government inspection and indeed governmental appointment of teachers? To the latter questions Mary answered an obstinate No, though many ecclesiastics thought she should nibble, as they did, at the governmental loaf dangled before them.[1] As for the old quarrel about "central government" and one central "noviciate", we can see today that given the existence of groups of two or three Sisters, who might not be able to go to Communion or even Mass for months at a time, she was certainly right in asking for them a proper *training*, which could be done only in some central house, and certainly there had to be a central "control" if these Sisters were to retain any kind of homogeneity. Besides this, it is false to imagine that she wanted her Sisters only to *educate*—that is, to "instruct" like other schools. She, and Fr. Woods, saw the terrible lack of almost everything in their Australia, and, when attacked because she received postulants who were not equipped to *teach*, she remembered the needs of prisoners, the aged, prostitutes—in fact, seeing the tremendous necessity, she wanted to help all equally (though concentrating on education), and possibly dissipated her forces. But that is the explanation of her accepting so many postulants who

[1] I might presume that while Catholic schools perhaps ought to do without Government assistance—as they still do in Australia (not that this is at all equitable)—they might well accept governmental inspection. Else they may not compare themselves with other schools, nor realize how much the *standard* of education is changing elsewhere. But, on the one hand, this may no more be a "live" problem anywhere; though, on the other, very small schools, like most of Mother Mary's, may have to do simply what best they can with the intractable material provided to them! In those distant, raw days in an inexperienced and on the whole anti-Catholic Australia, I think Mother Mary was right in resisting any secular control which would have followed secular financial aid, and trying to provide *some* education for the "lost" population of the Bush rather than none, even if it were given gratis, which involved the incredible personal poverty of her teachers.

might not be fitted for teaching, but might well be for other services. I think too, that she was egged on by the mercurial, indeed headlong and erratic Fr. Woods whom, often enough, she had to check, though always with her incomparable humility and gentleness. He ended by deserting her altogether. He was no hesitating "director" like St. Francis de Sales, who at times was (I think) almost amused to find he had been—all but imperceptibly—directed by St. Jeanne de Chantal! Parts of her story sound almost fantastic— certain Sisters posed as ecstatics and even produced bogus stigmata and, what perhaps was even worse, carried on a lying campaign against Mother Mary's high virtue. More- over, a bishop who, at first, had warmly encouraged her, became I think, mentally sick; and not least because she proposed to move the "mother-house" into a different diocese, showed great hostility to her. In the end, her Sisters were divided into "black" and "brown"; the former remaining under diocesan control, the latter being central- ized. Before she died she had the happiness of realizing how much they were loved and asked for all over Australia; but her early prayer had been fully granted—that she should "never find anything easy".

ii

There were of course innumerable good works other than educational ones of which we can mention a few; some were strictly defined in their scope; others were more adaptable to circumstances. I recall first the Blessed Marie de Sainte- Euphrasie Pelletier (1796-1868) who, while at school at Tours met the Congregation of Our Lady of Charity founded about 1641 by St. John Eudes for the rescue of fallen women and the protection of those in danger. She joined it and was Superior at twenty-nine. Sent to found a new house at Angers, she took over a "refuge" already existing there called the "Good Shepherd". But the moment she returned to Tours this new foundation nearly collapsed.

She went back as prioress and long disheartening disputes ensued. At last she realized that these would always continue if each house remained autonomous with no Superior General, no central noviciate, and no power of moving its members from one house to another. In the long run a practically new Congregation came to exist, the "Good Shepherd", known all over the world. Anticipating, I must mention the Countess Maria Droste zu Vischering, afterwards Sister Mary of the Divine Heart (1863-1899). Born in her parents' ancient castle on September 8, she was baptized next day. Her vitality was intense, displaying itself in hot temper, self-will and a hundred faults that she generously overcame; but also, in her generous friendships, her open-handedness and readiness to be first to express her sorrow if a quarrel had been her fault. Not till her Confirmation did she experience the certainty of a "vocation", though at first she thought it was for the Missions. None the less, she went on riding with her father, running races with her brothers; learning, with her mother and sisters, to visit the sick and lonely. Her parents knew of her vocation, but rightly, in view of her restless mind, which took relentless toll also of her bodily strength, her father wished her to postpone her decision till she was twenty-one. Even so, she hesitated about her destination till it became clear it was the "Good Shepherd", and she was "clothed" in January, 1889. True, she still had to control her vivid personality, but the largeness of outlook, love for freedom, gaiety and remorseless suppression of self-pity to be expected in a girl brought up as she was, were of incalculable value when she was called to manage classes of extremely difficult "children", as penitents and others are called in the "Good Shepherd". In 1894 she was sent to Lisbon, and the wrench when leaving her homeland, its customs and language, was greater than she had foreseen. In May she was appointed Superior of the house in Oporto. We may smile at the thought of the impact of the German spirit on the Portuguese temperament, but it was no matter for laughter for the poor Superior. The house was

destitute; the "enclosure" was ill-kept; discipline hardly
existed; collapse seemed imminent. Soon she transformed
the place, having learnt Portuguese very fast; as of old in
Münster she won the love of children who, you might have
thought, would never be attracted by someone so different
from themselves. Well, the early offer of her whole self to
God had resulted in her heart being "like unto the Heart"
of Jesus Christ, and this was *felt* by all. In 1896 she had to
visit the mother-house at Angers and went by way of
St. Teresa's grave. It was here, perhaps, that her more
"mystical" life really began. She had always known that
love without sacrifice was an illusion; now she perceived that
her sufferings would be great. After a visit to her home, she
fell sick of some spinal disease. Despite her pains, or because
of them, she received special graces from God, and on
August 28, 1897, saw "spiritually" St. Augustine, St.
Benedict and St. Gertrude, who called her "sister". And I
feel sure that those who read her "life" will feel that they are
back at the atmosphere of St. Gertrude. And they will be
right—somewhat later, she heard our Lord say to her: "You
are My Gertrude!" It is fascinating to observe the Devotion
to the Sacred Heart thriving in the freshness and spacious-
ness of the distant German Saint and revived in that of the
German Sister, as truly as it was in the quite different air of
the convent at Paray.

It was in the summer of 1897 that our Lord first made
known to her His wish that the world should be consecrated
to His Sacred Heart. Under guidance, Mother Mary of the
Divine Heart wrote to Leo XIII. No answer came. But
next year the call came to her still more urgently, and this
time the Holy Father let her know that he had been preparing
an Encyclical on the subject, and the consecration was fixed
for the Feast that very year. Her illness grew more intense
as her joy was increased. Long ago she had given up her
"tours" of the house in her wheeled chair, inspecting all in
detail. She was now shut in a little room with a window
looking down upon the Tabernacle. But she soon grew too

weak to lift her head. As the bells were ringing for the First
Vespers of the Feast of the Sacred Heart, she, its true
apostle, died.

Sophie de Soubiran (afterwards Marie-Thérèse) was born
on May 16, 1834, and passed a lonely childhood in her
ancestral home at Castelnaudary. Her upbringing was that
normal in provincial families of overwhelming pedigree—
austere, and loving. From the outset she was pious and hoped
for a vocation to some Order; but at first she flung herself
into the work of a local association for young girls whose
director was her uncle, Canon Louis de Soubiran. He was a
man of iron who brought her up on the basis of two prin-
ciples—first, she was to be ready to think she was always
wrong; and second, in opposition to Jansenism, that she
was always able through sheer will-power to do right. "You
must choose right—you always can—you constantly don't."
Had it not been for her perception of his essential affection,
she might well have been not only bruised but broken. This,
under far worse trials, she never was. Now Canon de
Soubiran wanted to create one of those curious "settlements"
called, in Belgium, *béguinages*, consisting of ladies who do
not want to become nuns nor yet to live in the "world" but
in a kind of devout and fairly comfortable oasis. Canon de
Soubiran took his niece to Ghent for a year's training and it
proved the unhappiest of her life so far. She was sure
that this was not her vocation, and yet had to assume that
she was "always wrong". In 1855 she returned to Castelnaudary and her little group found itself under the rigid
control of the Canon, becoming less and less like a *béguinage*,
which in no case was suited to the south of France. Sophie
was glad in so far as she was enabled to live more like a
Carmelite, which she had set her heart to. After a while the
buildings (which the Canon had forgotten) were completed
and a few children housed there. Almost at once, she had
made her vow of perpetual virginity in the sense of never
accepting even the purest joy for *herself*, and indeed, for years

she had but "flashes" of what might be called in any way peace of soul. In 1861, after careful consultation, she decided she must leave. The Canon, truly loyal to the will of God, offered no opposition. She left for Toulouse, and, directed by Fr. Ginhac, S.J., made two more vows—one, to do with God's grace what was the more perfect so far as she saw it; and to be *incapable* of possessing anything whatsoever, though obscurely foreseeing that she might be left one day not even a nun, but destitute and nondescript. But her heart began to be warmed by God's "mother-love". And she summoned such Sisters as were willing to follow her to form the nucleus of the future congregation of "Marie Auxiliatrice". Her ideal was that the Sisters should be as hidden, as small, as possible. Theirs was the Apostolate of Odds and Ends. They should help those whom no one else did—in the concrete, working-girls and shop-girls. Girls came in crowds—bed, meals, night-classes—yet all on the simplest though generous scale.

Suddenly, in 1867, a lady appeared as postulant, sent by a Jesuit priest. She was brilliant, imaginative, constructive, forceful—all that Marie-Thérèse felt *she* could never be. This Marie-Françoise demanded vast expansions. Let them invade France's great industrial centres! Only the Franco-Prussian war prevented their advance on Paris. They fled to England and in Kensington fifty of them lodged in a house equipped for eight. In 1871 they moved to Kentish Town, where, in a dilapidated building, on opening the door they found behind it a coffin and in the coffin a dead baby, left there who knows by whom. Finally, at Kennington, they looked after shop-girls, governesses, converts, and were settling down happily when it became possible to return to France. At once Mère Marie-Françoise, now "Assistant", began her enormous enterprises; Marie-Thérèse, aware that she did not understand business, trusted her while feeling that this grandiose policy was totally contrary to the spirit of Marie Auxiliatrice; by 1873-1874 the Congregation found itself in debt for over a million and a half francs and unable to prevent the debt from growing worse. Marie-Françoise put the whole responsibility on Marie-Thérèse whom she called, publicly, proud and ambitious, certain to draw down God's curse on all of them, and utterly unable to govern the society in any way. Crushed by such violence, Marie-Thérèse felt she ought to resign her superiorship, but foresaw that if she did she would soon enough be got rid of altogether. She went to see Fr. Ginhac, who telegraphed for the Assistant and forthwith fell victim to her fascination. Yes—the Mother General had better resign and not even enter any of her houses till the new General had had time to "settle down". One cannot exonerate the priest, hard-worked as he was, for having left Marie-Thérèse practically unaided, though it was he who had urged her to begin her work, and who now turned her loose in an alien world. She sought shelter in one convent after another—it was granted for a day or two; finally the Sisters of St. Vincent de Paul accepted her as inmate of their hospital at Clermont. Only once is there a cry of agony— she feels in a "mouse-trap that will not open"; and once a flash of the old aristocratic spirit—she will *not* become a "lady-boarder". "I would keep turkeys, rather!" The new Superior General suddenly reappeared. Would Marie-Thérèse go and be Superior in London? Only gradually did the poor Sister realize that the General wanted to concentrate in London, far away, all the Sisters who might resent her innovations, put Marie-Thérèse at their head, and thus ensure the cutting off of the London house from the French communities and so, its swift extinction. Marie-Thérèse said she would go anywhere she was told to, but not, she begged, as Superior. She was sure she could not *rule*. Finally she was accepted, definitely, at first, as a "lady-boarder", by the Sisters of Charity in Paris, but after a while, as a postulant. And there she died, an exile from the Institute she had founded, saying very slowly: "Come, Lord Jesus, come!", on June 7, 1889.

Almost at once, Marie-Françoise became still more domineering and more erratic. Seeing that her authority was waning, she shut herself up in a morose solitude and did needlework. Then she went to Rome and in 1890 wrote that she was leaving the Congregation and that it was no use looking for her. In *King's Daughters*, as long ago as 1921, when writing of Mother de Soubiran, I tried as hard as I could to find reasons for supposing that Marie-Françoise was in good faith. It was not known, at that time, that she was really a married woman who had run away from her husband (long afterwards he accidentally met her, demanded restitution of conjugal rights, and on her refusal, obtained a legal separation from her), so that her vows, as she must have known, were canonically null and her life had been a lie. In 1891 Marie-Thérèse's coffin was brought home to the great hospital at Villepinte near Paris and re-buried. And in that very year 1921, the then Mother General of Marie Auxiliatrice visited the tomb to pray there. To her amazement, a grave had been opened alongside of it, and in it was a coffin not yet covered up. It was that of the unhappy Marie-Françoise, who in old days had bought herself a grave there, and now had been brought, unaccompanied, to lie beside the relics of her whom she had treated so cruelly. More than that—the new grave had not at first been dug to the legal depth; the coffin had to be taken out and was laid for a while on the neighbouring grave—that of Marie-Thérèse. Such was the end of this sad tempestuous story. Marie Auxiliatrice woke up from her long nightmare and continues now to do her noble work in freedom. The purely spiritual life of Mother de Soubiran—she was beatified in 1946—was such that I hope her *Life and Letters* will become everywhere known.[1]

Other societies were formed for primarily spiritual purposes, that is, not having any specific work of external charity. Such was the Congregation of Helpers of the Holy Souls, founded by Eugénie Smet (Mother Marie of Providence,

[1] *Mère Marie-Thérèse de Soubiran* (Ed. Spes: Paris, 1936). Also *A Study in Failure*, translated by Dom T. Bailey, O.S.B., Prinknash Abbey. Hers was a life of total sacrifice, interior and exterior. She was asked for all and gave all.

1825-1871). Her "life" is exquisitely written by Marie René-Bazin—"She who Lived her Name"; and indeed where else will you find so pure a trust in Providence? You would say that she had but to ask and it was given.[1] If "expiation" is associated with Purgatory, we may allude, along with Eugénie, to Mère Marie de Jésus (Marie Caroline Deluil-Martigny) who founded the "Daughters of the Heart of Jesus" definitely in view of reparation for the "increasing Godlessness of our times". From childhood she had longed to shed her blood for our Lord, and on February 27, 1884, an anarchist broke into the convent-garden near Marseilles and shot both her and a companion. With her last words she forgave him. He had written only a few hours before to some newspaper saying what he proposed to do and that it was from hatred for religion as such. The same feeling for reparation inspired Emilie d'Outremont (1818-1878), a Belgian of splendid ancestry and great wealth; she married the no less illustrious Baron d'Hooghvorst. They had two sons and two daughters, but he died when only thirty-four, and then began for his widow a life rightly called "unusual". She began almost at once to found what was to be the Society of Marie-Réparatrice; but so long as her children were young or needed her, she seems to have taken an intermittent part in elegant society. Finally her two sons married and the two daughters entered their mother's Institute. Practically everyone, bishops included, was hostile to this new creation. The Baroness would do much more good in her position in the world . . . she had over-persuaded her daughters to follow her—she wanted to lay hands on their fortune. . . . This storm blew itself out; but perhaps all her life, especially towards the end of it, Mother Mary of Jesus passed through a "dark night of the soul", which was a much better reason for comparing her with St. Jeanne de Chantal and St. Frances of Rome than the mere fact that she was a holy widow and had founded a religious Congregation.

[1] This "life" falls also into the "missionary" category; see below. Its pages on China are entrancingly moving *and* amusing.

Connected with the amazing development of devotion to
the Blessed Sacrament in recent years is the career of Anne
Marie de Meeus (1823-1904). She too was descended from a
very ancient and wealthy Belgian family which suffered
much in the revolutions of the time. In 1843 she was horrified
by a visit to a parish priest living almost destitute—by the
sight of his pewter chalice, his rotting tabernacle—and found
that since the French invasion a hundred parishes were in
the same plight. She realized that an *organization* was needed,
but her director, Fr. Boone, S.J., kept her for long in check.
She was shown the constitutions of a French society of
"Nocturnal Adoration and Work for Tabernacles", enjoining a monthly Communion and a collection for corporals
and ciboriums. She expanded this notion until the Society
of Perpetual Adoration and Work for Poor Churches came
into existence. She did indeed settle into a fifteenth-century
chapel built in reparation for a Host that had been slashed
by a Jew, from which blood was said to have flowed. By
1852 the entire Belgian hierarchy approved of her work and
in 1853 it became an Arch-Association officially approved
by the Pope. It has always wished to catechize and to
instruct converts as well as to do its normal work. The usual
criticisms and jealous rivalries caused her the no less usual
torments; but in 1879 Leo XIII transferred the centre of
her work to Rome and thenceforward the destiny of the
Congregation and the Arch-Association was (allowing for the
normal set-backs) assured. In June, 1904, she fell sick; on the
15th a Sister having said to her: "My God, Thy will be done",
she added in a clear voice: "Not mine." She then died
without any struggle. This Congregation unites in many
ways the Adoration of the Blessed Sacrament with the most
practical work of making and distributing gratis all neces-
sities for worship to poor churches whether at home or (so
far as England is concerned) throughout the Commonwealth;
and no wonder that His Holiness Pius XII has said he wishes
that it should be established *in every diocese of the world*.

A close friend of Mère de Meeus was a Spanish lady who

has become known as the Blessed Maria Michaela of the Blessed Sacrament (1809-1865). She lived for some brilliant years with her brother, ambassador in Brussels and Paris, faithful all the time to prayer and penance and tireless service of the sick. She made various efforts to establish foundations for this purpose in Spain; met with every rebuff, but her "Congregation of the Handmaids of the Blessed Sacrament and of Charity" has outlived her. She died at Valence of the cholera which she and her associates were nursing.

Another society closely related to the cult of the Blessed Sacrament is that of Our Lady of the Cenacle. On Christmas Day, 1791, a child was born in a tiny village in the middle of France and was baptized next day. By sheer force of character he made his way to the priesthood and became the Abbé Terme. His very first priestly work was to preach a "retreat" or mission in his native village of Le Plagnal. His transparent sincerity and volcanic energy stood him in lieu of experience. In 1815 this priest of twenty-four was made curé of Aps, a place known only for the collapse of its Christian life. At least he would educate! Sister Claire, an ex-Presentation nun, with two others begins a school. Children pour in. The work spreads to other townlets. But in 1824 his bishop tells him to join a band of missionary priests with, for headquarters, La Louvesc where St. John Francis Regis was buried. During his first mission, he met Marie-Victoire Couderc, born on February 1, 1885, and baptized next day. The people of those uplands are, and have to be, indomitable. Rising at four she would battle through the snows of those appalling winters, make her Communion, do her marketing, return maybe at three, still fasting. In 1825 she was taken to that mission of Fr. Terme's. He recognized her force of character, her refinement, her quickness of wit and repartee, piously kidnapped her and sent her to Aps where she received the veil in 1820. Terme began to create a hostel for pilgrims to La Louvesc; he bought a territory and began to build a vast house—with no money to pay for it. A community was formed; the Sisters carried stone, mixed

the mortar, borrowed bread, and melted snow for drink.
Money always turned up to pay the workmen. A ribbon
industry was created; it succeeded, became a nuisance, and
was abolished by Terme. At twenty-three Marie-Thérèse
was made Superior. The winters were still appalling; they
had to burrow a tunnel of snow to reach the church. In
1829 Terme made his first Retreat. He returned, entered the
"refectory" where the Sisters were at supper and said: "I
have some news for you; but as it might upset some of you
I will keep it till after supper. Eat as usual." He then
marched up and down the room. Then he said: "Four of
you will at once go into Retreat. Make no comment! Not
a word—for or against. Anyone who allows herself a word is
answerable to me!" Then he gave them the Book of the
Exercises and a few sheets of paper: "Now make your own
Retreat!" His direction was austere, but he had his dry
humour. "I am travelling", he wrote, "with Fr. X, who is a
second St. Regis. I perceive therefore that Saints had their
faults and make other people pay for them. Observe that the
lives of the Saints mention only their virtues and keep quiet
about their faults!" "Never occupy yourself with what is
true but terrible. Leave alone the Foolish Virgins, the Idle
Servant, the Barren Fig-tree. . . . The Gospels contain also
the Prodigal Son, the Lost Sheep, Magdalen, Zacchaeus!"
He proceeded to tell the Sisters that they must themselves
give Retreats, though not mentioning that alarming name.
They began to do so, and the work had taken on firmer
contours; but neither then nor later did they undertake the
"direction" of souls. Instruction, yes; for women naturally
understand and are understood best by other women. Alas,
on December 12, 1834, Fr. Terme died. Anyhow, the purely
educational element in the Sisters' work was segregated and
the Sisters who were good at this were formed into a separate
Congregation, the Sisters of St. Regis. A period of confusion
was to follow, largely due, as so often, to wealthy benefactresses
determined on managing the whole enterprise to which they
make largesse. The first of these ladies (indeed, a second one)

after causing the utmost chaos and the departure of some of the most valuable Sisters, went away in 1840, lost her mental balance, started nineteen years of law-suits, wrote anonymous letters and ended by regarding herself as being in personal relations with the devil. Unhappily she left behind her a "Mme. Anaïs" who obtained an amazing ascendancy over such nuns as remained, including Mère Contenet, an admirable woman who took Marie-Thérèse's place when she was practically forced to resign the superiorship. There is no need to relate a distressing episode in which a Jesuit priest, Fr. T., became so bemused by Mère Anaïs's qualities (he thought she saw visions) as to call her the co-Foundress of the Cenacle and himself co-Founder. The Vicar General of Leo XIII, consecrating the altar of the Roman Cenacle, declared once and for all that while our Lady was the true heavenly Foundress and St. Regis the heavenly patron of the Society, Fr. Terme was its earthly Founder, while its earthly Foundress was still with them.

For forty-six years, then, the Foundress had been relegated into absolute obscurity; indeed, she felt grateful to be so much as "kept" in the Society. But never a complaint. Seldom has such suffering and such peace been imprinted on a human countenance as you can see in hers. When she lay dying, surrounded by those who had learnt to venerate her and to realize that in this death "something great was happening", she felt herself surrounded too by the loving souls in Purgatory—and where else had she been during more than half her life of over eighty years? She died on September 26, 1885.[1]

While I have no space even to mention many another beneficent "Institution", I cannot omit the Little Sisters of the Poor (our Nazareth Houses are derived from them). They were founded in 1839 not by the Abbé Le Pailleur, but in fact by Jeanne Jugan, a very simple Breton girl, born in 1793. She with two others began by looking after one old blind woman; but the work spread, miraculously, all round

[1] See *King's Daughters, I*, by the present writer, London, 1921.

the world. I think I am right in saying that their houses are
everywhere arranged in the same way, so that on entering you
know just where to turn to find what you want. At least, so
I have found them—not resenting, for once (so sweet is the
spirit of these Little Sisters), the sheer exportation of French
habits even to Australia. Also I think that they still live
entirely on alms, given in coins or in kind. They go to
collect these in ancient vehicles drawn by horses and driven
by coachmen no less ancient. I remember how, in a
Provençal house, a disgruntled old free-thinker—on the
whole, the Sisters look after the aged destitute—said: "They
give us scraps, and themselves have grand dinners." I
replied: "Get this into your thick skull. When *you* have
finished, it is *your* scraps that they eat." Also, how in a smart
hotel a Sister came in during dinner to "beg". A rich
vulgarian took a fish and threw it in her face. The other
diners growled. But the Little Sister (who had been, and
evidently still was, a "great lady") swept a superb curtsey
and said: "That was for me . . . now something for our
Lord!"[1]

I hope that these pages have not seemed a mere catalogue
of Institutions. The modernist, M. Loisy, said that it was
Institutions that "kept the Church going", not the faith of
Christians. But what save the undying Spirit in the Church
gave rise to those Institutions? We ought to be amazed at
the multitude of young men who (to look no further back
than the Renaissance and the increasingly corrupt centuries
that followed it) have gallantly resolved to serve God in
chastity, poverty and self-sacrifice "unto blood". But no
less amazing has been the continuous history of self-sacrifice

[1] I cannot resist recalling how in Styria, when Austria just after the first
world war was unthinkably impoverished, a beneficent society called the
White Cross reserved one evening for a supper given to "Offered Souls".
No other name could be thought of for these utterly useless (so man might
think) destitute men and children. During supper, the story of the multi-
plication of loaves and fishes was read to us, and the collection of fragments
that remained. An old man next to me said: "We are the fragments!"
His little grand-daughter said: "What will the dear Lord do with the
fragments?" He said: "The dear Lord *will keep them for His own table*."

on the part of women of all "classes" and in all nations, whatever the persecutions they endured. An Institution can become ossified, or dwindle, or die. And I have almost too much insisted that the cruellest blows struck at such Institutions were dealt from within them, or, very often, by the hands of "those who should have loved them". Even, it was their Foundresses who were hardest hit. Yet the ever-fertile Mother, the Church, continually creates what is needed at the hour. The Romans accurately spoke of the *singultus aquai*, the hesitation, sobbing, of fountains that leap, are oppressed by the load of air above them, but never cease playing. It is Christ's Spirit in the Church that creates the men and women who may begin the Institutions. I would like now to write a little about the extreme apparently opposite to the "practical" one; what is called "Mysticism" in modern times. Then I wish to write about the "missionary" urge, which is no degenerate successor to that of the medieval Franciscans or Dominicans, or the Renaissance Jesuits.

iii

Most divisions of Saints into "sorts" of Saints are artificial; still, there are some who can be labelled "officially" mystics, so to say—who are often in ecstasy, suffer the stigmata or other preternatural phenomena, though, we repeat, it is not because of these that they are held holy. Nor do we deny that an intense spiritual experience may produce purely physical or psychological (and abnormal) effects, or lead to misapprehensions, as when mystics reflect on their experiences and may interpret them awry. With this warning, we can 'recall a few instances even in the eighteenth and in the nineteenth centuries which denote the "mystical" life.

Anna (afterwards Crescentia) Höss (1682-1744) was born of very poor parents in Kaufbeuren, Bavaria. She made her First Communion when only six. She wished to enter the

local Franciscan convent, but could not do so without a
dowry. This was obtained by a strange Providence. Near
the convent was an uproarious tavern which distressed the
nuns, but they could not afford to buy it. The Protestant
burgomaster, however, did so, on the sole condition that the
"innocent lamb" Anna should be admitted even without a
dowry. This was done, but her penniless arrival was not
forgotten and she was treated in a most humiliating
way. Her very cell was taken from her in favour of a
moneyed candidate, and she was forced to beg one
Sister, then another, to let her sleep on the floor of her
room. Finally she obtained a dark little corner of her
own. At last a wiser Superior appointed her portress, a
post that she held for fifteen years. (It is curious how
many Saints have become so by way of the porter's lodge!)
Suddenly they realized her holiness and made her novice-
mistress and then, to her appalment, Superior. No wonder one of her watch-words was: "I would sooner give
up life than hope!" Her reputation as an ecstatic spread
far and wide and the convent was besieged with persons
of every state of life, including the highest in Church and
State affairs, asking for her advice. Her death was perfect
peace.

The Blessed Anna Maria Giannetti (1769-1837) was born
in Siena, but, after financial losses, went with her mother to
Rome, where both entered domestic service. Anna herself
married Domenico Taigi, a servant in the Chigi palace.
Both before and after this she was attracted by gay dresses
and frivolity, but, after meeting a Servite, Fr. Angelo,
underwent a deep "conversion" and soon began to receive
her strange experiences. It is said that she would see a
bright disc, slightly above the level of her eyes and to the
right; "in" this sat a woman between two "horns", and
across the disc figures of persons and events would pass as
though across the screen of a magic lantern. I cannot find
any adequate analysis of the genesis or symbolical meaning
of this. It remains that she devoted herself wholeheartedly

to her good but moody and unimaginative husband who recognized her virtue without understanding the heights of renunciation to which grace called her. Five of her children survived; and when the eldest son Camillo married a very domineering girl, Domenico admired how perfectly his wife preserved peace within the house. She mysteriously became very widely known and the highest personages in Church or State thronged her little house. Apparently it was her gift of prophecy that most impressed her contemporaries; but detailed instances of this are by now impossible to examine. What is clear is that her greater "consolations" occurred towards the beginning of her conversion; as so often, darkness, temptation and even calumny beset her later years. She died on June 9, 1837, within but a few days of Queen Victoria's accession, and she helps us to measure the enormous gulf between the English mentality of those days and that of a world of faith.

Simply for the sake of Italian names we must mention Rosa Carafa di Traetto (1832-1890) and along with her Catherine Volpicelli (d. 1894), for these two were closely associated in the organizing of the Servants of the Sacred Heart, interesting not least because they were women who, without vows and living in their own homes, yet had a regular noviciate and a Superior. Unconsciously, no doubt, yet substantially, they looked forward to the modern institutions of "secular" religious.

Zoë Labouré (1806-1876) would hardly have won attention had she not become a Sister of Charity, taken the name "Catherine", and received several visions of our Lady in the form made familiar by the "miraculous medal". This medal was first issued in 1832, but not until 1836 was a canonical enquiry into the authenticity of the visions instituted. A curious, perhaps unique, fact is that Catherine refused obstinately to appear before this or any other ecclesiastical commission. The only person who knew about her was her confessor and a M. Aladel who wrote a book about the origin of the medal. Its popularity was immediate, but was vastly increased by the conversion of the Jew, M. Ratisbonne, who had agreed to wear the medal and then had a vision of our Lady in similar form. Catherine lived from 1831 to her death at Enghien-Reuilly as portress and looking after the fowls, and the aged people whom that house sheltered. Only eight months before she died did she tell her Superior that it was *she* who had had the visions. Her authorities had, up to date, thought her "rather insignificant", matter-of-fact, unexcitable and almost apathetic. She was to be one of those Saints of whom no one knew anything—like St. Benedict Labre—but whose death was immediately followed by a perfect explosion of devotion. A proof that visions *as such* are no proof of sanctity may be seen in the life of St. Bernadette, who has been canonized, and in that of the two children of La Salette, about whom the question of heroic virtue has never arisen. On the other hand, we may hope that the two children of Fatima who have died, Francisco and Jacinta, may indeed be placed above our altars; of the surviving "seer" naturally nothing can be said. Indeed, as for St. Gemma Galgani (1878-1903) whose physical sufferings were so terrible as to recall St. Lydwina of Schiedam, and whose "stigmatic" career was as astonishing as anyone's, the Sacred Congregation of Rites not only refrained from passing any judgment upon such phenomena, but said that no such judgment ever would—or could—be made. The loveliness of her life is quite independent of them. I have no room to describe the life of the Blessed Clara Moes (1832-1895), born in Luxemburg. She, amid astonishing visitations, insisted that if extraordinary graces "do not lead to God and His life, they sanctify neither the soul that experiences them nor those who behold them". There are many other ecstatics of this period that we could mention, and many of extraordinary self-sacrifice and prayer, e.g., the Venerable Théodolinde Dubouché (d. 1863), whose life of exquisite virtue is the more wonderful because both her parents were "dead to the Faith" and in all her environment only one clerk was plucky enough to go to Mass. She had in fact to hide her own visits to the church, so did her family try to detach her from Christian belief and even morals. She was told that the "passions were an essential element in life and that no one could escape from them". She wished to become a nun, but was told that her apostolate must be within her own home, and indeed, quite marvellously, she brought her mother and then her father, a sister and a cousin, back to religion. It was she who in the "year of revolutions" itself, 1848, created the Paris Congregation of Reparation and Adoration of the Blessed Sacrament (see p. 155), and also collaborated with St. Julien Eymard in founding his own Congregation of the Blessed Sacrament for priests and men. As she died, she exclaimed three times, "I see!"[1]

The story of St. Bernadette Soubirous (1844-1877) almost vanished into that of Lourdes itself, which is just what she would have wished. That story is too well-known to require even a summary here. We need but recall that God chose a child who was slow-witted enough, who could not learn her catechism, whose parents lived partly through the father's fault in real destitution, and who was herself caused to bring to light the source through which so many marvels were to take place, only at the expense of her own great humiliation —she had to try to drink from it and rise with her face all muddied and was told to eat of the vegetation that grew beside the oozing drops so that all thought she had taken leave of her senses. Then came the day when the Vision declared that she was the Immaculate Conception. One would say that as from now her innocence begins to become holiness. Stared at, mobbed as if she were a 'wild animal' on show, she could but agree when they told her it would be

---

[1] There are so many names I would like to mention, like that of Mme. de Montaignac (d. 1885), who did heroic work for the spread of devotion to the Sacred Heart: or along with this aristocratic woman, Maria Agnes Steiner, a Tyrolese (1813-1862), a very poor worker in the fields, who ultimately did much to restore the discipline of Poor Clare convents in many a town. But the list would be interminable.

better to leave Lourdes altogether; she tore herself, sobbing, from the Grotto which had been her heaven, and exchanged the Pyrenees for the flat lands of Nevers and a new kind of humiliation, the kind yet calculated snubs she received in her convent. Gradually, she was treated more gently; they need have no fear for her humility. The asthma from which she had always suffered grew worse; she was constantly sick and had to sit, gasping for breath, on the side of her bed. At last she died, murmuring the words that had meant so much to her—"Holy Mary, Mother of God, pray for us poor sinners...."

The short life of St. Thérèse de Lisieux (1873-1897) is known throughout the world and has had an astonishing influence. We are frequently told that it is a proof that "anyone can be a Saint", because she spoke often of her "Little Way"; she worked no miracles, did no extraordinary penances, and had no ecstasies (though, once or twice, some abnormal psychological experiences). None the less, no one can call her life an easy one. Oddly enough, both her parents had wished to be "religious"; but they met and, in 1858, married and had eight children, of whom four died. Thérèse was very small and extremely weak; her mother died when the child was four and a half; her father (he had retired from business and was fairly well-to-do) had plenty of time and inclination to spoil her, had that been possible. She was gay, obstinate and very affectionate and liked the ordinary toys— doll, skipping-rope, toy-oven and piano, and kept canaries in a cage. Already when only nine she asked to enter Carmel and was of course refused. Her father took her to Italy and they were presented to Leo XIII. She had been told on no account to speak to him; but she seized hold of his hands and begged him to let her enter Carmel. Leo smiled, blessed her, and evaded the petition. Yet in 1888, she actually entered, aged fifteen, and was "clothed" a year later. Now we must recall that her "Little Path" was trodden within a Carmel, which means a life of very great austerity. Further, her Superiors, doubtless to "keep her humble" (as was done to Bernadette), treated her very severely indeed; still, they trusted her, and made her "mistress of novices" when still incredibly young. Interiorly, her "testing" was very bitter—she had a protracted spell not only of desolation but of temptation to doubt everything. During her last illness her bodily suffering was quite terrible, so that the "little way" of simply *disregarding self* was also a very lofty one. The demand for her canonization was world-wide and immediate; all rules had to be set aside, and it occurred in 1925. For the first time since 1870 the Dome of St. Peter's was illuminated.

I cannot resist writing of a humble but enchanting "mystic", Sister Marie-Marthe Chambon, who lived from 1841-1907, the daughter of very poor, hard-working field-folk, near Chambéry; she was born and baptized the same day (March 6). When she was eight or nine she "saw" our Lord on Good Friday, bleeding and torn, "but He did not say anything to me". At her First Communion, September 8, 1850, she saw the Holy Child, who said that when she received Communion it would always be "like that". Later on a Sister asked her if He had a white frock—blond curls? "Oh Sister", cried this very simple peasant, "It isn't like that. One can't *say* those things, don't you think?" Since then she always "saw Him", even when at field-work. Once, she "saw" our Lady—and often at other times; but *that* time, it was "special", "*c'était notable*". She was accepted in 1862 by the local Visitation convent; she told her father she was to go next day; he fell on his knees exclaiming, "God preserve us!" But off she went, her clothes in a parcel, and unable (as she remained) to read or write. In the convent she was very homesick. "My mind kept going down there to my parents. But whenever I noticed it, I reined myself in. . . . I was very frightened of being dismissed. I was so clumsy— I didn't even know how to light a fire! It always smoked. . . . I kept saying: 'My good Jesus, keep me! Oh my good Jesus, please keep me!'" She used to say: "My good Jesus, with all your graces, you leave me all my faults." He agreed . . . so did the others; she was so "rustic" as to make them laugh; poor memory, quick temper; a certain obstinacy allied with narrow "village" views. A young Sister once told her as a joke (!) that she was not pretty: "didn't you know that?" "Oh yes, I should say I do! But, do you see, it rather hurts to be told so. . . ."

As from 1866 she realized that much was being asked of her. Our Lord wished her to sleep on the floor; Superiors refused leave for this "eccentricity". But she suffered from complete insomnia till the leave was granted. Other almost incredible penances followed. Her director was a Canon Bouvier, for thirty-two years confessor at the Visitation. When people came from Savoy to consult the Curé d'Ars, he would say: "Why come to me? You have the Visitation chaplain!" He and others impress me as genuinely circumspect and reticent; but when the Sisters wrote down what our Lord "said" to the Sister, they often did it in so conventional a style as to carry no conviction. In 1874 she received the stigmata in her feet; only gradually did she obtain that the flow of blood should lessen. For four years, she ate nothing save Holy Communion; but her strength increased; she did the normal house-work; her place was again laid in the refectory. Despite her great devotion to our Lord's Five Wounds, she never gave up her love for the Holy Child, and here we reach some of her authentic sayings. She asked Him to help her wash up, to lay the tables, which He did. She would shut the door, because she thought the others would see Him. He kept recommending childlikeness to her. "We are living the Holy Childhood together, you and I. . . . *Nous faisons ensemble la Sainte Enfance*." "Aren't you pleased with Me? (He said.) *Aren't* I helping you well!" He told her also to contemplate her unworthiness. "How could I help doing so? But all the same—be my Light, else I could never keep that promise." She was criticized for her daily Communions, especially as she did not seem so very holy. When Pius X gave his wide leave for this, she cried gaily:

"Aha! What will you say *now*? Are *you* all Saints? . . . You must discover the Tabernacle everywhere." We pass, with her, into a world of holy fairy-tales, by which I mean that it does not matter much if the anecdotes be "objectively" true, for it shows how she felt about things. Having collected raspberries, it was the turn of plums; still, she felt she must go back to the raspberries. "But, dear Lord, it's useless. I took them all yesterday." Still, she found plenty more. "My child, I put them there to give you the pleasure of giving them to the Sisters." When she was refectorian, they chaffed her simplicity. "What was the colour of Henri IV's white plume?" "Oh, Moiselle, you must ask your mistresses. *I* never went to school!" She would beg pardon rather disconcertingly when she had been clumsy—"My dear Sister", said a very busy nun, "don't you see that this is *not* the moment for apologies . . .?" So she apologized for apologizing. She knew she had her faults: "Well, yes, on earth we aren't angels! Everyone knows that—our Lord too. No, we aren't angels!" "Doesn't it tire you to kneel fasting all the morning?" "But one doesn't *know* one is. One doesn't think about that sort of thing." "But aren't you very tired *afterwards*?" "Oh no, not that one is always very clear where one *is*." In 1875 a new Archbishop was making his first visitation, and the usual yet incredible event took place. Certain Sisters told him things that they thought "odd"—"intolerable"—in Marie-Marthe. He made no enquiry, but denounced her publicly, and stopped her daily Communions. This was so great a shock to all that when Canon Bouvier interceded for her, the interdict was revoked and all went well.

None the less, a final purgation began. She often thought she was deluded, gave bad example, was a cross to her Superiors, was lost. She had long periods of complete blankness—*elle faisait pitié à voir*. Some of these younger inexplicable Sisters tried experiments—one burnt her (like Bernadette) with a candle; another drove a pin "fairly deeply" into her, as the Avignon lady did into St. Catherine. She was unconscious of this. When she "had nothing to do", she "let herself slide into God." "Then there isn't anything more, no more time, we are together . . . *on est ensemble*." After 1888, her notebooks (in which they wrote down what she said) were given to a new chaplain who kept them to himself. As from 1906, she suffered terribly, even physically. During Midnight Mass she cried out: "My Jesus—all, yes, all—but not *that!*" The meaning can be only guessed. In 1907 she had to be kept tied in an armchair, else she slipped forward. "Come", she said often, "but come quick!" On March 21, she died. Her photo shows indeed her knotted fingers, but also an expression of extreme suffering, dignity and calm—more than mere death.

iv

The Church has always been a "missionary" Church, even before the daring expeditions of St. Paul. But there have been times when this side of the Church's apostolate has been specially noticeable—when for example the earliest Franciscans and Dominicans penetrated into the Far East; when the Jesuits played a heroic part in the great sixteenth and seventeenth century revival; and in the modern world, after the tragic events of the late eighteenth and early nineteenth centuries. It would be unfair not to mention the name of Pauline Jaricot (1799-1862), of Lyons; she herself went to no foreign mission, but inaugurated that astonishing organization, "The Propagation of the Faith", which *popularized* the whole idea of Missions oversea, till by now almost every religious Congregation has its own missions—in Africa, in China; precarious as their fate has increasingly become. It is clear that I cannot even enumerate all the societies at work in the Missions; after a few brief allusions I hope to devote rather more pages to four or five personalities, because, as I said, I do not want to end this book with a mere catalogue of names.

I must concentrate first on the missionary work of an

amazing woman—Pius XI even called her "the first woman missionary"—Anne-Marie Javouhey, born in 1779 of an agricultural Burgundian family. During the Terror she catechized, and, said the old curé when he returned, "transformed the village". She felt that she ought to found a religious Order. Impossible! Still, she did enter a convent, but was so miserable that on the very eve of her vows she had to tell her parents she could not make them. She had dreamed that her cell was full of children, black, white, yellow, and that St. Teresa said to her: "These are the children I will give you!" Yet, till then she did not even know that not everyone was "white"! After other abortive experiments, her father gave her part of his house where she and a few companions might start to work for children. This could not be permanent. She looked towards Chalon in the diocese of Autun, saw the Bishop, and so impressed the local officials that they obtained Napoleon's authorization of her "Religious Association of St. Joseph". This was in 1806, and the rapid arrangement was presumably due to the recognition that education had been ruined in France by the Revolution and that children were growing up savages. Other houses were founded—too swiftly for the solid formation of novices. A central quiet home must be found and was discovered in a deserted monastery at Cluny— hence the name "Cluny" added to St. Joseph's. In 1815 Mère Javouhey went to Paris and created a storm by using the "Lancastrian" system which was denounced as foreign, and religiously indifferentist.[1] Well, the Government ordered catechism and Catholic prayers where the system had been introduced, and Mère Javouhey went on using it as a temporary expedient. But I will say no more about the development of her Institute

---

[1] Joseph Lancaster, a Quaker, invented in 1796 a monitorial system for a school established in 1803, though an Anglican, Mr. Bell, claimed that *he* had invented it. The master appointed a more advanced pupil as "monitor" for ten others. He himself instructed the monitors; they, their groups of ten. Thus a minimum education was given cheaply to large numbers. Lancaster, not Bell, wished for undenominational schools.

within Europe so far as education as such is concerned.

Meanwhile her personality had so impressed itself on all, that when the *Intendant* of Bourbon Island (today, Reunion) came to Paris to ask for educational help in his colony, he resolved to meet her, and the Minister of the Interior actually told her that she and her Sisters were required for *all* the French colonies. In January, 1817, four Sisters sailed for Bourbon and arrived in June; four more followed after a year. The work prospered; in 1819 the Government asked for Sisters also in Senegal, where the island of Goree and a churchless, schoolless "capital", St. Louis, were the only "colonized" parts and terribly demoralized; nor did officialdom like its inertia being disturbed. In fact, the new Prefect Apostolic, who had arrived with the nuns, not only, after six weeks, desponded and sailed home, but put the whole place, nuns included, under an interdict, so that for two years they were deprived of Mass and the Sacraments. This seemingly lunatic action has been explained as due to a wish to show the officials that if they would not play up, they should have no help, educational or medical, at all. But in 1822 Mère Javouhey came herself to Senegal and at once summed up the situation with uncanny accuracy. She realized the character of the Natives—inflammable, no doubt, but affectionate, childish, unstable, indolent; yet their graver vices and even diseases were too often a European importation. She had long hoped for a society of missionary priests, and the desolation of Senegal convinced her yet again of its necessity; but France itself suffered from lack of priests and there was not much missionary spirit there. Yet she looked even further—to the creation of native priests such as recent Pontiffs have so earnestly asked for. Meanwhile a new Prefect Apostolic had come—and also left. The nuns depended for their Sacraments on visits from the priest at Goree. At least there was no second interdict! In spite of this, she used her childhood's agricultural lore to initiate a vast Christian colony at Dagana; and General MacCarthy, governor of Sierra Leone and Gambia, called her thither. Yellow fever broke out—she shared in making mattresses and sheets; she baptized, and herself buried the already putrefying dead, and was more than once so sick as to be despaired of. But in 1824 the French Sisters, firmly backed by the Government, obtained her return. Foundresses cannot afford to be away too long![1]

Meanwhile the Institute was being asked for from Cayenne to Pondicherry. It is certain, on the one hand, that the French Government was only too glad to have such willing, competent and inexpensive assistants as the nuns; on the other hand, Mère Javouhey did not think of the world *exclusively* as a religious mission-field, nor simply as colonies to be civilized (still less, as colonies *within which* the Whites had to be catered for); she thought of each man, and of society, as "wholes", as to be supernaturalized *as* "wholes", and not as asking from the Missionary *only* supernatural assistance while being left, so far as "nature" went, in the condition in which they had been found. Thus you find her planning an enormous territory on the river Mana in Guiana, which should be practically a new "Paraguay", populated by troops of orphans with whom France could not cope (they did not come); by colonists who would come, but for a limited period (many came, but most returned) and by Natives with whose ultimate emancipation she was concerned. You find her dealing with agriculture, drainage,

[1] I just mention an exasperating but characteristic incident. To stabilise her Institute, she had asked for an approbation from Rome. She received a most laudatory reply, but was correctly told that the application must come through her bishop. At least three French bishops had warmly encouraged her, but, still tinged with Gallicanism, did not wish to ask, nor in fact asked, for anything from Rome. Now a French Superior, exceeding her powers, had appointed a Mère Thaïs as Superior of Bourbon. Mère Javouhey saw she was quite unfitted for government and sent a Mère Bathilde and then a Mère Rosalie to replace her. Thaïs refused to resign—Mère Javouhey, she announced, had no authority till Rome had confirmed the Institute: the Sisters were not "religious" at all. The Bourbon officials backed Mère Thaïs, relegated Rosalie to one desolate parish, and wrote home that Mère Javouhey was a domineering would-be autocrat. The French Government was well aware of Mère Javouhey's forcefulness, but also, that she knew how to remain within her rights, and her charity and humility. But communications were slow: it took three years to adjust matters: since then, Reunion has prospered, not least owing to the self-sacrificing work of the Sisters.

building, kinds and quality of wood or soil, digging a huge canal. There was no limit to the work she imposed on herself. Alas, vested interests were against her; the Government was extremely corrupt; slave-owners had no intention of freeing their slaves; joy and sorrow were mingled in her soul. She returned to France after four years, meaning to come back again after one. But not only she had to make sure of the spiritual, educational and material well-being of her Institute, now grown so large, and to bring its statutes up to date, but she was confronted by a new and acute form of an old difficulty. Certain bishops began to insist in various ways that St. Joseph of Cluny should be wholly in diocesan control. The Bishop of Beauvais appointed a priest as "Superior of Temporalities" of the Institute and said that all finance must be given over wholly to this priest and to himself. Mère Javouhey rightly said that this contravened the arrangement made between herself and the civil and ecclesiastical authorities in 1827. The Bishop was annoyed and put the Paris Archbishopric against the Institute. But a conflict was started by the Bishop of Autun which was defeated by its own violence. He was a Mgr. d'Héricourt, a Marquis, who at twenty-six left the army for the seminary, where after two years of study he was ordained, and after two more, became bishop. He was determined to be autocrat in his own diocese, but went further. Not only he resolved to alter the constitutions of the Institute in all sorts of ways, but declared that the bishop in whose diocese a noviciate was, must be Superior General of that entire Congregation, and that there must be only *one* noviciate, i.e., within *his* diocese. But this meant that if the Congregation had houses in other dioceses, his authority would extend also into those dioceses, which their bishops would not like at all. He displayed every form of cajolery and threat, foreshadowing not only the closure of all French houses outside his diocese but of those in the foreign missions, where the Prefects Apostolic were also all too ready to wish to have absolute power over any religious congregation there, but

could certainly not have permitted houses to subsist if one
French bishop had supreme control of them.   Mgr.
d'Héricourt, sharing the general disinclination to appeal to
Rome, did not hesitate to appeal to Caesar; but the Government made him understand very clearly that the statutes of
1827 remained in force and that the considerable changes
he had actually had printed were invalid. The King, Louis
Philippe, told Mère Javouhey that he was quite willing to
intervene personally in her favour; but this generous woman
did not wish to be the occasion of ill-feeling between Church
and State, nor would she ever appeal to the latter against the
former.   However, on the eve of her next departure for
Guiana, the King ordered Mass to be celebrated in his
private chapel that her enterprise might be blessed. She,
and all the royal family, attended it. The slave trade was
abolished in 1833; but it was seen that slaves needed to be
educated into freedom. Mère Javouhey toiled at this in her
colony of Mana, building on the foundations of prayer,
marriage and home, and work. Here the undying hostility
of slave-owners was encountered. Unhappily, young and
headlong priests added to her difficulties, and even wrote
appalling calumnies about her to lay and clerical officials
both in the colony and in France.   Naturally Bishop
d'Héricourt intrigued against her with the utmost energy,
and finally she was, personally, forbidden the Sacraments.
On her return to France in 1838 the Sacraments were at once
restored to her; Beauvais and Paris became friendly to her;
the Bishop of Autun alone remained implacable. There is no
point in entering into this controversy; after a final paroxysm
of hostility, the Bishop found everyone against him, and he
was destined to die only a few days before Mère Javouhey
did, in whom he suddenly realized that she acted from
"conviction", not "caprice". This suffices to show how he
himself acted from pure imperceptiveness, and that autocracy
does not know what to do when it encounters firmness joined
with humility. It was noticeable how, when the abrupt
emancipation of the slaves in 1848 threw the mass of those

in Guiana back into idleness and almost savage life, the population of Mana remained true to their homes and work, and continued to regard Mère Javouhey as alike their Mother and their Governor. Her incredible labours in gradually breaking down bad traditions and preparing for a true civilization should have earned for her a primary place in the history of Emancipation; but for that, textbooks themselves would have had to recognize that the spiritual life alone can civilize. And if the infamous expulsion of the religious Congregations in 1903 dealt a severe blow to education by closing her houses not only in France but, often enough, in the colonies to which, it was said, anti-clericalism should not be exported, it is we in the North who were among those who chiefly profited by the Sisters' exile; and today, at least for the time being, the Sisters of St. Joseph of Cluny are working all round the globe, true to the spirit of their Foundress, who died on July 15, 1851. Her Cause was soon introduced, and she was beatified in October, 1950.

As for the south-eastern coast of South Africa, I have room but to say that in 1847 an "Eastern Vicariate" was made and placed under Bishop Devereux, who introduced the first nuns into South Africa. Their home was Grahamstown. He applied in 1848 to the Assumption Sisters (p. 137) and a misunderstanding arose. In this new world, new methods would be needed; nuns must turn their hand to everything; he thought that the Superior General realized this—only, she begged, let the new foundation be under French protection and preserve its "national French character". The nuns sailed; Bishop Pompallier too with nuns for New Zealand was on board (p. 189); English, French, Flemish, Dutch, German, Maori were studied. Conditions were deplorable. Was a nun sick? The doctor was busy, smoking. The very crew revolted against the food; they began to live on whale-flesh. Cholera forbade them to land at Teneriffe; at Praya, they were ordered back—Americans had recently landed and carried off some women. A slaver sailed up, but retreated at sight of guns. A mutiny broke out—the Bishop wrenched a musket from a murderer; finally, knowing Algoa Bay, he enabled the captain—who measured his whereabouts with a teaspoon—to land the ship safely. On board had been the Assumption nun, Mother Gertrude, Josephine de Henningsen, descended from northern kings, enormously tall, destined to experience two revolutions, two Kaffir and two Boer wars—she "loved the whistle of bullets". She was born in 1822; she argued it out before her First Communion whether to be a Catholic or a Protestant, and decided the former was "more self-sacrificing". In Grahamstown she opened a free school and a day and a boarding school which prospered exceedingly; but alas, the life she and her community perforce, and by the Bishop's orders, had to lead in raw South Africa differed too profoundly from the Parisian life, so the former had to be severed from the European family, which in any case (it seems to me) was not matured enough to send out Sisters in no way prepared to be flexible. In 1850 the Natives "ate meat" and besieged the town into which 10,000 refugees came pouring. The nuns spent their time in the church, nursing the wounded, laying out the dead. These Sisters were given guns; Mother Gertrude, having practised broad-sword with her brother, received a cavalry sword. After this war, much had to be rebuilt; much invented. She generously co-operated with the Jesuits, the Trappists, the Dominicanesses. In 1896 she was sent home to attempt a reunion with the French houses; but the Paris portress, terrified by her stature, deep voice and massive walking-stick, took her for a man and fled shrieking. She returned to Africa and died, after great pain heroically endured, in 1904. I have liked to finger, in Grahamstown, the irresponsive strings of the harp she installed there (a heroic laywoman had already taught children at least to play correct notes on a "dumb" piano— so hungry were these poor expatriates for *some* "culture"!); but today nuns of very many orders are like St. Hildegarde, teaching the souls of Natives and in-comers alike to make music to the Lord.[1]

Modern times too have had their Martyrs. During the period of the French Terror, the triangular blade of the guillotine flashed ceaselessly up and down; and for the few who have been canonized innumerable others must have perished for their faith despite the accusations—so closely copied in our own times—of being "enemies of the people" and "conspiring against its sovereign rule". When the Carmelite nuns of Compiègne were arrested they were not allowed any defence, but were accused of just those crimes. Ten choir-nuns, one novice, three lay-sisters and two extern-Sisters were guillotined on July 17, 1794, and their bodies thrown with one thousand two hundred and eighty-two others into a pit. None the less, England possesses many of their relics, since they were imprisoned with the English Benedictine nuns from Cambrai; these were allowed to return to England and did so wearing the secular attire which the Carmelites had been made to put on when they left Compiègne. With these we must rank the eleven Ursuline nuns who were executed at Valenciennes in October, 1794, and with these too how many must have been welcomed into heaven, having died of starvation or sickness in their prisons.

[1] In the *Southern Cross*, February 5 and 12, 1947, there was an account of Sister Mary Evangelista, by Mr. Justice S. Solomon. She was born in Bavaria in 1890 and entered the Congregation of the Teaching Sisters of the Holy Cross. In 1907 she was sent to South Africa. It is too early to give a full description of her life: enough to say that she spent the last seventeen years of it in Alexandra Township on the edge of the Johannesburg munici-pality. She suffered throughout from such agonizing illnesses that you might have thought they would have sufficed both to occupy her and sanctify her: but her work among Natives was incessant: she seemed to know each of them, and all of them worshipped her. In 1922, on the eighth day of a Novena, she was, it would seem, miraculously cured of a ghastly illness—her whole body was a mass of sores and she vomited blood daily. As they not seldom did, her doctors said she was quite incurable. This illness had lasted six years. Her cure was instantaneous and complete. On August 18, 1947, she died, having received Extreme Unction some fifteen times during her life. Towards the end she endured the *spiritual* "purification by temptation" from which souls like hers never seem exempt. Her life will certainly, some day, be seen as an integral part of the spiritual history of South Africa.

Yet at this very time France especially was sending missionaries out to the East; and while, naturally, most of those who were martyred were priests or men catechists, yet we find names of women too—especially in China and Annam—the widow Agnes Tsao-Kuy (1856), who was only thirty and was born of Christian parents; the Blessed Agnes Thanh, the catechist Lucia Y (1862), Martha Wang (1861); in a new outbreak of persecution as from 1873, we know of the young maiden Thu and her little sister—only four—buried alive together (we read of this in a letter written in 1888); in the Boxer rebellion of 1900, in the Chinese province of Kan-su, all the Chinese Sisters were bound to trees and pierced with swords and spears; one survived, but so mutilated that she looked hardly human (we are reminded of the Martyrs of Lyons, p. 2 ff); two-thirds of the girls and children were killed; numbers were sold off to Mohammedan slave-dealers. A specially remarkable list of Korean martyrs could be compiled—in 1801 women of exalted rank were killed by poisoning and in other ways; others followed, one not yet twelve years old; another, fourteen; another seventeen; two sisters, Columba and Agnes Kim, were martyred together, and a whole series of others whose determination to vow their virginity to God seemed to infuriate the Koreans even worse than their faith—the cruellest enemy of Agatha Tsien was her own brother—and once again we are back in the period of the early girl-martyrs of the Church, this time with no legendary admixture to distract us.

Nothing is more impressive than the way in which Japanese Christians remained true to the rudiments of their Faith from the earliest days, even though no priest was left to support them. Early in the nineteenth century there was a new series of executions; and between 1867 and 1873 there was again a period of appalling persecution; and we could make further lists of women's names from the history of Damascus (1860) and from that of Russia, especially during the first and second partitions of Poland (1773, 1793) and the persecutions of Catherine II, Nicholas I, Alexander II. Even had I space, I would not exhibit the hideous details of the tortures inflicted during those times. They would be quite capable of arousing in us feelings of retrospective hatred and vengefulness. Yet I cannot but add that contemporary history has hardly been less bloodstained, nor its tale of mass-murder and expatriation less horrible. It was, however, reserved for our time to invent the breaking down of the *mind* both by drugs and in other ways; and, if we are to find grace to be as brave as our remoter or nearer ancestors, should we be called upon to suffer as they did, we must prepare for that by exorcising from our indignation all evil recrimination; we must rinse out from our souls every drop of gall; we must in short begin to realize what is meant in the Our Father when we ask to have our sins forgiven us *as we* forgive those who have sinned against ourselves or our fellow men.

Comparisons of worth, as between holy persons, so between religious Institutes, must be deprecated; but the Franciscan Missionaries of Mary certainly occupy a very special place. Helen de Chappotin (1839-1904) was inspired with the idea of a vocation by Jeanne Jugan, the true Foundress of the Little Sisters of the Poor (p. 158), who came to Helen's home to beg. But the path was not clear. She tried to enter the Poor Clares; her health gave way. She actually did enter Marie-Réparatrice (p. 154) and in March, 1865, was sent to the Madura Mission in India, having taken the name of Mary of the Passion, and actually was made Provincial of the three houses there. But difficulties arose, in spite of initial success, so acute that Mary was deposed from her position, rivalries and a storm of slander broke out, and the very existence of the group which surrounded her was threatened. Either they must accept impossible conditions imposed from Europe, or leave Marie-Réparatrice. Neither the chief nor later biographers consent to "draw aside the veil" which covers these quarrels, save indeed to hint that certain native Sisters refused to agree to European discipline; so the real origins of this schism, for such it became, remain unknown to us. Enough to say that Mary left for Rome not only still under the protection of ecclesiastical authority in India, but surrounded by the lamentation of the poor Indians who worshipped her and, long even after her death, recalled her with love and homage. In 1877, as a matter of fact, Pius IX sanctioned the continuance of the Sisters who had remained attached to Mary as the nucleus of a definitely Missionary Society and suggested that a noviciate be opened for it in France. The next part of her existence is concerned with her ever closer connection with the Franciscans and with the renewed difficulties that beset her. It is quite amazing how many groups of "missionary" Sisters had come into existence during the nineteenth century, and how closely many of them were linked with the Franciscans, into whose great family Mary and her companions were after some time incorporated. What should not by now surprise us is that despite the favour shown to her by Popes, Cardinals, prelates and many another, a new storm of calumny blew up so fiercely around her that she was again deposed from her office and only after some time did Leo XIII insist that the situation be cleared up once and for all. In 1884 a decree was issued saying that she who had always been a Mother should be recognized as also the Foundress and Superior General of a Congregation. The last adjustments between her and Marie-Réparatrice had been made. No shadow had darkened her perfect humility, resignation and charity. Already Cardinal Lavigerie had asked her help in Africa; it had been her duty to remain in Rome. Now, 1885, she accepted his renewed call and opened a house in Tunis and felt herself in the steps of St. Augustine and St. Vincent de Paul, and was unknowingly the predecessor of Charles de Foucauld in the northern regions of that vast continent. Next year, Rome acceded to requests from Ceylon and even the British Government asked for the nuns to take charge of the great hospital at Colombo, and in four years, native postulants were presenting themselves. Soon enough the Sisters were asked for from

China and then by a Goan bishop, and now they felt themselves heirs of St. Thomas and of Xavier.[1] Clearly I cannot
give details about the development of this Congregation
(or of any other!); it went forward despite the consistent
ill-health of the Foundress; despite cruel persecutions in
China itself; perhaps *because* of its truly Franciscan poverty.
In 1892 it crossed the Atlantic to Canada. And in 1947 the
Sisters had three hundred and fifty houses in all five conti-
nents and were as practical—they inaugurated printing-
presses and workshops—as they were prayerful. I would
like to emphasize their work among lepers, for whom at that
date there were thirteen asylums; and their great eagerness to
train candidates alike for the native clergy and native
convents![2]

Well aware of how much I have left out (most notably,
St. Margaret Mary Alacoque, St. Louise de Marillac, and
St. Sophie Madeleine Barat) I would like to conclude with
a reference to three women, at once highly "personal", and
"representative".

It may, as we said, seem strange that we confine what we
say of St. Madeleine Sophie Barat (1779-1865) to but a few
lines, seeing that it was she who founded the Society of the
Sacred Heart in which Mother Philippine Duchesne (1769-
1852) was after all her daughter, though so eminent a
one, and since it was really its Foundress who (along with
others) revived Catholic teaching in French schools after a
disastrous period of degeneracy and revolution. However,
the nuns of whom we are now writing are definitely
missionary nuns, and St. Madeleine Sophie's work was done

[1] Four Catholic Orders were already working there: the Sisters of Charity
since 1862 (I trust the *Life of Sister Xavier Berkeley of Spetchley* (see p. 142) is
very well known: a fascinating account of missionary work in China); the
Carmelites and Helpers of the Holy Souls at Shanghai, and the Canossian
Sisters at Hankow.

[2] There is a Congregation of "Medical Mission Sisters" entirely devoted to
medical work in which it is likely that both religious and clergy will be
allowed to share more actively than once was canonically permitted. The
history of the Franciscan Missionaries of Mary can be read in Georges
Goyau's *Valiant Women*, translated by Mgr. G. Telford, 1947.

at home, and consisted largely in the creation, safeguarding and consolidation of her Society. Philippine was a Burgundian, born at Joigny; she was entrusted for her "formation" to her elder brother Louis, who was, if not Jansenist in doctrine, at least a severe task-master; it is a real miracle that the relentless education that he gave her did not leave her cowed in soul. That this did not happen was due, under God, to a certain Fr. Varin, who, like others, was looking forward to the restoration of the Society of Jesus. Meanwhile he was Superior of the Fathers of the Sacred Heart, whose Society led up to that restoration. But he was anxious to found a teaching Order for girls, and it was in Madeleine Sophie that he discovered his first recruit, and indeed in 1802 made her, though only twenty-three, its first Superior. Despite incredible difficulties, from within and without, the Society of the Sacred Heart prospered and went overseas, into Asia, America, and became cherished throughout our own island, till in 1864 St. Madeleine Sophie knew she was exhausted. On May 21 she came into a room where the Sisters were assembled and said she had wanted to see them that day, "for on Thursday we are going to heaven". That would be Ascension Day, and to that they thought she was alluding. But next day she suffered a stroke, and on May 25, Ascension Day, she did indeed leave this world where she had worked so hard.

Rose Philippine Duchesne was born at Grenoble, grim among mountains and rushing torrents. The Duchesnes lived in an appropriately austere house in a public square. The men were upright, uncompromising, in municipal or parliamentary positions. The house was chilled by "liberalism"; the child's father gave up the practice of his religion; her mother was, if not Jansenized, rigid in her affection. Philippine was taught a masculine religion; she read Roman history to a sister sick in bed; but a missionary widened her horizons by tales of Louisiana and lit a flame in her soul. She went to school at the Visitation convent of Ste-Marie-d'en-Haut, founded by SS. Francis de Sales and

Jeanne de Chantal themselves, and by fourteen she was wanting to be a nun in a world illuminated by the gentler light of the Sacred Heart. But she loved dancing, though she attacked her minuets "as though they had been an algebraic problem", and she was fond of music and painting. She did not speak of her vocation till, at seventeen, she asked to visit her old school, and, once there, said she would never leave it. The "Duchesne character" was such that no one hoped to dislodge her; but the France of 1787 was in such disquiet that her father insisted that no vows should be taken as yet.

In fact the American War of Independence was inflaming imaginations; the writings of Voltaire and Rousseau, the dull though well-meaning King and the extravagant Austrian Marie-Antoinette had set the land in a ferment. Grenoble, refusing to abolish its parliament in accord with the royal decree of 1789 which convened the Estates General at Paris only, led the revolution; its parliament met, in fact, in the house of Casimir Périer, Philippine's uncle. She was brought home; in 1791 religious houses were suppressed and the nuns scattered. The Terror followed; the family escaped to a factory of theirs in the country; a priest applied for a post there, rose to be foreman, and Mass was secretly celebrated every day. In 1793, Mme. Duchesne died. Philippine spent some time with an irascible old grandmother and began to learn how to control her own headstrong temperament. She returned to Grenoble, organized a society of "Ladies of Mercy", visited prisons and the sick and risked the guillotine a thousand times over. But Robespierre fell; she proceeded to organize the city's little street-boys—by now mere savages—till in 1801 she obtained the return of Ste-Marie to its proper use. But the house was derelict; the few aged nuns who consented to accompany her departed; her first enterprise collapsed.

She then opened a school. A Fr. Rivet said that his sister might join her and bring more children; he also spoke of a new Society founded at Amiens, dedicated to the Sacred Heart and devoted to education. Fr. Varin, its co-founder, visited Philippine and wrote to Mme. Barat, Superior at Amiens, that in Philippine she would find one worth seeking to the ends of the earth. Madeleine Sophie Barat visited Grenoble, accepted the idea of fusion, and a Fr. Roget put them all into a fierce Retreat and for a year, I think, continued to form the Sisters, seeking to soften the rather inflexible Philippine and mitigate her tendency to ask from others as much as she did from herself. All took their first vows in 1805. But ever since a pilgrimage to the tomb of St. Francis Regis she had longed to go to the foreign missions. So had Mme. Barat, but since she, clearly, had to stay at home, perhaps Philippine would be the one to go! Meanwhile she must wait, and did so, in fact, twelve years, teaching, tending the sick, looking after the external affairs of the house—and praying; children who had in the evening stuck bits of paper to her dress as she knelt, found them still there in the morning. At last the Bishop of Louisiana visited them. Philippine implored to go back with him to America. Refusal after refusal—and at long last, assent.

In 1817 she and four others set sail. In 1818 the heaviest armed brig was 200 tons—this was a sailing-boat. The crossing was atrocious. In the Bay of Biscay they tossed, terribly sea-sick, for a week with hatches battened down. Off the Azores, a privateer; in the tropics, more gales— twice their portholes burst open and they were flooded out; also, they suffered from scurvy. Mère Duchesne's spoken prayer resolved itself into the words: "My God, for You!" On May 25 they entered the muddy Mississippi. Delay followed delay. Bishop Dubourg's introductory letter had been lost. After six months' inactivity in New Orleans, they decided to go to St. Louis. So, in a tiny ship, with no due accommodation, through sad majestic forests where cypresses were weirdly festooned with Spanish moss, between hidden rocks and whirlpools or floating rafts of lumber, without bell or buoy, continually passing rotting boats like carcases in the desert—after six weeks they reached their goal.

At first they found no house. All the same, in next to no

time, a school. Barefoot children arrived, by some Catholic instinct, in throngs. In four months, they were held fit for First Communion. Everything seemed provided, though everything was lacking. The cow-house had to be cleared out —Mère Audé, ex-great-Court-Lady of Napoleon's heyday, had charge of *that*. "I never expected", said Mère Duchesne, "to run short of water on the banks of the Missouri". Yet that river was at times entirely frozen over; even the milk in pails had to be broken up with axes and of course they had to cut their own wood. Alas, Mère Duchesne was no linguist; she *could* not learn English! But her great preoccupation was with the Indians, about whom she had no illusions, any more than about our own civilization, which, then as now, was killing off so many others. They emigrated to St. Charles, Florissant.

Picture them—especially if you know the highly-organized convents of that Society in Europe—trekking behind recalcitrant cows uselessly tempted by apronsful of maize—nuns stumbling through thorn-bush and finally depositing themselves in a log-cabin eighteen feet square with a loft above it—it was the nuns who had the loft; the children, the room. Philippine asked for reinforcements. None could yet be sent, such was the extension of the Society in France. Mère Duchesne fell sick and received the Last Sacraments; another Mother broke her leg and endured a long fever. Mère Audé, responsible for the sick *and* the school, was laid low. The chaplain died suddenly. But a number of first-rate American girls arrived as novices—all persevered. "This trying time will pass, dear Philippine", Mère Barat kept writing, though also she kept insisting that missions must become self-supporting. Those who in fact arrived to dedicate their lives knew well that the lovely solitudes, where sunlight dappled the waters through magnolia-leaves, were pestilent with malaria, and that lonely scattered priests needed almost as much help as the devout but fluid-minded negroes. "My soul is alone", wrote Philippine, "I have no interior comfort; I long for support . . . for someone to lean on; but there is no one!" (This, from the indomitable Philippine Duchesne!) But she wrestled on in prayer, while she mended the socks of undomesticated priests and even taught them how to cook their dinners. A child's discarded cotton frock did duty for a nun's veil; a cassock, for a cloak.

In 1822 Mère Duchesne was able to make the journey to Grand-Coteau. It was horrible, of course. Mud-clogged rivers; fetid water; nothing to eat. But "the progress", she wrote to Mère Barat, "that the girls have made is phenomenal". One, indeed, who arrived aged eighteen, knew nothing of God, swore like a trooper, smoked like a man, cared only for the company of blacks; but now made a daily meditation. After three years of "unalloyed happiness", Mère Duchesne returned with one companion, Teresa Pratt. Their cart-horse sank breast-high into mud; an ox-wagon took them through mosquito-infested swamps till the water was deep enough for them to join a steamer. Changing boats, they embarked on the last four hundred leagues. Philippine had caught malaria; now they found that she, like the captain, the first mate, and a passenger, all had yellow fever. These died on the second day; their bodies, with a young Frenchman not even dead, were thrown onto the banks. Soon, Mother Duchesne too with her companion was put on shore to die. They had nursed the sick till their strength gave out. In the end, a stranger offered them a bed—it proved to have been his wife's who had died of the fever three weeks before—nor had the sheets been changed. They recovered and set sail again but ran aground—the river had sunk, and they actually passed the wreck of their original boat. The boilers had burst, and thirteen of the passengers and crew had died of the accident or the fever.

Home at Florissant, she felt that disaster impended. And indeed, a layman had made off with funds belonging to the Bishop; the nuns, who had been his friends, suffered every calumny; pupils were withdrawn; the Sisters' work was ridiculed as quixotic. However, a colony of Dutch Jesuits

arrived, having walked the four hundred miles from George-
town, begging their way. They provided great spiritual
encouragement—perhaps paradoxically; the Superior was
as "rugged" as Mère Duchesne. He refused her absolution
for so long that she rode off to obtain it from a gentler priest
ninety miles away. And, having differed from her as to where
a mat should go, he would not give her Communion the
next day—the feast of the Sacred Heart.

New foundations followed—the nuns had to be scavengers,
masons, carpenters; one establishment was opened on a
foundation of eight dollars. How easy, in such circumstances,
to be *heroines*—how difficult, in the gracious artistic houses
of a homeland! However, there were now eight houses in
Louisiana; Mère Barat appointed Mère Duchesne to visit
and co-ordinate them. And a new trial—there were those
who argued that she had no authority; her position was a
false one—she could criticize but not legislate. Mère Barat
was in fact disappointed that Philippine had not been
authoritative enough! She was, perhaps, too loyally
"conservative" and did not guess that not all could be done
in young America as it had been within the ancient etiquette
of France. She felt this herself, and longed for oblivion.
Detachment was indeed forced on her not only by the closing
of houses due to floods or cholera that brought death to one
Sister after another, but she herself thought she was going to
die. Yet, bowed with age and sickness, she worked incessantly
in the garden or at needlework, and add to this her many
hours of prayer—she might answer eight or nine Masses in a
morning. Her own prayer was of extreme simplicity. "I
never could reflect on anything in detail", she said: "I am
unaware of sub-divisions when people speak or preach at
length, I sum it all up in a few words. Methods and
considerations only distract me." But she nursed one hope
—in 1837 Mère Barat wrote to her: "My affection for you,
dear Philippine, never has and never can be diminished . . .
never can I forget what you have suffered and done. When
I can send someone to take your place, there will be no

reason why you should not come home to die." But she was never to see her friend again.

And before her death, Mère Duchesne experienced a curious interlude. Mère Barat sent to represent her in America a Mother Galitzin, of princely descent, brilliant, apt to "pounce" upon decisions, with all Mère Duchesne's early authoritarianism but as yet unsweetened by the long patient suffering, the self-effacing heroism of the older nun. Very soon, she removed Mère Duchesne from all posts of responsibility and sent her to St. Louis, but again very soon she sent her with four others to Sugar Creek to work among the Indians. The dreams of youth were realized! Two miles from the camp, a cloud of a hundred and fifty Redskins swirled towards her at full gallop and in all their war-paint—feathers, quills, shells—all that enchants school-boys and enchanted no less the old nun and renewed the spirit of thirty years ago. After salvos of musket-fire, the Chief and seven hundred of his braves shook hands with each nun in turn. Alas, even though her life was spent almost wholly in prayer, so that she was named by the Indians "the praying woman", the conditions were too rough for her, and she was recalled to St. Charles, where in fact she died on November 18, 1852, aged eighty-four.

I have singled out only the "missionary" aspect of Mère Duchesne's life, and have hardly mentioned some of the domestic trials which befell her, nor have I done more than allude to that interior life of prayer which made her exterior heroism possible. Such trials will probably be part of the normal purification of a soul; such prayer will always be necessary in one who is seeking perfectly to carry out God's Will. The America that she knew has long since passed away; her Indians have all but ceased to exist. It is the work she did in *that* America and, for a brief space, for *those* Indians, that I have wished to recall.

Suzanne Aubert de Laye, Mère Aubert (1835-1926), was born into a "large" tradition; great-uncles of hers had been archbishops or presidents. Better, she had been friend of St. Madeleine Sophie Barat and was cousin of the Blessed Philippine Duchesne, friend too of St. Julie Postel (p. 133) and of Mlle. Tamisier who inspired our Eucharistic Congresses, and of Pauline Jaricot who initiated the Association for the Propagation of the Faith and was well known to the Curé d'Ars. Moreover, her mother had blessed Peter Chanel, the Marist peasant-priest who sailed for the Pacific the year before Suzanne was born; he was martyred on Fortuna Island in 1841; and Bishop Pompallier, first Vicar Apostolic of New Zealand, was a close friend of the family. They wanted to marry her off; she said "No"; the Curé d'Ars looked hard at her and said she was right. She proceeded—incredible audacity then!—to study medicine; she followed lectures, hidden in an alcove. She learnt nursing under the Sisters of Charity. At twenty she told her recalcitrant father that she would go whither her vocation called. During the Crimea war, she worked on the transports, and afterwards in France during the cholera scourge. Meanwhile, she studied botany! In 1859 Bishop Pompallier asked for help in New Zealand. The Curé d'Ars had prophesied, in detail, that such was her vocation. In 1860 they sailed in a whaling-ship, reeking with whale-fat, and the journey took twenty weeks! (It was in this ship that Bishop Devereux, too, sailed with nuns for South Africa, p. 137.) On December 30, Auckland gave the nuns a rapturous welcome.

Bishop Pompallier made Sister Aubert (as she was now called) begin a Maori orphanage in which a Maori girl, niece of the Great Chief Rewi Mangiapoto, helped her much; but she felt she ought to visit every accessible *pau* (village) and was sure that the Maoris would be like "chivalrous medieval knights" (about which she was optimist—past, or present?). She won her way, though the Tohungas (priests of a fanatical tribe) decided to bewitch her. These great copper-dark men, grass-kilted, tattooed in powder-blue, their tongues lolling out, advanced on her. She made the sign of the Cross—they retreated "as by bomb-blast". She became at home in those reed-clad houses with wide-winged gables painted indigo, dull red and white; she developed immensely her knowledge of botany; during the Maori wars she refused, rightly, to return to France.

From 1871 she spent twelve years with the Marist Fathers at Hawke's Bay; but in 1884 she was sent with some St. Joseph Sisters to Hiruharama (Jerusalem) on the Wanganui river. Travelling south from Auckland, did she pass through the volcanic zone, more active even than now? Did she see the pits of boiling muttering mud; the jets of silvery water hurled up into the exquisite sky; the petulant pools, cascades and fountains—sapphire, emerald, amethyst —so hot as to eat in an instant flesh from bone should you touch them—tossing themselves about among tortured rocks? As to that, perhaps I was luckier than she; but that was not what she was looking for. Anyhow, canoeing down the Wanganui she will have seen the mighty kauri trees and their golden gum, the loveliest tree-tall ferns, fleeces of crimson flowers, and will have heard a new music of birds—about which New Zealand's truest poet, Eileen Duggan, has exquisitely written. Desperately poor—alms were slow in arriving at places that no one could *imagine*—the Sisters became doctors, agriculturalists, school-teachers, above all spiritual *forces*, and in 1892 Mother Aubert's little community (she could not help becoming a leader!) was made into a diocesan Congregation under the aegis of Our Lady of Compassion. Meanwhile, she developed native medicine; not only all the islands sought for her remedies but the sick pilgrimaged to Hiruharama till a home had to be built for the aged and for incurables and another for orphans or abandoned children. At last, in 1900, she had gone to Wellington, opened her Home for Incurables, and was the first to institute district nursing and a crèche.

The work began (literally) with half-a-crown, with a pram (obtained on credit) for collecting food and clothes, and no beds (anyhow none for the Sisters!). But in next to no time, new houses had to be opened. At Island Bay, a reservoir was an absolute necessity. Yet how pay for carting gravel and cement up such a hill? But by now Mother Aubert was *understood*. Men of all classes and all creeds, "from Lord Plunket to the humblest labourer, removing their top hats or their tweed caps", flocked to the place and joined in the work. 1910 was the Golden Jubilee of her arrival in New Zealand. Wellington's citizens, led by the Governor, Lord Islington, packed the Town Hall amid scenes of incredible enthusiasm, to offer £2,000 to this little nun in her blue serge and peasant's cap (with hair still plentiful beneath it), with her calm eyes, firm lips and sudden smile, and her chuckle "as of a gnome, but a very good gnome!".

In 1913 she left for Rome to obtain papal approbation for her Institute. There were the usual ecclesiastical delays; there was an appalling earthquake; war broke out. She nursed, impartially, the victims of both tragedies. Not till 1920 could she return to New Zealand, being now eighty-five. At once she flung herself into new creative work. Did she regret being no more able to concentrate on Maoris? As always, she followed God's guidance; still was her smile "a permanent free cure for pessimism and cynicism". She still rose at five; one bitter winter a visitor found she had no fire. "We can't afford fires; work makes warmth!" In 1926, she was ninety-one; she lived for her daily Communion till, on October 1, 1926, she died. Four days later, all Wellington—one might say, half New Zealand—was at her funeral. The Maori "Goodbye" was:

"Loving greetings to our beneficent Mother Mary Joseph. Go, Mary! Go, Lady! Go to our Father and our ancestors! Go to those who held the Faith in the days when you lived amongst us and ministered to our bodies and our souls. Go, Mother of the orphan and the poor! Go to our Lord. He has prepared the way for us to reach His kingdom in heaven. We are your children. All the People."

Only two years later I was privileged to visit her houses. And, a little later, to re-visit them and see how rapidly they had grown. Yet, as always, I feared that as things become institutionalized, taken over by Governments (I don't think that her creations were, but sooner or later a de-personalized officialdom will want to control all activity), the *kind* of heroism that was Mère Aubert's will become impossible. Success, so often, is suicide. Well, we must have a new sort of heroism! We *must* have heroes (and, of course, no less certainly, heroines!). Mère Aubert may have been disconcerted if she knew of Maoris being knighted and becoming legislators. Amen. But may they never cease to be real sons of that noble race, the Maoris, nor melt into some nondescript "civilization" such as Europe, just now, is confusedly offering to so many.

St. Francesca Saveria Cabrini was born on July 15, 1850, in a Lombard farmhouse, youngest of thirteen children. Her father was a "Cristianone"—a "hundred per cent. Christian". Her mother rose early, prayed for an hour, went to Mass, spent the day seeing to the house and the children, and when they were asleep prayed for another hour. The child was baptized on the day of her birth—and the three Francis's—of Assisi, Xavier and Sales—seem to have dowered her with their special gifts of love, zeal and tender strength. After a while she was entrusted to her sister Rosa, fifteen years older than she. Rosa not only had opened a school in their house, taught catechism, offered it as subject for examination, but, when an inspector asked her if she did not know that catechism had been abolished, answered that of course she did, but had no intention of obeying such a law. She used to plaster down Francesca's golden curls, lest she should grow vain. "Never, never", Mother Cabrini was to say, "will my hair turn white! My sister oiled it far too much!"

Rosa wanted to be a nun. Her mother said, "Make your home your convent." Francesca turned her dolls into a community, which behaved very well. She put dolls into paper boats and sent them sailing down the Lambro—missionaries off to China. When they fell in, she envied them their martyrdom till she fell in herself. This gave her a long-lasting anti-water complex—little did she guess how often she must cross the Atlantic! She was tiny, with a little round face and short nose, and so shy that she dared not raise her eyes. "But the day came", she was to say, "when I had to keep them wide open and see everything!" When she was thirteen a missionary came and related his adventures in the East. The child took fire. "You?" cried Rosa, "You—so ignorant, a missionary?" Snubbed, she contented herself with poring over geography books and took a teacher's diploma. Her spiritual life grew so rapidly that the local rector, if she asked advice, would simply say: "Go and tell that to Jesus." Thus she learnt "to lean on no one but Himself". In 1870, both her parents died.

Smallpox broke out; she nursed the sick and caught it but recovered. She tried to be a nun, but was "too small and weak". Suddenly her Bishop said: "You are to be a Missionary Sister. I know of no Institute for such women. Found one." Not knowing how to, but obedient in will, she at first opened a school for children who flocked there. She was as competent in the class-room as in the kitchen. A nucleus was being formed for the future Society. In 1881 a draft of a Rule was offered to the Bishop. In 1888, he approved of it. This occurred in the little town of Codogno, where prudent people criticized her. Had she not already and audaciously urged that all, who could, should receive Communion daily? When imagination terrified her, she repeated: "Control that Fool of the House! Do you suppose you will always be asked to do what you *can*?" And long later, some prelate echoed this: "Do you think that God is going to ask you only for *what is possible*?"

The Missionary Sisters of the Sacred Heart began to spread—even to Milan. The Bishop, now old and con-servative, wished to keep the Sisters for his diocese, but

Mother Cabrini went to Rome where the Foundress of the Franciscan Missionaries of Mary (p. 180) welcomed her. But—she had no credentials. She went to the Cardinal Vicar; might her Institute be approved? Out of the question. Might she wait, and open a school meanwhile? She might wait, but, no school! She waited, and prayed. The Cardinal sent for her. "Are you willing to obey?" "At once, Your Eminence." "Then you will open not one school in Rome, but two." In extreme poverty, this was done. The Cardinal visited the nuns, saw a statue of our Lady with a crown lying beside her, and asked when it was to be put on. "She is waiting", said Mother Cabrini, with sanctified impertinence, "for him whose heart she has changed." It was Friday, "but", said he, "these nuns turn any day into Sunday." The decree of approbation was granted with extraordinary rapidity and put into her own hands.

The Bishop of Piacenza had inaugurated a mission for emigrant Italians in New York, and asked and asked that some of these nuns should be sent there. "New York is far too small for me!" she exclaimed. China, not civilized America, filled her dreams; pagodas, not sky-scrapers. But the Bishop said, "Off you go!"; and Pope Leo, "Not East, but West!" Seven Sisters then crossed the Alps and embarked at Havre. One thousand five hundred Italian emigrants were on that ship. As it sailed all sang the *Ave Maris Stella*. At last, after a distressful voyage, they arrived. But—the Italian priests who welcomed them had forgotten to find lodgings; these were discovered in a slum, but Archbishop Corrigan of New York disapproved of the scheme and said they had better go straight back to Italy. This time Mother Cabrini could present overwhelming credentials and said she would stay. But the tact that went with her firmness—and which caused her to be ranked with the greatest Generals or statesmen of the world—won her friends all round. In no time she could go where the police could not. She revisited Italy—was told that an American

Jesuit noviciate was to be sold—would she return and buy it? She did so, with seven more nuns, the ship having to anchor amid icebergs to mend its engines. On a second visit to Italy Leo held her hand affectionately and insatiably asked questions. Back she went with twenty-eight more Sisters, most of them meant however for Nicaragua. On the way there hurricanes drove the ship into real peril. The Captain, who found Mother Cabrini sitting on the floor and grasping the legs of a sofa, owned to his alarm. She went off and prayed; he altered his course for the open sea; all went well; but next day the coast was strewn with wreckage. The passengers organized a concert to celebrate. "Yes, if we may provide the first item!" Quaint concert, which began with two hymns written by this nun! They crossed the isthmus; at last she saw Chinese; also negroes. She experienced typhoid, earthquakes, and reptiles that terrified her half out of her wits. Moreover, the convent was attacked at night because it sheltered illegitimate children.

She returned to the States by small ships, having to change as many as nine times in twelve days. At Rio San Juan she was so ill—henceforward she always was!—that they thought she had yellow fever. But Governments visited her when she could not visit *them*. In New Orleans, where eleven Sicilians had recently been lynched, she opened her convent in a tenement full of negroes, of midnight orgies, with putrid water, and, for kitchen, a heap of bricks in a yard. Yet soon she could buy the entire house and make a splendid centre there. Back to New York. She was asked to take over a hospital which other Italian nuns had failed to manage; they had returned to Italy. It had an enormous debt. She took it over, for she saw our Lady with her sleeves rolled up, saying: "*I* am doing the work that you won't." But after a year she had to say she could not work the hospital gratis, *and* pay off the interest on the debt, *and* get rid of the capital. Apparently people were shocked that she should mention money; she was told to leave in ten days.

She took the dying to the public hospital, but hired two houses in which she placed ten persons who refused to leave the Sisters. A storm of abuse—there was no gas, no water; food must be heated on a stove; there was but one table in the surgery. And yet—by now, 500,000 patients must have been treated there; the Senate has allocated moneys to it; doctors have actually dismissed colleagues who demanded fees; it is, in short, the famous Columbus hospital. The Institute now numbered two hundred Sisters in fourteen houses.

She returned to Rome and Leo XIII often received her. Once, when two Sisters were going to Brazil, "Brazil!" he cried, "how vast a field! Let us work, Mother Cabrini; let us work and what a heaven will be ours! Heaven is made for people who work like you. Courage, Mother; work till death." At his door, he turned, and repeated, "Let us work, Mother Cabrini, let us work!" She thereupon opened other houses, including a rest-house for her exhausted Sisters—the one sort of house *she* never used. But, a thunderbolt. Her Sisters in Nicaragua had already experienced three revolutions, followed by epidemics; another broke out, and they were told to leave the republic within two hours. They descended to the shore, hedged with soldiery lest the lamenting population should rescue them. Suddenly a Sister remembered she had left her slippers behind. The entire cortège was held up. Thereafter, when Mother Cabrini was giving the most serious parting advice to Sisters, she would always add: "And be *sure* to remember your slippers!" A flotilla of boats followed the Sisters in their ships, with gifts not least from the Indians. Soon enough, the Nicaraguans begged them to return. But no; they had better learn their lesson. It was Benedict XV who brought them back again. I make no pretence of cataloguing all Mother Cabrini's creations, but I like to recall that she returned to South America down the Pacific coast and had to cross the Andes into the Argentine. They went on mules through heavy snow, 24,000 feet above sea-level. Once they had to be slung like sacks over a crevasse. Asked, in a shelter-hut, to write their impressions, they did so cheerfully, but duly added that the peaks of perfection were even higher and harder to climb than the Cordilleras. She reached Buenos Aires, and once more Rome. "How can you endure such fatigues?" asked Leo. "I am strong, but I could not stand it. True, I am old, but I am stronger than you!" Next time she was too ill to present herself; but he sent her oranges from the Vatican gardens, which did her more good than any medicines.

It is pleasant to know that she arrived in England in a "golden sunset", and that here, almost alone, she experienced no insults, anti-clerical or other. Within a fortnight, helped by the Bishop of Southwark (afterwards Cardinal Bourne) she had opened a house in South London! From Liverpool she sailed back—Colorado, California—as conscious of the intoxicating loveliness of nature as of the horrors of mining towns. She was a miraculous "business woman", foreseeing even where railway lines would go. In Chicago, finding that building operations were in a horrible mess, she dismissed, out of hand, "architects, contractors and foolish (though wealthy) friends". She became her own contractor. From August 1904 to next February she supervised the building of the enormous new hospital, choosing men from among the unemployed, and herself giving them their orders. When the hospital was opened, she was carried shoulder-high to the platform. "To whom", cried the inaugurating doctor, "do we owe this great work? To that little woman!" And the doctors themselves were delighted to accept her rules, even when she reserved forty-three wards for the indigent, and said that service there must be gratis.

But in 1905 it was the Silver Jubilee of the Institute. It numbered by then one thousand five hundred Sisters in fifty houses; five thousand children were in her schools; impossible to reckon the sick in her hospitals; at least two hundred thousand emigrants regarded her as their mother; when yellow fever or smallpox or typhoid broke out, these were the Sisters, who, as a matter of course, were sent for;

they dealt fearlessly with the most hardened prostitute, and miners found a few minutes' talk with them more cheering than an hour in a saloon. The prisoners in Sing Sing sent them an illuminated Jubilee address. Meanwhile, when a new hospital was started in Chicago the neighbours, objecting to these Catholics, cut the water-pipes which flooded the house and then froze; drenched the doors with petrol and then set fire to them. The nuns thought the best plan was at once to go and live there, and their neighbours did indeed draw the line at murder.

But by now she was sixty and tired to death. She had wanted to resign—Rome ordered her to remain Superior-General for life. The Sisters declared they would all willingly die if but she might live. "What", she asked, with truly Italian dry humour, "would be the good of that? What should *I* do, if all of you were dead?" A Spanish Cardinal handed her the decree, and with even more caustic humour said: "Having heard that you have done so badly, we give you a little longer in which to do better!" Impossible to relate her final foundations and the civic honours which befell her. In 1914 war broke out; she had arranged new sites for such houses as should have to be evacuated. "Manage", she said, "to save everything—even your slippers." In Paris and London, she gave her houses to be domiciles for troops or the Red Cross. She was sent for to found an orphanage in Seattle, discovered a hotel for sale and drew up the contract. The usual opposition. Orphans? Intolerable! Banks, intimidated, refused to advance money. She had a statue of our Lady learning to read from a book held by St. Anne. On it she wrote the exact sum needed. "Now", she charmingly said, "our Lady can't help seeing it all the time!" And in a day or two a Scandinavian bank offered her all she needed. She then proposed to make a hospital, not an orphanage. The Bishop vetoed this; but the day came when not only the orphanage but a hospital—eight storeys high—ranked among Seattle's finest monuments.

But by 1916 she was definitely sick. Yet in December, she asked that new habits should be made for herself and all the Sisters. For her, the act was symbolical; "all things" were about to be "made new". On December 22 she remained in bed, but transacted business and asked a Sister to brush the floor, especially round the arm-chair where she usually sat. At 11.40, a Sister came to ask her a question, which she answered; she returned at 12 but found the door locked. "Good", she thought; "Mother General is getting up", and she went to the refectory, leaving another Sister by the door. In a few minutes this Sister ran into the refectory—Mother Cabrini had felt the end was imminent, had risen, rung the bell, unlocked the door, and relapsed into her chair. Before doctor or priest could come, she had died, serene as ever. She lay in state in Chicago till December 26, and was then taken to New York. Enormous crowds awaited her and the coffin lid had to be lifted, that they might see her features, still unchanged. She was canonized in 1946.

CHAPTER VII

CONCLUSION

THE FIRST thing we shall notice is, surely, the amazing variety of women who have become "Saints". Queens and princesses, shepherdesses and servant-maids. Noblewomen who rode a-hunting, and the wives or daughters of little shop-keepers. Ex-courtesans, and girls immaculate from childhood. Sublime ecstatics, and manageresses of hospitals or schools. Martyrs, whose flesh was torn to pieces; and women, young or older, who suffered not only at the hands of brutal governments but at those of their "own household". Impossible, then, for the most wise, or the most foolish, to risk an opinion about sanctity in our own days, in what sense it reproduces or differs from that in by-gone centuries. The Church never ceases to be "Holy", and that adjective must be taken also in its active sense— *sanctifying*.

There are, however, certain "ingredients", so to say, in sanctity which hold good from the times of the earliest Martyrs to our own—however variously sanctity may manifest itself (or lie latent) as civilizations change. One is Self-Sacrifice, which you will watch from the days of SS. Peter and Paul down to those of St. Thérèse of Lisieux and to the doctrine proclaimed by our Lady at Fatima.

By "self-sacrifice" I do not mean the fierce penances that certain Saints imposed on themselves when conscious of the terribleness of sin and of the Passion of our Lord; it is hard to imagine our Lady, in her old age, being called to anything of that sort. But her "Lo me, the Handmaiden of the Lord" began her life as Mother of God and has never ceased throughout her Motherhood of ourselves. The total abdication of her self-will to God's. At one moment, this led her literally up the hill of Calvary; but that was an affair of one day, however terrible; her total self-abdication lasted all her life. The Liturgy never fails to associate with her those who "loyally stand with her beneath the Cross". In some way or another those who would be closely with Christ must have their heart pierced by a sword, as hers was. So I have not disguised, indeed I have emphasized, the sufferings endured by holy women, at the hands of those who both thought themselves and *were* virtuous. So difficult is it to attain to the *total* self-abdication we have been speaking of; to be wholly rid not only of the seldom acknowledged sin of jealousy and that instinct of possessiveness which may mislead even parents who think they want to do the very best for their children, or priests who are convinced that they are seeking only to serve their parish, or those who found or direct some enterprise.

Another permanent ingredient in sanctity is prayer. Here again we meet the paradox that Prayer has been at times the subject of acrimonious dispute. It baffles the imagination how men could argue about the sublimer forms of prayer while offending, at least outwardly, so gravely against charity. Let us at any rate rejoice that the Church has always prayed; and also, that some of the greatest Saints during maybe long-drawn periods of their lives have been unable to make use of any but the driest, most laborious forms of prayer dutifully and even irksomely recited. It is no less true that God may lift the soul far above all normal experience; but ecstasies and the like *are* not sanctity nor necessarily even the marks of sanctity, and they offer all sorts of opportunities for delusion or misinterpretation to those who suffer from or witness them. Perhaps we are less inclined than of old to attribute fictitious "ecstasies" to the direct action of the devil; but our knowledge of psychological maladjustment is enormously increased; and the Church always judges of sanctity by what can be known of the person concerned and his or her virtues independently of abnormal phenomena. But it is good for us to be reminded that we live, so far as our normal awareness goes, on the mere fringe of spiritual reality.

Another element permanent in the genuine Saint is the desire of an "apostolate". Nothing is more surprising than the immense influence exercised by Saints who lived, one might have thought, completely withdrawn from the "world"—in desert-tombs, on columns, behind grilles—could have had no influence; yet how great, in reality, was that influence; how wide their apostolate; perhaps the stimulus towards interest in "foreign missions" given by the short, hidden life of St. Thérèse of Lisieux has been as great as any.

Here then are forms of the essence of sanctity, which is the entire transference of the will from self to God.

It is clear, then, how these remain unalterable however much exterior forms may change. We saw how the modification of "enclosure" in the interests of free movement, which had defeated St. Francis de Sales or Mary Ward, has now become nearly normal. If, as seems likely, the Church is to pass through yet harder times, we may see the progressive abandonment, at any rate out of doors, of the "religious habit"—every detail of which used to be clung to almost like a dogma of the faith—and it may become usual for women of "dedicated lives" to earn their own living during the day, as many already do. The Holy Father has quite recently legislated for a new form of "religious life" called "secular". Maybe that instead of sacrificing (in the sense of "doing without") as many of the contents of the world as possible, we shall learn so to use them to the maximum that they all become part of an offering, a true "sacrifice", acceptable to God. Notice that this does not mean a dilution of the idea of "sanctity"; on the contrary. In old times the "grille" was regarded as essential because womanly virtue could not, it was thought, be trusted in so wicked a world. The idea may, by now, seem to us unworthy. It remains that virtue must be even stronger and more resolute today, if the ideal is to be maintained without so many safeguards. And after all, our Lady lived in no "enclosure", wore no special dress, never deviated from her vision, was always to the utmost "the Lord's handmaiden".

It is with regret that I finish this book and the association it made possible with so many holy memories—or rather, presences; for the Saints are not over and done with. I can but repeat that, first, I have not wished to attribute official holiness to anyone about whom the Holy See has not yet pronounced its decision; and again, that I am sure to have made many mistakes which, I hope, I shall be enabled to rectify later on; and perhaps above all, that I am quite conscious of having spent much longer over certain personages than over others. This was because to some extent, as I said, I thought them more picturesque and likely to lay hold of the imagination, and also, because they came from various lands and addressed themselves to their vocation in different ways. We must pray that countries where the Catholic tradition has been lost, or has never existed on the national scale, may become rich in Saints and provide a yet greater "cloud of witnesses" to the battles of their own compatriots— for the conflict between God and Evil can hardly but become intensified.

INDEX

THIS INDEX contains the names of most of those who have been mentioned in the above pages. They have not all been canonized, and it is difficult to be sure of all who have been officially beatified, since beatifications have of recent years proceeded very rapidly, and there is—and in fact can be—no up-to-date record of all such events. Nor was it always easy to know in what order to put these names. For some Saints are better known, to the public, by their surnames; thus we are sure that more would recognize "Mother Barat" than "St. Madeleine Sophie"; others cling to their popular name—thus it is no good writing "Soeur Marie-Bernard" and not "St. Bernadette". Others refuse to drop their surname, like St. Mary Magdalen de' Pazzi, St. Catherine Ricci, Blessed Anna Maria Taigi. So I have not tried to be consistent, but shall say, for example, St. Crescentia Höss, but St. Catherine *of* Siena, *of* Bologna, *of* Genoa, and so forth.